Vegas
Golden Knights

Vegas
Golden Knights

How a First-Year Expansion Team
Healed Las Vegas and
Shocked the Hockey World

Joe Pane
with Deke Castleman

and contributions from
Andrew Uyal and John L. Smith

HUNTINGTON PRESS
LAS VEGAS, NEVADA

Vegas Golden Knights
How a First-Year Expansion Team Healed Las Vegas and Shocked the Hockey World

Published by
  Huntington Press
  3665 Procyon Street
  Las Vegas, NV 89103
  Phone (702) 252-0655
  e-mail: books@huntingtonpress.com

Copyright ©2018, Joe Pane

ISBN: 978-1-944877-21-7
$16.95US

Cover Design: Laurie Cabot & Tanya Maynard

Cover Images: front: Marc-André Fleury, ©Cal Sport Media/Alamy.com; back: "The Knight," ©Shawn Hickey Photography

Inside Photos: Dreamstime.com: Hockey Stick ©Oleg Magurenco; Hockey puck ©Nikolai Sorokin; Vegas Golden Knights team logo ©Mohamed Ahmed Soliman; Alamy Stock Photos: ©ZUMA Press, Inc., pgs 1, 4, 7, 8, 10, 11, 12, 13, 16; ©Ken Howard, pg 4; ©MediaPunch Inc., pg 4; Shutterstock.com: ©Kevork Djansezian/AP/REX/Shutterstock (6370416ah), (6488113a), pg 2; ©AP/REX/Shutterstock (8610794a), pg 2, (9126779m), (9122775j), pg 6, (9135900b), pg 7, (9493141b), pg 8; ©Karl B DeBlaker/AP/REX/Shutterstock (7524981o), (7524981q), pg 3; ©Jeff Chiu/AP/REX/Shutterstock (9658641c), pg 3; ©Ross D. Franklin/AP/REX/Shutterstock (9695492c), pg 5, (9695454a), pg 10, (9707306ao), pg 14; ©John Locher/AP/REX/Shutterstock (9707306o), pg 7, (9486116a), (9697178be), pg 9, (9707421b), pg 14, (9723151ad), (9723151ac), (9723134an), (9723151ae), pg 15; ©Gene J. Puskar/AP/REX/Shutterstock (9358561u), pg 8

Production & Design: Laurie Cabot & Tanya Maynard

Acknowledgments

Even though my name is on the cover of this book, I would like to acknowledge a few others that helped it come to reality.

Anthony Curtis, who at a Fourth of July barbecue took the time between his burger and a beer to consider the idea of having LasVegasAdvisor.com cover the Vegas Golden Knights.

Deke Castleman, my editor, polished my Brooklyn version of the English language, game after game for 102 games, and completed this book.

Cheryl Jennings, a Las Vegas resident who prior to 2017 had never attended a NHL game in her, life but caught VGK fever through my blogs. I want to thank her for helping with the proofreading and for editing suggestions.

Eric Tosi, Alyssa Girardi, and Sage Sammons of the Vegas Golden Knights communication department for access to the players and coaching staff.

To my dad and best friend, for just knowing that once

you go hockey, you're hooked for life. I hope you get to read this in heaven. If not, I'll have a copy for you when I get there.

Finally, to the Golden Knight players and coaches who created this amazing story that united and healed an entire city while, bringing worldwide attention to Las Vegas and the NHL. Thanks, guys.

Contents

Author's Note 1

Prologue 3

Chapter 1: The Groundwork 7

Chapter 2: The Players 45

Chapter 3: The Preseason 83

Chapter 4: The Season 97

Chapter 5: The Fans 213

Chapter 6: The Playoffs 237

Chapter 7: The Bookmakers 287

Chapter 8: The Cup 301

Chapter 9: The Records 327

Epilogue 343

Index 347

About the Authors 357

Author's Note

I've been a rabid hockey fan since my dad took me to my first game at Madison Square Garden when I was nine years old and growing up in Brooklyn. That was when and where my lifelong love of hockey and the New York Rangers began, and it continues to this day, nearly 60 years later.

Though hockey has the smallest fan base of all the major sports, it is by far the most loyal. Why? Mainly, hockey is a family sport. A fan's grandfather, or even great-grandfather, was the first follower of one of the original six National Hockey League teams. He handed down his love of the sport to his kids, who handed it down to their kids, who really had no choice but to do the same with their own. (A side benefit: It sure makes Christmas shopping easy.)

Hockey also has the Stanley Cup. It was introduced to the sport by Frederick Arthur Stanley, 16th Earl of Derby — London-born, Eton and Sandhurst educated, and Governor General of Canada where he and his wife Lady Constance Villiers became avid hockey fans and steered their two boys into amateur leagues. It was a family affair — then as now. In 1892, Stanley awarded a silver cup to Canada's top team, though he called it the Dominion Hockey Challenge Cup. Since then, it's been revered by seven generations of fans.

The Vegas Golden Knights represent many things to many people, all of which I discuss at length in these pages. But to me, what underlies the incredible outpouring of acclaim and devotion has been the chance not only for families, but for an entire city and even parts of the world, to become hockey fans *at the same time*, rather than having the tradition passed down, which is tough to do with a year-old team. In my opinion, this powerful imprint helps to explain the intensity of the VGK's impact.

I've attended NHL hockey games in countless venues in a couple dozen cities in two countries and I've found the passion and allegiance of the fans to be about equal. Most arenas are filled with season ticket holders who attend most, if not all, of the 41 home games. I always thought that Madison Square Garden had the most fervent fans. But in my entire life, I've never seen the likes of what this Las Vegas team unleashed.

I dedicate this book to the fans brought together by the Vegas Golden Knights and to the powerfully unifying force that is hockey.

Prologue

On November 6, 2017, when Toronto Maple Leafs' forward Zach Hyman crashed into Max Lagacé, the fourth-string goaltender for the Vegas Golden Knights, Max appeared shaken up. Everyone involved with the National Hockey League's Sin City expansion team held its collective breath. The VGK's fifth and final goaltender under contract was Dylan Ferguson, who'd turned 19 a couple months earlier—a scary moment for the fans, even scarier for the VGK organization, but scariest of all, perhaps, for Dylan Ferguson.

Twenty-four year-old Max Lagacé had kicked around the American Hockey League and ECHL for a few years before signing with the Vegas Golden Knights as a free agent. He'd been called up from the Knights' AHL affiliate after Marc-André Fleury, the team's first-string goaltender and shining star, was sidelined with a concussion more than a month earlier. In the ensuing 11 games, second-stringer Malcolm Subban went out with a groin injury, third-stringer Oscar Dansk went down with a leg injury, and Lagacé found himself starting his first NHL game on Halloween against the New York Rangers.

A fourth-string goaltender playing 15 games into a season is usually a good indication that the rest of the schedule will be painfully long. This would seem especially true for a first-year expansion team.

No one had high hopes for this ragtag collection of cast-offs in their inaugural year. In Las Vegas, we were all hoping for a decent showing and praying that the city would support the NHL's newest franchise enough to make hockey a success in the desert. Many of us had seen the struggles that the Arizona Coyotes, in another desert location, faced since they entered the league: multiple ownership changes, poor attendance even from a state with a large snowbird population, and constant whispers about relocation. Heck, there was even a strong rumor that Arizona was the team that would come to Las Vegas.

As Max Lagacé gathered himself in the third period, the Golden Knights were playing the last game of their longest road trip on the schedule, the sixth in nine days with four of the six played on back-to-back nights. They'd lost three, tied one, and trailed Toronto at the end of the second, outshot 31-6 in the two periods.

They'd had a strong start, setting records: the first expansion team in the NHL's long history to win six of their first seven games and even after three losses in a row on the road, the second expansion team in NHL history to play the fewest games before achieving their ninth win. But at that moment, the Knights were occupying what turned out to be the most ominous interlude in their celebrated, though short, story. If Max had to leave the game, he'd be replaced by the *fifth*-string goalie, the shoe that the sportswriters and talking heads and bookmakers had been waiting for 15 games to drop.

Max took up his position in front of the net, finished the game, and the rest is the stuff of sports lore and glory.

Is there a more overused idiom than "team of destiny?" Even if there is, it's usually the *last* statement about a team that was destined to win a big sporting event, such as the Philadelphia Eagles' victory over the favored New England Patriots in Super Bowl 2018. In this case, however, it's the least thing that can be said about the Vegas Golden Knights.

Sure, the VGK were the team of destiny in the National Hockey League's 2017-2018 season. But many of their first-year expansion-team accomplishments — ticket prices, merchandise sales, media attention, fan adulation, and, most of all, record setting — applied not only to the NHL, but *all* major-league sports.

Beyond that, because the first home game was played only nine days after and barely a long block away from the site of the worst mass shooting in U.S. history, the Knights had to embrace the stigma and horror of it. In essence, they set out to heal Las Vegas, to turn themselves into the antidote to Stephen Paddock and the savagery that he perpetrated on the Route 91 Harvest Festival.

And by the time the VGK were winning playoff games, then whole series, finally becoming one of two teams to vie for one of the most coveted trophies on Earth, the support for this team had gone viral. They were the subject of tweets from—and sold merchandise to—fans in more than 100 countries. The fantastic journey that this team was on grew into an enormous cultural phenomenon, especially for such a transient and skin-deep city like Las Vegas.

The Vegas Golden Knights, in the end, transcended hockey, all of sports, Las Vegas, and the U.S., to enfold the whole world. There will never be another triumph quite like the one that this book chronicles.

Chapter 1
The Groundwork

Las Vegas has been in the Maloof family blood for nearly 90 years, though the first 15 or so were in Las Vegas, New Mexico. Joe G. Maloof, the grandfather, emigrated from Lebanon and settled near relatives in northern New Mexico where he opened a general store. Right after Prohibition, he got rights to distribute Pabst Blue Ribbon beer. After that he picked up Coors and other beer, wine, and alcohol suppliers and set up distribution points throughout New Mexico.

After Joe died, his sons, George and Mike, moved the expanding business to Albuquerque in the late 1940s. George parlayed the liquor distributorship's success into other major ventures, including ownership of First National Bank of New Mexico and the National Basketball Association's Houston Rockets. In 1980, when George passed away suddenly of a heart attack at age 57, his wife Colleen and their two oldest sons, 25-year-old Joe and 24-year-old Gavin, assumed the reins of the businesses.

George Jr., fourth of the five Maloof siblings, attended UNLV where he majored in casino management. After graduating in 1987, he began raising money to open a casino in North Las Vegas on Rancho Drive. The Fiesta debuted in 1994 and George's brothers and sister began getting involved in southern Nevada.

At the time the Maloofs owned the Rockets, they met Gary Bettman, a lawyer for the NBA. Later, the Maloofs also owned the NBA's Sacramento Kings from 1998 until 2013. That's a long story for a rainy day, but when they sold the Kings for $535 million, brothers Joe and Gavin started looking for a new opportunity in the major leagues. They'd kept in touch with Gary Bettman, who'd risen through the NBA ranks to become general counsel and senior vice president, in pursuit of a team for sale or in an expansion market— and continued their twice-yearly phone calls when Bettman became commissioner of the National Hockey League.

In addition, in 2008, George Maloof, who by now had built the uber-hip Palms Hotel-Casino a mile west of the Las Vegas Strip, was making a list of big events the Palms could host—movie premieres, concerts, the NBA All-Star Game, and various awards shows, including the NHL's. Once again, the Maloofs connected with Bettman. The NHL moved its awards show to the Palms in 2009; it will remain in Las Vegas at least through 2021.

At the same time that they were selling the Kings, the Maloofs found out that MGM Resorts was building an 18,000-seat arena. Joe and Gavin looked at each other and said, "What about an NHL team to play there?"

"In a hundred and fifty years, Nevada never had a

team," said Gavin Maloof. "I didn't *think* it would work; I *knew* it would work."

How could he be so sure? On one hand, the conventional wisdom held that hockey was most popular in places where you can actually play the game. The naysayers pointed to the Arizona Coyotes, based in Phoenix, which consistently ranked near the bottom of the NHL in attendance.

On the other hand, perhaps Gavin Maloof's confidence had something to do with the 2.3 million residents in the Las Vegas metropolitan area, many of whom come from cities with hockey teams. He knew of the market research indicating that 130,000 hockey fans, making $55,000 or more, live within 35 miles of downtown Las Vegas. He was certainly aware that Las Vegas is a town of big-time sporting events, such as heavyweight championships, PGA tournaments, NASCAR races, Professional Bull Riders World Finals, the National Finals Rodeo, the National Basketball Association's Summer League, and the World Series of Poker, and that an NHL team's home season consisted of 41 big-time special events. He was also no doubt familiar with the fairly long and little-known history of hockey in the neon desert

The Las Vegas Thunder was a team in the International Hockey League in the 1990s, playing their home games at Thomas and Mack Center, the 18,500-seat arena for the University of Las Vegas-Nevada. They were known for an interesting roster of players that included Wayne Gretzky's younger brother Brent, 17-year-old Radek Bonk who played 13 seasons in the NHL, even a female goaltender, Manon Rheaume, who appeared in two games in 1994. They finished first in their division two out of their six seasons and made the playoffs in five; they had such a rabid following that the Thunder drew more fans to the Thomas and Mack than the popular UNLV Runnin' Rebels basketball team. When the T&M Center wouldn't renew the Thunder's lease in 1999, the team folded. I still see old-timers here and there around the city, proudly wearing their white-and-silver-on-blue Thunder jerseys with Boom Boom, the ferocious polar-bear mascot, lightning bolt in one hand and hockey stick in the other.

Four years later, another hockey team, the Las Vegas Wranglers, won the hearts of the Thunder fans. The Wranglers were an expansion team in the East Coast Hockey League (now the ECHL), who played in the Orleans Arena for 11 seasons between 2003 and 2014. The Wranglers set all kinds of league records, including the longest win streak (18), highest winning percentage over five seasons (including on the road), fewest penalty minutes in one game (0), and the first team to post three consecutive seasons with more than 100 points. They also made the playoffs in 10 of their 11 seasons, going all the way to the final (the Kelly Cup) in 2007-2008 and 2011-2012. They averaged just under 5,000 tickets sold per game and, like the Thunder at Thomas and Mack, folded only after the Orleans failed to renew their lease and they couldn't find anywhere else to call home. The Wranglers were Las Vegas' second-longest-lived professional sports team, behind the Las Vegas 51s Triple-A baseball team, now in its 38th season.

So an NHL team finding a fan base in Las Vegas wasn't, perhaps, as far-fetched as the naysayers initially believed.

When the Maloofs went to see their acquaintance, hockey commissioner Gary Bettman, about an expansion team for Las Vegas, they said, "We want to be sure it's a halfway decent team. We don't want a typical money-losing expansion club."

Bettman told them, "You have to show us two things. First, you have grass-roots support. And second, you have the arena."

Joe Maloof later summed up the meeting. "He didn't say yes. But he didn't say no."

The Maloofs returned to Las Vegas, started planning the campaign to sell 15,000 season tickets to locals, and made the deal with MGM for a lease on the arena. In an interview, George Maloof gave "a lot of credit" to Jim Murren, chairman of the board and CEO of MGM Resorts, and Bill Hornbuckle, president of MGM. "Just getting the arena built with no public money was a great accomplishment. They didn't give away anything by any means, but they did make us a fair deal for hosting the team."

After the first exploratory meeting with Bettman, the Maloofs' attorney knew an attorney who had a client interested in owning a major-league sports team. When they first heard the name Bill Foley, the Maloofs thought he was interested only in a football team, so they didn't see him as a serious partner possibility. But it turned out that he also had an interest in hockey. In early 2014, they struck a partnership deal, then they all went to New York, where the Maloofs introduced Bill Foley to Gary Bettman.

Seventy-four-year-old William Foley II spent the first few years of his life in Austin, Texas—not exactly a hotbed of hockey. But his father was in the U.S. Air Force and Bill Foley moved for the first of a half-dozen times when he was six—to Ottawa, where he learned to ice skate and play street hockey, also known as "shinny." For three years, he was a member of little neighborhood teams that skated on the frozen ponds of southeastern Canada. He likes to say he's been "all over" hockey ever since.

Foley graduated from the United States Military Academy at West Point in 1967 with a B.S. in engineering; according to Wikipedia, in his spare time as a cadet, he invested in the stock market and earned $40,000. Apparently, he liked to gamble even then and was good at it. From there, he switched branches to serve in the Air Force. Sent to Seattle to monitor military contracts with Boeing, by his mid-20s, he was negotiating deals in the hundreds of millions; he achieved the Air Force rank of captain.

He earned an MBA from Seattle University, then a law degree from the University of Washington in 1974. While practicing in Phoenix, specializing in corporate and real-estate law, Foley brokered a deal between Fidelity National Title Insurance Company and a small underwriter in Tucson. That led to control of Fidelity National in 1984 in a $21 million leveraged buyout. For the next 20 years, through a reported 100-plus mergers and acquisitions, Foley and investors turned Fidelity National into the largest title-insurance company in the U.S., a Fortune 500 company with a $4 billion market cap and $7 billion in annual revenues. Fidelity National is headquartered in Jacksonville, Florida, where Foley flirted with buying the NFL's Jacksonville Jaguars. He remains the Chairman of the Board of FNF, but he and his wife Carol now live in Las Vegas, spending summers in Montana.

Though title insurance helped Foley to achieve an estimated net worth of $600 million, he found it boring and started expanding his business interests. He served as CEO of CKE, Inc., parent company of Carl's Junior, and bought a 40,000-acre cattle ranch and resort, along with a ski resort and restaurants, in Montana. He also began investing in distressed wineries from California to New Zealand; his Foley Family Wines is based in Sonoma, California. One of his wine labels is Wayne Gretzky Estates—another nod to hockey.

But perhaps Foley's deepest connection to hockey was via his neighbor in Whitefish, Montana: Murray Craven.

Craven is a veteran of 18 NHL seasons, having played on six teams starting in 1982. He retired in 2000 and he and his family moved to a house on Whitefish Lake; when the Foleys bought a summer house on the lake, Bill and Murray became friends and golf partners.

For years, Craven had encouraged Foley to consider buying an existing hockey team, but as he told Dan Rosen, a senior writer for NHL.com, "It was a dead issue for a long time"—until one day out of the blue, Foley announced that he was planning to bring hockey to Las Vegas. From then on, Craven helped Foley navigate the maze of an NHL expansion team.

In a 2016 profile, *Worth* magazine wrote, "Foley has earned a reputation as a skillful and tough executive with an eye for a bargain, a talent for building value, and a passion for cost-cutting. He's deeply involved in all aspects of his businesses. That way, he says, 'If there's a failure, it's my fault.'"

At the time that Bill Foley and the Maloofs were formalizing the idea of bringing a pro-hockey expansion team to Las Vegas, Foley spoke to Scott Burnside, a senior writer at ESPN, and said that he planned "to be hoisting a Stanley Cup within eight years of seeing the first puck dropped on National Hockey League ice on Las Vegas' famous Strip." He added, "I don't care what it takes." Not long after, Foley changed the eight years to what became a mantra: "Playoffs in three, Cup in six."

Burnside, who probably knew that the claim was just a marketing pitch, as the team needed to sell 720,000 seats (18,000 times 41 home games), called Foley's plan "a speck on some distant hockey horizon." It certainly seemed like a longshot at the time. The NHL hadn't expanded beyond 30 teams since 2000 (the first year for the Columbus Blue Jackets and the Minnesota Wild). And in his first week as mayor of Las Vegas in 1999, Oscar Goodman, the mob lawyer turned Vegas politician and cheerleader, had visited the NHL's Gary Bettman—just he and two showgirls he took with him everywhere—in New York to discuss the possibility of bringing its first major-league team to Las Vegas, with no luck.

On the other hand, the Las Vegas Arena (now T-Mobile) had broken ground seven months earlier and the Foley-Maloof partnership had a lease agreement with the arena owners, MGM Resorts and Anschutz Entertainment Group (AEG), which owns the NHL's L.A. Kings.

The plan to receive approval from the National Hockey League and the owners of the 30 other teams called for Foley and the Maloofs to solicit support for professional hockey in Las Vegas from individuals and small businesses—not casinos and other big business—via open letters, word-of-mouth, a website, and personal appearances all over the city. If enough people committed in principle, they'd then be asked to put down deposits on season tickets.

The NHL was looking to see strong grassroots support from workaday locals, rather than counting on the casinos to buy up large blocks of tickets to use as comps, tourists taking in games for a new kind of entertainment, or fans of visiting teams following them to Sin City. Las Vegans were limited to eight tickets per person. Basing preliminary approval on a trial season-ticket drive to test the Las Vegas market was unusual, to say the least. But the ticket drive, dubbed Vegas Wants Hockey, was on.

Three days after the Atlanta Thrashers received NHL approval to relocate to Winnipeg and become the Jets in 2011 (for a $60 million relocation fee to the league), 7,158 season tickets were sold in a pre-sale; the remaining 5,842 were purchased online—*in the first four minutes* that they became available. It took another 17 minutes to process them and complete the sellout.

Las Vegas hockey had an uphill battle compared to Winnipeg, but Commissioner Gary Bettman was in attendance at the February 10, 2015, press conference at the MGM Grand in Las Vegas, where Bill Foley launched the Las Vegas hockey team's season-ticket sales.

The website VegasWantsHockey.com, in conjunction with a call center to handle queries and ticket purchases, was the main vehicle advertising the estimated per-game prices for seats: from around $20 for the nosebleed section up to $220 for center-ice "club" seats. The deposits for season tickets, in increments of one, three, five, and ten years, were for 10% of the actual prices. The goal was to secure 10,000 deposits and no time limit was imposed.

Another angle on it started out as the Las Vegas Founding 50: If you joined the group and sold 60 season tickets, you'd serve on the team's advisory board. It caught on so quickly that it had to be expanded to the Founding 75, which included poker pro Daniel Negreanu; boxing champions Mike Tyson and Floyd Mayweather; Derek Stevens, owner of several downtown casinos; star DJ Steve Aoki; and Steve Sisolak, chairman of the county commission and candidate for Nevada governor, who wrote the ceremonial first deposit check.

George Maloof remembered, "We'd worked on it for nearly three years. It was challenging, but we were also surprised by how quickly ticket sales picked up."

More than 5,000 tickets were sold within two days and 9,000 within a month. By March 30, VegasWantsHockey.com had reached its goal of 10,000 deposits from individ-

Poker Pro Superfan

Daniel Negreanu is one of the world's best-known and most successful poker professionals. He was inducted into poker's Hall of Fame in 2014; he's the second all-time money leader in live tournaments ($39.7 million cashed); he has six World Series of Poker bracelets and 105 cashes ($17 million); and he's won two World Poker Tour championships with 23 cashes ($6.4 million).

Negreanu grew up in Toronto, so like I am with the New York Rangers, he's a diehard and long-suffering fan of the Maple Leafs, which haven't won a Stanley Cup since 1967 (at 51 years, it's the longest current Cup drought in the NHL), which was also the last time they played in the Finals. Also like me, as a life-long hockey fan, when he first heard that Las Vegas was getting an NHL team, he immediately jumped on the bandwagon.

One of the original Founding 50, Negreanu bought 16 season tickets. Four of them are in Section 6, 11 rows behind the benches at center ice. He donates the other 12, in the upper deck, to Bill Foley's charity, the Folded Flag Foundation (which provides grants and scholarships to the wives and children of U.S. military and government personnel who died in service) and Cambeiro Elementary, whose underprivileged students get to attend hockey games.

On theathletic.com, Michael Russo wrote that Negreanu is known by everyone as the "mayor" of Section 6. "He is still largely the face of poker. And he has quickly become the most identifiable celebrity spokesman for the Golden Knights." ♣

uals and announced the second phase of the drive, aimed at casinos, banks, and other big companies that might buy blocks of tickets for their biggest customers, employee incentive-travel perks, and sponsorships. Also around that time, Bill Foley bought a house and office property in Summerlin, a sprawling master-planned community located 12 miles west of the Las Vegas Strip in the western Las Vegas Valley.

By May 15, deposits on 13,000 tickets had been received and on September 19, 2015, seven months after launching the drive, the season tickets were sold out: 16,000 for the 2017-2018 hockey season. Some deposits were for tickets for a quarter or half of the season, while many buyers no doubt planned to scalp the tickets on the resale market. Even so, it was a remarkable show of support—given that the T-Mobile Arena had only 17,500 seats and wouldn't even be completed for another six months, not to mention that the nameless team was still waiting for approval from the NHL.

So would the NHL even allow a Las Vegas team?

On the no side, Nate Silver, a statistician and baseball writer known for successfully predicting the outcomes in 49 states in the 2008 U.S. presidential election and all 50 states plus the District of Columbia in the 2012 election, enumerated the reasons that Vegas should *not* and probably wouldn't be selected as the new home of the NHL's 31st team.

First, Canada, which has only seven NHL teams, should

get an eighth; our northern neighbor, with one-tenth the population of the U.S. (less people than California) has just as many hockey fans. Second, the NHL teams in the smallest American markets—Nashville, Raleigh, Columbus, Tampa, Miami, and Phoenix—tend to lose money, often in the millions every year. Third, Silver downgraded the Foley market research from 130,000 hockey fans to 91,000, even fewer than Nashville's lowest in the NHL 146,000, or Seattle's 241,000 and Quebec City's 530,000, both also angling for expansion teams. And fourth, Silver's research found that Vegas wasn't especially supportive of the previous hockey teams, calling the Wranglers' attendance "middling" and citing the Las Vegas 51s as having the lowest attendance in the Pacific Coast League. Finally, he noted that the irregular hours of the workforce, mediocre public transportation, and abundant competition for entertainment dollars would depress attendance at sporting events. Contrary to his legendary prognostication prowess, it wasn't Silver's finest hour.

He didn't mention a couple other possibly prohibiting factors: Las Vegas is a warm-weather city with few ice-skating options and has limited parking options at its arena on the Las Vegas Strip, not to mention a built-in bias against paying for parking (the recent implementation of paid-parking on the Strip created one of the largest uproars in recent Vegas history).

Another objection Silver didn't foresee that proved true during the first season was what I started calling the "Vegas hangover," but the term that caught on was the "Vegas flu," in which teams that arrived a day or two early would suffer from the city's legendary distractions.

And, of course, there were the implications of a professional sports team playing in the sports-betting capital of the country.

On the yes side, the NHL needed at least one team in the Western Conference, which had only seven teams each in the Central and Pacific Divisions, compared to eight teams each in the Eastern Conference's Atlantic and Metropolitan Divisions. And Las Vegas had a good central location, with the L.A. Kings and Anaheim Ducks less than a four-hour drive away and the Arizona Coyotes less than five hours.

Also, the NHL already had a successful relationship with Las Vegas. Since 2009, the league had held its awards show in various venues around the city, where it became a much grander event, with an enhanced red carpet, hosting more celebrities, players, and coaches, and fans happy to attend.

But most of all, there was the buy-in, as we say in Vegas. The value of an NHL franchise had soared since the last time teams had joined the league in 2000, which was a lot higher than in previous expansions. In 1967, the NHL doubled in size, from six to 12 teams; Los Angeles, Pittsburgh, St. Louis, Philadelphia, Minneapolis, and Oakland, California, each paid $2 million to join. In 1970, the Vancouver Canucks paid $6 million. In 1979, four former World Hockey Association teams merged with the NHL, adding Edmonton, Quebec City, and Winnipeg; those teams paid $7.5 million apiece. The San Jose Sharks ponied up $45 million in 1991 and the Ottawa Senators and Tampa Bay Lightning paid the same price the following year. The price increased to $80 million when Nashville was awarded a team in 1998. Atlanta (1999) and Minnesota (2000) also paid $80 million.

The price for Las Vegas to join the NHL swelled by more than six times—all the way to $500 million. The half-billion-dollar price tag was, in part, meant to separate the men (who were serious about bringing the NHL to their market) from the boys (who couldn't afford it). Bill Foley, by all accounts, didn't flinch.

In addition, the willingness of Las Vegas' prospective team owners to shell out a half-billion dollars to become the NHL's 31st team was a sign of the league's enormous financial success since the days when it charged $2 million and even $80 million in expansion fees; that hard-nosed businessmen like Bill Foley and the Maloofs were ready and able to pay it was a sign of how profitable they were gambling on the team to become.

That $500 million would be divvied up among the 30 existing teams. Each would receive a nice $16.67 million windfall, which according to Scott Burnside of NHL.com, "didn't have to be shared with players under the current collective bargaining agreement." In return, the teams had to surrender one player each to the new franchise. Great deal, right?

Time would tell.

On June 24, 2015, after a Board of Governor's meeting at Bellagio a few hours before the NHL Awards ceremony at MGM Grand, Gary Bettman announced that the league would accept applications for expansion for the first time in more than 15 years.

On July 20, Bill Foley submitted his application for a team in Las Vegas. The NHL also received an application from Quebec City.

Phases Two and Three of the application process were completed in early September; in late September, Foley appeared before the Board of Governors to make a presentation and answer questions about his bid for a team.

Then, nothing.

"We went for months without any real indication that we were going to get it," Murray Craven told Dan Rosen.

In the meantime, however, the Zamboni Room was built at the new arena to house the ice-resurfacing machine and the process of laying the ice itself continued — based on nothing more than optimism that the building, which opened on April 6, 2016, would house the team.

Finally, on June 7, the Executive Committee officially recommended an expansion team for Las Vegas and on June 22, almost exactly a year after receiving the application, on a unanimous vote at the Board of Governors meeting on a 109-degree day in "Sin City," the NHL granted Las Vegas its expansion franchise.

Even then, local sports fans were bowled over. They clearly remembered that, mere years before, a major-league sports team for a city with such a transient population and stigmatized by legal sports betting was considered an impossibility.

Almost immediately, the Maloofs stepped back. "Once

T-Mobile—Built for Hockey

On May 1, 2014, MGM Resorts International and AEG broke ground on what came to be known as T-Mobile Arena directly behind New York-New York on the Las Vegas Strip. The $375 million arena opened a little less than two years later, on April 6, 2016.

Murray Craven, VGK senior vice president, told Dan Rosen of NHL.com that the "race to Las Vegas" for a major-league hockey or basketball team was all predicated on an arena. "If there's no arena in place," Craven said, "it's a non-starter."

Since T-Mobile started the whole puck sliding for the Vegas Golden Knights, the arena was built primarily for hockey. For a building that seats 17,500 hockey fans, it's intimate enough that the fans on the upper level are much closer to the action on the ice than in many hockey arenas around the world.

It also features one of the largest locker rooms in the NHL at 10,000 square feet, complete with meeting rooms and offices, a video theater and player's lounge, skate sharpening, and a sports-medicine area.

Of course, on the more than 300 days a year when hockey games aren't being played at T-Mobile, customized seats provide clear sight lines for other sports, including basketball, Ultimate Fighting Championship, WWE, and Professional Bull Rider events, along with concerts, beauty pageants, and award shows. ♣

the tickets were sold and we were awarded the franchise, our involvement in the process pretty much ended. We felt like we'd done our work by bringing the team here," George Maloof said. "We're still heavily invested in the team, of course, but one guy has to be in charge. It's too hard to rule by committee in this business, or in any business. The day to day is all Bill Foley."

As one of his first operational decisions, Foley hired George McPhee as the general manager of the new NHL organization.

Sixty-one-year-old George McPhee grew up in Canada and attended Bowling Green State University in Ohio, where he played hockey and won the 1982 Hobey Baker Award, given to college hockey's best player. After a stint in the Canadian Hockey League, where he helped win the Adams Cup with the Tulsa Oilers, he was an undrafted free agent when he signed with the New York Rangers and made his first NHL appearances during the 1983 Stanley Cup playoff. He remains one of two players in the league's history to score three goals in a single post-season before ever playing in a regular-season game. His career in the NHL lasted seven years with the Rangers and New Jersey Devils.

McPhee's first administrative job in the league was as director of hockey operations and alternate governor of the Vancouver Canucks, which played in the 1994 Stanley Cup Final, losing in seven games to my beloved New York Rangers. In 1997, he became the general manager of the Washington Capitals. In his first season, the Capitals reached the Stanley Cup Final for the first time in its history, only to lose to the Detroit Red Wings in four games. McPhee managed the Capitals for 17 years, during which time they topped their division seven times and set a franchise record for most points in a season (121). McPhee also drafted Alex Ovechkin, their all-time leading scorer, in the 2004 draft. McPhee left the Capitals at the end of the 2014 season.

A little more than a year later, he went to work as vice president and alternate governor of the New York Islanders; he left the Islanders when he was hired by Bill Foley as the general manager of the new Las Vegas expansion team. Almost immediately, McPhee hired Kelly McKrimmon as his assistant general manager and executive vice president of hockey operations; McKrimmon played at the University of Michigan and in the Western Hockey League and had been with the WHL's Brandon Wheat Kings as the head coach, general manager, governor, and owner for 30 years.

As the NHL's 31st GM, McPhee confronted any number of major challenges when he went to work for the Vegas organization as its first employee. He had to lay the foundation for the team—build the front office with personnel in hockey and business operations; the coaching, scouting, equipment, and medical staffs; finance, legal, and marketing; ticket sales and service; media relations and team services. He had to find an AHL affiliate for player development. He had to build a practice facility. He had to gauge the Las Vegas fan base. He had to hire a scouting staff to prepare for the expansion draft and the regular draft, both scheduled for the third week in June 2017.

Nick Cotsonika from NHL.com wrote, "When you aren't taking over an existing team with an existing infrastructure, that means you have to build an infrastructure from scratch down to the smallest, most mundane details. You can't draft players before you fill out a hockey operations department to evaluate them, and you can't fill out a hockey operations department before you figure out everything from pensions, health-care plans, and car allowances to cell phones, computers, and the software on the computers. At one point, McPhee wondered who was going to draft the contract for a new employee. He said to himself, 'I guess I am.'"

On the other hand, McPhee was building a franchise from ground zero, straight from scratch. He wasn't taking over an established team, with long-time employees and players, some bad contracts and a history of mistakes, a distinct and long-running culture, and all the other baggage.

Better yet, McPhee worked for extremely savvy and highly respected owners with deep pockets whose main goal was to build a first-class organization and win the Stanley Cup in six to eight years. He could also look forward to a brand new 17,500-seat $375 million arena right on the Las Vegas Strip, surrounded by tens of thousands of hotel rooms, and his $25 million practice facility in Summerlin, near where he lived, was also going up fast.

Perhaps best of all, he could establish his team not only in his own image, but also where he believed the league, and the game itself, were going. He could combine older, more established, and more experienced guys who knew the ropes, in particular goaltenders who can single-handedly save and win games, with younger, faster, hungrier players in an all-around effort to balance immediate success against long-term development.

Finally, after establishing the infrastructure of the Vegas hockey organization, George McPhee was ready to start erecting the edifice of the team.

By slightly altering the rules of the expansion draft, Gary Bettman and the NHL had responded to the request from Bill Foley and the Maloofs that their team would have a chance to be successful early on without having to go through the typical five- to seven-year development curve because it didn't have any good players to start. That was big. And McPhee was locked and loaded.

About those rules.

A lot was said and written about how the 2017 expansion draft was biased in favor of the new Las Vegas team. Many fans of the other teams liked to believe that, thanks to the $500 million league entry fee, the "fix was in" — the NHL, wanting its product to succeed in new markets, handed instant and automatic success to Vegas by way of liberalized expansion-draft parameters.

As everyone knows, "It's supposed to take years to build a Stanley Cup contender — nurturing top prospects after they're acquired in the draft, retaining good players with lucrative long-term contracts, and supplementing rosters with free agents," wrote Carol Schram in *Forbes*. "Successful teams are supposed to build winning cultures over many years, with veteran leadership groups that keep the dressing room united. History matters."

Well, welcome to the present—and future. The NHL made no bones about its goal: to make the Las Vegas expansion team competitive in its first year. As such, they tweaked the rules leftover from the last expansion draft.

In 2000, when the Wild and the Blue Jackets entered the league, the existing teams were allowed to protect either one goaltender, five defensemen, and nine forwards or two goaltenders, three defensemen, and seven forwards—14 skaters and a goaltender or 10 skaters and two goaltenders. In the 2017 expansion draft, the teams could protect either one goaltender, three defensemen, and seven forwards or eight players from any position and one goaltender—10 skaters and a goalie or eight skaters and a goalie. Also, any player who had a no-trade clause in his contract couldn't be exposed to the draft.

The fine-print rules called for Vegas to select one player from each of the 30 teams with a combined value of at least 60% and at most 100% of the salary cap. The 30 teams also had to leave unprotected, at a minimum, two forwards and one defenseman who played a minimum of 40 games the previous season or 70 games over the previous two seasons. Finally, Las Vegas could participate in the 2017 NHL entry draft with the same selection criteria as the third-to-last team in the league.

What did it all mean? In a nutshell, the 30 teams had to expose a number of good players, especially younger guys who saw a lot of ice time, but were yet to be granted no-move contract clauses. It also forced the league's general managers to make their moves based more on the future than they normally might have, especially in terms of upcoming free-agent deals, but also with possible trades for players and entry-draft picks. Finally, it gave George McPhee, no stranger to assembling teams after doing exactly that with the Washington Capitals for nearly two decades, a golden opportunity to cherry-pick from a deep pool of players stockpiled over the 17 years since the last expansion draft.

In many games of strategy, such as poker, chess and cerebral board games like Risk, the player who can think the furthest into the future to determine immediate tactics and long-range strategy generally wins. And it's roundly acknowledged that George McPhee's expert eye fashioned an expansion team that in the words of *Sporting News'* Brandon Schlager, "has become a case study for tactful opportunistic management."

The teams' lists of protected and unprotected players had to be finalized by June 17, 2017, and Las Vegas' selections would be announced a few days later.

In the meantime, the team's practice facility was feverishly being built.

The commemorative shovels were engraved with "Vegas Hockey/Practice Facility, October 5, 2016." The team hadn't been named yet, but training camp leading up to the NHL preseason would begin in 11 months. In that time, a team practice facility, along with its corporate offices and a community ice center, had to be completed and operational.

But even coming as far as the groundbreaking ceremony was something of a victory. The location of the facility changed three times, necessitating alterations in schedule and budget; the final location required some radical redesigning. Originally, it was announced that Clark County would fund 100% of the construction costs from its parks budget and the team would rent space for two hours a day, but along the way that flipped to 100% privately funded. Negotiations over the lease with the Howard Hughes Corporation, which owns the land, delayed the final deal for weeks and the permit process added time onto that. So construction didn't begin for a full month after groundbreaking.

The practice facility was the baby of Murray Craven, whom Bill Foley hired as a senior vice president shortly after he made George McPhee the general manager. Craven began his professional hockey career with his hometown Medicine Hat (Alberta) Tigers in the Western Hockey League when he was 16. Two years later in 1982, he was drafted (17th overall) by the Detroit Red Wings and spent four years shuttling between the WHL and NHL, until he was traded to the Philadelphia Flyers just before the 1984-85 season. In his first year with the Flyers, he helped lead the team to the Stanley Cup Finals, losing to the Edmonton Oilers. After seven years in Philadelphia, Craven played for four more teams before retiring in 2000; he appeared in 1,071 NHL games, including three losing appearances in the Finals. He also represented Canada in the 1990 and

1991 International Ice Hockey Federation World Championships.

"So it's safe to say that Craven has seen every iteration of an ice rink there is in the world," wrote Shawn P. Roarke in the *Golden Knights Yearbook*. "Those experiences made him a natural to be in charge of designing the new practice facility."

Amazingly, as is everything about this story, the 146,000-square-foot facility in Summerlin (Howard Hughes' mother's maiden name) opened slightly ahead of schedule, though the budget went up in $5 million increments from $15 million to around $30 million.

Nearing completion, the team and City National Bank, based in Los Angeles with four Las Vegas branches, inked a multiyear partnership deal that included City National's name on the arena. The financial particulars weren't disclosed, but the sponsorship, no doubt, helped defray the building's opening and maintenance costs.

Like many graduates of military academies, Bill Foley's years at West Point left an enduring mark on his consciousness. Early on, he spoke of his new hockey players in military terms. "They're warriors. They're soldiers. They get hurt. They lose teeth. And they're back there on the ice. It's the same culture I learned at West Point. It's all about being a team, not being an individual, and working together for a common goal."

Another way his Academy days manifested was in the name of its athletic teams, the Black Knights. The word "knight" had resonated with him ever since. As he wrote in an open letter to fans and Las Vegans, "The Knight always advances and never retreats." One of Foley's companies, which provides tech, data, and analytics for the mortgage and real-estate industries, is called Black Knight Financial; originally, Black Knight Sports and Entertainment was the name of his hockey-team company. Naturally, observers predicted the name of the team would be the Black Knights, but the "Black" part was unpopular with local hockey fans as a name for the neon-oasis' team, so it was shortened to Knights, with a new modifier yet to be selected.

In the meantime, the Vegas daily newspapers took straw polls to name the team. The *Review-Journal* offered up a number of gambling-related names, such as the Black Jacks, Keno Runners, Snake Eyes, and High Rollers, but they didn't amuse the league, which made it known that gambling terms and team names didn't mix. Other local variations included Flamingos, Scorpions, Hitmen, Outlaws, Jokers, Bighorns, Miners, Monsoon, Sinners, and Saints. Outlaws won the *R-J* poll; it was also the name of an early Las Vegas hockey team that played for three seasons in the early 1970s in the Independent Teams League at the old Ice Palace in the Commercial Center, Las Vegas' first large-scale shopping district; the Ice Palace doubled as a concert venue in the days when rock 'n' roll was mostly unwelcome in the Entertainment Capital. Aces won the *Las Vegas Sun* poll (it later became the name of the Vegas Women's National Basketball League team).

The Big Poll

LasVegasAdvisor.com, the gambling-centric website of the publisher of this book, ran its own poll that received 3,300 votes. The top five were Aces, High Rollers, Rat Pack (an apt name, I thought, for drafted players), Scorpions, and Wild Cards. Other top vote-getters included general gambling terms like Flush, Bluff, Dealers, and Croupiers, sports-betting terms like Moneyliners, and slot machine terms like TITOs (standing for ticket-in ticket-out, the slot machine payout vouchers), along with Vegas inside jokes like Barbacks, Impersonators, Resort Fees (a major bone of contention with savvy visitors), and Bumper-to-Bumper Traffic.

I especially liked the 86ers, adopting the term for getting kicked out of a bar or backed off at blackjack for card counting. But my favorite was the Stickmen, the perfect combination of hockey and craps: Hockey players use sticks to control the puck, while at crap tables, the stickman controls the dice with a bent and elongated stick. ✤

ESPN came up with a few names of its own: Bones, Sin, Nordique, and of course Strippers.

The reported finalists for the Knights' adjective were Golden, Desert, and Silver and all were trademarked in August 2016. Nighthawks was another name on the list, though it was only mentioned in passing as a backup plan—too close to the Chicago team's name, Blackhawks.

Finally, on November 22, five months to the day after the NHL announced the franchise, an estimated 5,000 fans packed the plaza fronting T-Mobile Arena, with hundreds more looking down on the festivities from the New York-New York parking garage, to see Bill Foley reveal the name of the team: the Vegas Golden Knights. "My whole idea," Foley said, "was to create a name that epitomized the warrior class. The knights are the top of the line in terms of defending the realm, the unprotected. This is all part of the culture we want to create with the hockey team."

First came the local fallout. The negative reaction was almost universal. The locals couldn't see what "Golden Knights" had to do with Las Vegas—except perhaps for being a nod to Excalibur, the 4,000-room hotel-casino across the street from the home arena. Sports talk radio was full of head-scratchers and dissenters, both call-ins and talking heads.

Barry Petchesky, writing for Deadspin, the sports news and blog site, led the charge: "Too bland to be respectable, not whimsical enough to be memorable." Petchesky didn't like the idea of a modifier at all. "As a general rule, adjectives are minor league. 'Rays' is so much better than 'Devil Rays, and 'Ducks' infinitely preferable to 'Mighty Ducks.' I can see a future where they drop the 'Golden' and everyone is better off for it."

One wag commented, "Golden Knights sounds like a themed sex room at a bad Vegas hotel."

Then came antagonism from the Army, whose parachute team has been called the Golden Knights for 55 years and has performed in more than 16,000 shows.

As soon as Foley unveiled the name the Golden Knights, Army officials began "reviewing the situation." More than two years later in mid-January 2018, the Army requested that the U.S. Patent and Trademark Office deny the hockey team's trademark application.

An article in *The New York Times* quoted the request: "The hockey team's name and mark are confusingly similar in sound, meaning, and appearance to its own, the team's similar color scheme adds to the likelihood of confusion, and the Army would be damaged if the mark is registered, because it would falsely suggest a connection between the Army and the hockey team."

The VGK offered its rebuttal: "We strongly dispute the Army's allegations that confusion is likely between the Army Golden Knights parachute team and the Vegas Golden Knights major-league hockey team. Indeed, the two entities have been coexisting without any issues for over a year and we are not aware of a single complaint from anyone attending our games that they were expecting to see the parachute team and not a professional hockey game."

In the meantime, the VGK and the Army met to try and form a joint-use agreement, where both sides could continue to use the name.

Reportedly, the VGK cleared "Golden Knights" with Clarkson University in Potsdam, N.Y., the College of Saint Rose in Albany, New York, and the University of Central Florida, all of which use Golden Knights as the name of their athletic teams, which could support the Vegas team's contention that they can all co-exist without confusion.

At the same time that he unveiled the team name, Bill Foley also brandished the logo, designed by the Adidas graphics team: a slate-gray-and-gold medieval helmet superimposed on a gold-embroidered black background and a face protector that forms a "V" in the negative space.

This, too, received a fair amount of pushback, especially a little later when the team first displayed the uniform.

No less an arbiter of the national aesthetic than a fashion writer at the *Washington Post* summarized the reactions online: "It. Is. Hideous," and "The team hasn't played a game yet and already took its first 'L.'"

Deadspin damned it with faint praise in the headline, "The Vegas Golden Knights Uniforms Are Pretty OK." The short opinion piece concluded that they're "... so unflashy, they look like create-a-team jerseys from a video game."

"I don't know," a sports fan wrote in a comment box on Deadspin. "I have reservations about this team's willingness to fight hard for a championship, because that logo just isn't angry or snarly enough."

Steven Heller, former art director of *The New York Times* and co-founder of the New York City School of Visual Arts, disagreed with that comment. He wrote that the logo was "a tad menacing in a *Game of Thrones* sort of way and has a militancy, a kind of fascist quality to it." Still, Heller added, "It's a clever brand and a clever use of the icon. I can see it appealing to many people in and of itself, just on the strength of the image."

A Canadian marketing professor also defended the look. "Normally, it takes longer for a team to find that combination of performance and the right-looking logo that people are proud to wear. [The VGK] got it right from Day One."

GM George McPhee weighed in on the plus side. "It's

clean, it's symmetrical, it's kind of bold, and it stands for something."

Bill Foley further explained, "The goal was to create this logo and uniform based on strength and power. It represents going forward, never giving up."

Privately, no doubt, Foley and McPhee could live with whatever early criticism came their way, as merchandise and apparel sales, thanks to effective marketing and saturation distribution, were brisk from the start.

On April 13, 2017, George McPhee hired his head coach, Gerard Gallant.

One of 11 siblings, Gerard Gallant was dubbed "Turk" by a brother or two for his pastime as a toddler of running around the family basement, chasing turkeys raised by his uncle; to this day, that's what he prefers to be called, even by players. "I'm just Turk," says the 54-year-old VGK head coach. "Everywhere. Same guy in practice, on the bench, in the room, at home."

He was also known in his pro-hockey days as "Spuddy" or "Spudsy," having come from Prince Edward Island, the potato capital of Canada. Alex Pruitt, a writer for *Sports Illustrated*, commented, "Between Turk and Spuddy, the coach is some cranberry sauce short of a Thanksgiving dinner."

The Gallant mom, Rosie, ran the snack bar at the ice rink in Summerside, the town on PEI where the family lived; the story goes that Gerard and his friends swept the stands in exchange for extra ice time. He was remembered as a better-than-average skater and tough as they come. He played for four junior teams in Canada before he was drafted by the Detroit Red Wings in 1981 in the sixth round, 107th overall.

He appeared in his first American Hockey League game in 1983; only 19, he was the youngest skater on the Adirondack Red Wings. He was a rookie for the Detroit Red Wings in the 1984-1985 season. In December of the following season, Gallant's jaw was broken during a fight with Dirk Graham of the Minnesota North Stars; it had to be wired shut for six weeks. "I always felt that if I got in a fight in the first period, I had a better game," Gallant says. "And it was easy pickings back then — ten guys on every team who liked to fight." He fought in nearly 50 games between 1986 and 1989.

Playing mostly for the Red Wings and Tampa Bay Lightning, Gallant logged four seasons in a row with 30-plus goals and 200-plus penalty minutes. During his skating career, he amassed 480 points over 615 games and served 1,674 total penalty minutes, more than 80 full periods worth. After a career-ending back injury, he retired in 1995 at the age of 32.

Turk Gallant moved right into a new career behind the bench, returning to coach his hometown team, the Summerside Capitals, in the Junior Hockey League. He moved up to coaching in the majors: the International Hockey League in 1998, the American Hockey League in 1999, and finally the National Hockey League, starting as an assistant coach in 2000 for the Columbus Blue Jackets in their inaugural year. Gallant was named head coach of the Blue Jackets in

2004, then fired early in the 2006-2007 season. From there, he went to the New York Islanders as an assistant coach for two seasons.

After three seasons in the Quebec Major Junior Hockey League, Gallant spent another two seasons as an assistant coach with the Montreal Canadiens before being hired as the head coach of the Florida Panthers following the 2013-2014 season.

In the 2014-2015 season, the Panthers finished with a 47-26-9 record and made the playoffs for the first time in four years, though they lost in the first round. Gallant was also a finalist for the Jack Adams Award as the NHL's best coach that season. But after starting the 2016-2017 season with an 11-10-1 record, Gallant was fired. He later said that it wasn't a surprise; he didn't expect to make it until Christmas due to a management shakeup. But it was a somewhat ignominious sacking—Turk and his longtime assistant coach Mike Kelly were outside the Carolina Hurricanes' PNC Arena after a game, waiting for a chauffeured car that never arrived, which led to a well-known photo of him climbing into a taxi that he and Kelly had to flag down.

Gallant insists he's never changed as a coach. He speaks softly, if at all, during practices. He's considered calm and patient for a head coach, fair-minded and forgiving, but demanding of the players' work ethic. Players have to earn their ice team, so they realize it's nothing personal if they're benched. At the same time, he likes to see his team having fun. He rarely shows up in the locker room. He respects the players and doesn't embarrass anyone in public.

One interesting offshoot of his philosophy is that Gal-

Coach Gallant and the Florida Panthers

In his second year as the head coach of the Florida Panthers (2015-2016), Gerard Gallant led his team to a franchise-record 103 points and the second Atlantic Division title and fifth playoff appearance in its history. Gallant was also a finalist for the Jack Adams Award, given to the coach who most contributes to his team's success.

Twenty-two games into the following season, the Panthers had a winning record of 11-10-1 while battling key injuries since game one. After blowing a two-goal lead in a loss to the Carolina Hurricanes on the road in Raleigh, Coach Gallant was fired. It was reported at the time that Gallant and the Panthers' owners had a deep difference in philosophy: Gallant wanted bigger players; the front office wanted faster players. Gallant was literally kicked to the curb and had to hail a cab, then make his own way home from the road game.

Of course, Florida's trash turned out to be Vegas' treasure, as Coach Gallant's accomplishments with the Golden Knights were celebrated around the world and recognized by the NHL when he was selected as coach of the year and presented the Jack Adams Award. ♣

lant hates numbering his lines. Early in the season, he referred to what everyone else calls the "fourth" line as the "energy" line, which he wasn't afraid to match up against the top line of any opposing team. He knows what to expect from players and they know what to expect from him. Since he doesn't change, there are no surprises.

This was especially important when it came to coaching a team that began the season as an afterthought, a collection of players thrown together, literally dropped off at his door step, in hopes of winning a respectable number of games in their first year. And don't think he didn't use that, from the first day of training camp to the end of the Stanley Cup Finals, to incentivize 20-plus players, strangers in a strange land with bruised egos and no idea what system they'd be employing in their major-league games.

Obviously, as events later proved, Turk Gallant's system, and his style of coaching, took the team, the league, and the world not only by surprise, but by storm.

Meanwhile, back at the expansion draft ...

Like a professional Las Vegas "advantage player" who sits down at a casino game only when he has an edge, GM George McPhee tried to stay several moves ahead of his 30 counterparts. To fill out his 37-man roster, he chose — or had handed to him — hot young prospects with current credentials and future potential, strong veterans who could contribute to first-season success, low-ego team-oriented players who could provide a steady hand for an abandoned bunch of throwaways, and post-season stalwarts for whom playoff-bound teams might come calling as the trade deadline approached — or might help his own team make a deep run.

As the details of the deals emerged, the wheeling and

dealing looked like the world's largest single-table poker game, where the chips were unprotected players, existing contracts, entry-draft selections, free agency, salary caps, and trade fodder, with backroom maneuvering, behind-the-scenes intrigue, side deals, and subplots going on all over the figurative green felt.

McPhee also had aces in the hole and up his sleeve during the process, in a position to act as a middleman for teams that fancied a valuable unprotected player. He could select him in the draft, then flip him to the highest bidder. That thickened the plot with a revolving cast of characters—introducing them with the unstated intention of dealing them off immediately. No doubt McPhee also called some bluffs and picked some pockets by agreeing *not* to draft certain available players. At the same time, the expansion draft and deal-making left holes in the 30 teams, the filling of which necessitated even more arrangements and trades and transactions.

Oh, and a lot of this was going on before the Golden Knights were officially *in* the league, which didn't happen until March 1, 2017, after the last installment on the $500 million payment cleared the NHL's bank account. Until then, McPhee was making what were referred to as "gentlemen's agreements" and "agreements in principle." I can only imagine the scrambling to ink official deals before the trade deadline occurred at three p.m. *on the same day*. And all this involved just skaters. How many millions of *dollars* discreetly changed hands? Only the general manager in the midst of this maelstrom knows for sure.

The whole business assumed efficiencies in this unique

marketplace, but plain old miscalculation presumably called some of the shots too. Some teams gave up more than they needed to in order to protect overvalued players; others underestimated assets that they should have held in higher esteem. And the expansion situation surely laid bare any number of skeletons in NHL closets—grudges, resentments, grievances, feuds, personality conflicts, and all the baggage that comes into play in the politics of sports.

The real fun began on June 17, 2017, when the 30 teams released their official lists of players they were protecting in the expansion draft. The next day opened the Golden Knights' 72-hour window to pick their 30 players according to the NHL rules—a minimum of 14 forwards, nine defensemen, and three goalies.

"We kept having to get on the phone to talk to a team, then another team calls in and another team calls in," McPhee told Dan Rosen. "We were all taking notes, but we were talking to thirty teams and it was a real challenge to keep things in order, trying to remember what you said in your last conversation."

Early on June 21, the roster was finalized among the teams, but then the VGK had to call the players; those calls were made on the 20-minute ride from the office at City National to T-Mobile and the rehearsal for the NHL Awards show held live that night. "McPhee, McKrimmon, and Gallant split up the calls, but sometimes they called the same player twice," Dan Rosen wrote.

The VGK roster was announced on national TV and in front of 10,000 fans at the show held at T-Mobile. From there, McPhee and company boarded a chartered flight to

Chicago, where they started preparing for the NHL Entry-Draft, held on June 23 and 24, from which they made 12 selections, including three first-round picks.

"There was a lot of pressure there," McPhee commented, in what might have been the understatement of the Vegas Golden Knights inaugural year.

So, who were these players, anyway?

Chapter 2
The Players

How do hockey players, or participants in any sport for that matter, feel about being exposed by the team they play for in an expansion draft? It's often difficult to discern the truth from spin, in which professional athletes — and most people in the public eye — are expert, but it's not hard to imagine all the conflicting emotions they must feel.

Some, no doubt, are pleased and relieved that they'll have a chance to move to a new team and be given the opportunity to shine in a way that's been limited with the organization for which they're now playing. But most, I suspect, see it in the opposite way. They're aggrieved that their team considers them expendable; they fear they'll be playing for a typical losing expansion team; they have to learn a brand new system with a couple dozen other guys they don't know and who don't know the system either; and they might have roots in their existing city and don't want to uproot themselves and their families by moving to a whole new scene.

And what about the players exposed to the draft and not selected? Now they're left, perhaps, in the most precarious position of all: The old team can do without them, but the new team doesn't want them.

And how, George McPhee had to wonder as he mulled over his selections—one player from each team, so many goalies, so many defensemen, and so many centers and wings—would his drafted players feel about moving to Las Vegas?

In his press conference addressing the draft, McPhee provided a little preview of his sales pitch to the players he wanted: a state with no income tax and a city with nice weather in hockey season; an easy commute to the practice and game arenas, both brand new state-of-the-art hockey facilities; a fun city in which to live; and rabid support from 16,000-plus fans who cared enough about their city's first professional sports team to lay down deposits on four-figure season tickets long before anyone could be sure that Las Vegas would even get the team. Still, the new general manager painted a picture in which his players would be as comfortable as possible, so they could focus on playing well and winning.

After the draft as the team started coming together, the Vegas Golden Knights consisted of some Nashville (James Neal), Pittsburgh (Marc-André Fleury), New York (Oscar Lindberg), D.C. (Nate Schmidt), Detroit (Tomas Nosek), Florida (Jonathan Marchessault), Vancouver (Luca Sbisa), L.A. (Brayden McNabb), Buffalo (William Carrier), Dallas

(Cody Eakin), and Calgary (Deryk Engelland).

That was a big part of what made this team Las Vegas' team: It's a lot like the melting pot that Las Vegas itself has always been. Ever since the first criminal casino owners and operators, from New York, Chicago, Kansas City, L.A., Saratoga Springs, Miami, and dozens of other gambling hot spots, turned legitimate once they crossed the Nevada state line where gambling was legal, people from around the country and the world have gravitated to Sin City for excitement and action, opportunity and possibility, a place to start over and reinvent themselves. And now it would do the same for, of all things, major-league hockey players.

The team's core skaters are profiled in this chapter alphabetically. I'd never presume to order such a cohesive unit in any other way.

Among the top three oldest players on the Vegas Golden Knights at 33, Pierre-Édouard Bellemare was born in Paris and began his professional career in France before playing in the Swedish Hockey League from 2006 to 2013. He's fluent in French, Swedish, and English.

He was signed by the Philadelphia Flyers in June 2014; he played in Philly for three seasons, appearing in five play-off games in 2016 with the Flyers. He was picked up by the VGK when Philadelphia exposed him to the draft.

Bellemare was extremely popular with his teammates and as a locker room leader all season long, he earned an

"A" (for alternate captain; the team had six alternates and no "C" for captain) on his jersey. He could always be seen before games pumping up his teammates, and after games congratulating them on victories on their way off the ice. His penalty-killing and shot-blocking skills were an integral piece of the success of the Golden Knights.

Pierre-Éduourd and his wife Hannah had their first child, a son named LeAndré, in January 2018; he missed the Knights' two-game road trip to St. Louis and Chicago for the event.

Ryan Carpenter, 27, was one of only four Americans on the Golden Knights. He played for Bowling Green State University in Ohio; he was named Rookie of the Year on the team. He signed as an undrafted free agent with the San Jose Sharks in 2014 and played that season in the American Hockey League for the San Jose Barracuda, where he led the team in points and assists and earned the AHL's Yanick Dupre Memorial Award for community service. Carpenter made his NHL debut in 2015 with the Sharks, which gave him a two-year $1.3 million contract six months before he was placed on waivers (San Jose made his contract available to any takers) and was immediately grabbed up by the Golden Knights.

Carpenter was one of the VGK's few players who didn't begin the season with the team. He was also a healthy scratch for a number of games as he learned the system and tried to find his place. He seized an early opportunity and earned a place in the regular rotation, scoring six goals in nine games. His game cooled off a bit in the latter part of the season, but he scored nine goals and earned 13 points over his last 22 games. Awesome for a waiver pickup!

Twenty-four-year-old William Carrier comes from Quebec and played in the Quebec Major Junior Hockey League from 2010 to 2013, when he was drafted in the second round, the 57th overall pick, by the St. Louis Blues. He was traded to the Buffalo Sabres in 2016, made his NHL debut in November of that year, and scored his first goal that month. Left exposed by the Sabres, he signed with the Golden Knights in the expansion draft.

Carrier has top-end speed and was the most physical player on the team until Ryan Reaves was acquired at the trade deadline. He missed some games due to injury, but on the ice, he made his presence felt, pursuing the puck and landing glass-shaking checks. His physicality was on full display in the postseason during the sweep of the L.A. Kings.

You can pick out Cody Eakin pretty easily; he stands out with bright red hair. Now 26, Eakin comes from Winnipeg.

His father played professional hockey before becoming a police officer. His uncle lasted 18 seasons as a pro, mostly in Europe; he appeared in 13 NHL games for the Detroit Red Wings in 1985-1986, where he was a teammate of Gerard Gallant.

Cody played major junior hockey in the Western Hockey League from 2006 to 2011, with a couple stints in the American Hockey League in the Washington Capitals organization (he was drafted by George McPhee). He made his NHL debut with the Capitals in November 2011 and scored his first goal three days later against the Carolina Hurricanes.

The next year, he was traded to Dallas and spent the next five years playing for the Stars. The center had two 16-goal 19-assist seasons (2013-2014, 2015-2016); he also scored 19 goals and earned 40 points (2014-2015). In the 2016-2017 season, he played less due to injury and what was considered inconsistency and scored only three goals. In 2015, Eakin was also a member of Canada's team at the World Championships; the team went 10-0 and won the gold medal.

Eakin was exposed to the expansion draft by Dallas and acquired by the VGK. He appeared in 80 games for the Golden Knights in their inaugural season.

At 36, Deryk Engelland was definitely the elder statesman on the Vegas Golden Knights, having played in the NHL for 18 years. Indeed, midway through the 2017-2018 season, he celebrated his 500th career NHL game. It was even

The Salary Cap

The salary cap in the NHL is similar to those in the other major-league sports. The cap numbers and details vary, but the premise is exactly the same. A limit is placed on player salaries to prevent richer teams, usually those in larger markets, from throwing money at the best performers, giving them an unfair advantage over the teams in smaller markets.

Since George McPhee was starting from scratch, he wanted to protect the VGK's enviable position of being far below the NHL's $75 million team ceiling. In addition, he couldn't predict how his misfits would crystallize. As such, one of his key strategies, reportedly, was to leave himself a fair amount of wiggle room by limiting his player contracts to a year or two, so as not to saddle the VGK with expensive long-term commitments.

Then he ran into a problem that NHL general managers dream about: The team gelled so solidly under Gerard Gallant's coaching style that McPhee saw the wisdom of holding the team together. As early as Thanksgiving, he signed Brayden McNabb to a four-year contract. In January, he locked up Jonathan Marchessault for six years. After his breakout year, William Karlsson will no doubt receive a hefty offer to remain in Vegas, as will a number of other core players who become free agents when their one-year contracts expire.

"Winners get paid," wrote Carol Schram of *Forbes*. "It may not be long before the Golden Knights find themselves struggling with the same salary-cap issues that plagued the Chicago Blackhawks after their young team won a championship in 2010." ❖

more impressive, considering he also played more than 500 games in the American Hockey League.

Engelland, who comes from Edmonton, played in the World Hockey League (Moose Jaw Warriors), the American Hockey League (Lowell Lock Monsters, Hershey Bears, Reading Royals, and Wilkes-Barre/Scranton Penguins), the ECHL (Las Vegas Wranglers), and even the GET (Rosenborg, Norway) before arriving at the National Hockey League (Pittsburgh Penguins) in the 2009-10 season. He played for the Penguins, in a limited role, for five seasons, then spent another three with the Calgary Flames. His three-year contract was expiring, so the Flames exposed him to the expansion draft.

When Vegas selected him, some thought it was just a sentimental pick, given that Engelland lives in Vegas where he met his wife and played for the Las Vegas Wranglers. However, George McPhee knew he was getting a solid penalty killer in the defenseman, who has no problem sticking up for his teammates when things get hairy.

With the VGK, Engelland had a career year in assists, points, and shots on goal, proving that his game had evolved offensively in addition to being a valuable defenseman. He was also a mentor to his young defensive partner, Shea Theodore. The two developed into a solid pairing, who often found themselves on the ice during crucial moments in a game. And he became the face and, in some respects, soul of the team, when he asked if he could deliver the opening-night speech. His teammates selected him to accept the Western Conference Championship trophy; he was also personally nominated by the Knights for two leadership awards, the King Clancy Memorial Trophy and the Mark Messier Award.He won the Messier.

Nineteen-year-old Dylan Ferguson was the youngest player to see ice time for the VGK in its inaugural season.

Born in Vancouver and raised on Vancouver Island, he played in the Saskatoon Midget Hockey League in the 2012 though 2015 seasons before being drafted by the Kamloops Blazers in the World Hockey League (166th overall). In 2017, Ferguson was selected 194th overall by the Dallas Stars in the NHL entry draft, but two days later, he was traded to the Vegas Golden Knights and signed a three-year entry-level contract as the fifth-string goaltender.

Who knew that Ferguson would get called up as Max Lagacé's backup after Marc-Andre Fleury, Malcolm Subban, and Oscar Dansk were all injured in a 10-game stretch? He appeared in one game during the season, in which the VGK were losing to the Edmonton Oilers 7-2; he played for nine minutes and gave up one goal on two shots. The shot he stopped was by NHL superstar Connor McDavid; barely 21 himself, McDavid reportedly said to Ferguson, "Nice stop, kid."

Ferguson was sent back down to Kamloops when Malcolm Subban was re-activated.

Not quite as vintage as Engelland at 33, Marc-André Fleury is, nonetheless, one of the NHL's best-known veterans. He comes from Quebec, where he met Véronique Larosée when they were 15; they've been together ever since and have two daughters, five and three. Of all the names Vegas announced on expansion-draft day, Marc-André Fleury was certainly the most notable and received the largest ovation.

Fleury played a few years in the junior majors in Canada; in the 2002-2003 season, he played so well that he was the first pick overall in the 2003 entry draft, acquired by the Pittsburgh Penguins. His 13-year career in Pittsburgh is the stuff of legend, winning the Stanley Cup in 2009 and back-to-back in 2016 and 2017, though in the 2016-2017 season, he shared goalie responsibilities with Matt Murray.

Just hours before the trade deadline in 2017, Fleury waived his no-trade clause, knowing it almost certainly meant that he'd be selected by the Vegas Golden Knights in the expansion draft. He spent the rest of the season as the Penguins' number-two netminder, though he played a big part in Pittsburgh's second consecutive Cup. He hoisted it in his last game for Pittsburgh.

After being drafted by Vegas, Fleury penned an article for *The Players Tribune*. In it, he expressed his deepest gratitude to the Penguins and the city of Pittsburgh. He also mentioned being excited about the next step in his career with the Golden Knights—though many pundits and fans believed Fleury would fade into obscurity in the midst of expansion-team woes. Then came the VGK's first game in Dallas, where the superstar goalie stopped 45 of 46 shots on the way to a 2-1 victory.

Fleury led Vegas to two more victories before the VGK's first loss to the Detroit Red Wings. In that game, he was run over by Anthony Mantha during a rush to the goal and suffered a concussion that kept him out for the next 25 games. Surely, this would spell the end of the Golden Knights' season, right? Wrong. In a combined effort from Malcom Subban, Oscar Dansk, Max Lagacé, and emergency backup Dylan Ferguson, Vegas surprised the world by going 16-8-1 during Fleury's absence.

The number-one goalie returned to action in a losing effort in overtime against the Carolina Hurricanes, but posted a quality performance, stopping 35 of 37 shots. Fleury's return to action came just in time, as the VGK's next game was against the Penguins in Vegas. He faced only 25 shots in the game, stopping 24 of them and leading his Golden Knights to an emotional victory over his former team.

The next five days saw two more big games, starting with a victory over the Florida Panthers (Coach Gallant's former team), then the first-place Tampa Bay Lightning. Fleury was back in top form.

In the remaining months of the season, Fleury played the best (statistical) hockey of his life. When the regular season ended, he boasted a 2.24 goals-against average and a .927 save percentage, both career highs.

When the Golden Knights entered the playoffs, they

faced the Kings in Round 1. Pundits proclaimed that the playoff and Stanley Cup experience of the Kings was sure to be the demise of the Fleury-led Knights in their inaugural season. Instead, the VGK goalie somehow got even better. During the four-game sweep, he posted two shutouts and the second best statistical series by any goalie (behind only Pekka Rinne) in NHL post-season history, with an unreal save percentage of .977 and a 0.66 goals-against-average.

He continued his playoff success in the Knights' next series against the San Jose Sharks, with two more shutouts, one of them coming in the series-clinching Game 6 in the Shark Tank. As soon as the Pittsburgh Penguins were eliminated by the Washington Capitals in Game 7 of their second-round playoff series, many Pittsburgh fans immediately switched allegiances to Marc-André Fleury's new team.

He continued to roll against the Winnipeg Jets in the Western Conference Final, where he posted a 1.50 goals against and a .956 save percentage.

Alas, Fleury's otherworldly postseason effort could not carry through the Stanley Cup Final, as Washington seemed to do what no one else could: get pucks into the Flower's net. In his postgame interview following the Cup-clinching loss, Fleury notably apologized to the Vegas fan base for not being able to bring home the championship. Of course, the city of Las Vegas and Golden Knights fans everywhere knew that Marc-André had nothing to apologize for after setting career numbers for himself and leading the most successful expansion team in history. Indeed, the VGK signed him to a three-year $21 million contract extension.

Erik Haula, 27, comes from Finland. He came to the U.S. to attend Shattuck-Saint Mary's, a 160-year-old boarding school in Faribault, Minnesota, where he had a strong season on the hockey team. From there, he went to play for the U.S. Hockey League in Omaha, where he was named to the All-Rookie and All-Star teams. He attended the University of Minnesota for three years, skipping his senior year after being drafted (seventh round, 182nd overall) by the Minnesota Wild as a freshman.

Haula spent five seasons with the Wild, appearing in all 13 of their playoff games, helping them get to the second round for only the second time in franchise history. When it came time for the expansion draft, though, the Wild knew they were going to lose a quality asset, as veteran center Eric Staal and young defenseman Matt Dumba were exposed to the draft, along with Haula. Haula agreed to a three-year $8.25 million contract with the VGK to become the required pick from Minnesota; the Wild sweetened the deal for Haula by offering prospect Alex Tuch, steering the Knights away from Staal and Dumba.

This worked out well for Vegas, as Haula established himself early in the season as the team's second-line center. He proved himself much more than simply a quality asset, scoring 29 goals, second only to William Karlsson. Haula's goal total, like many of the other players on the team, shattered his previous high of 15 goals in a season. Erik also led the team in third-period goals, making plays when they needed to be made.

In Game 2 against the L.A. Kings, Tuch scored the first goal for Vegas. With less than five minutes remaining in the second overtime, Haula scored a goal off of what looked like a broken play to put the Kings away 2-1, en route to the clean sweep. Thank you, Minnesota Wild!

Thirty-year-old defenseman Brad Hunt comes from British Columbia. He played college hockey for Bemidji State University in Minnesota, where he went to two NCAA tournaments, which included advancing to the Frozen Four in 2009; he also earned several individual awards. He played for the Chicago Wolves, Oklahoma City Barons, and Bakersfield Condors in the American Hockey League and the St. Louis Blues, Edmonton Oilers, and Nashville Predators in the NHL. He then signed as a free agent with the VGK.

Hunt had an outstanding game against the Columbus Blue Jackets on January 23, picking up two assists and scoring his first goal of the season. With that goal, every VGK on the roster had tallied at least one.

Expansion drafts usually mean second, or even third, chances for NHL players. No one seized that chance with more vigor than 25-year-old Lars William Karlsson who hails from Marsta, Sweden. In two full seasons with Columbus, "Wild Bill" was a bottom-six, penalty-kill, and second-unit power-play forward. In those two seasons, he scored a combined 15 goals.

When he came to Vegas, Karlsson worked his way up to the top line and on the team's first power-play unit. With the increased ice time, he had a breakout season, scoring a stunning 43 goals—more than seven times his previous season total of six. Only Alex Ovechkin and Patrik Laine scored more goals in 2017-2018.

Of those 43 goals, four were scored when Vegas was down a man. One of those was among the best goals of the season in the league, an incredible shot between his own legs at full speed, completely fooling San Jose Sharks' goalie Martin Jones.

By the end of the season, Karlsson also led the league in +/- with +49, followed by his linemates Jonathan Marchessault and Reilly Smith, who were numbers two and three,

---

What Do the Plus and Minus Scoring Symbols Mean?

The +/- system is a way of tracking the effect both offensive and defensive players have on a game (you'll often hear references made to a player's "rating"). A player is awarded a + if he's on the ice when his team scores at even strength or shorthanded. A - is given to a player who's on the ice when the opposing team scores at even strength or shorthanded. ❖

respectively, proving the dominance of Vegas' top line.

Karlsson played in the Swedish Hockey League from 2009 to 2014 and was drafted by the Anaheim Ducks in 2011 in the second round, 53rd overall, but didn't make his NHL debut for the Ducks until October 2013, scoring his first and second goals in his second game. Toward the end of the 2014-15 season, he was traded to the Columbus Blue Jackets.

Due to the completeness of Karlsson's game, many observers questioned how such a player lay dormant in Columbus for years prior. Some say he didn't get enough ice time in Ohio. But it may well have been the chemistry of the Knights, with Karlsson fitting perfectly.

His regular-season success carried through to the playoffs, where he scored another seven goals. It wasn't a league-leading number, compared to Alex Ovechkin's 15 and Winnipeg's Mark Scheifele's 14. Vegas, though, was getting more scoring contributions from the rest of the team, while Scheifele accounted for 35% of his team's scoring.

William Karlsson epitomized the mentality of an expansion team. He seized his opportunity and proved himself to be a star-caliber player in all facets of the game. He even popularized the phrase the "Golden Misfits," referring to his castoff teammates coming together for a history-making season. Karlsson was credited throughout the year with originating the moniker, but at the Awards ceremony following the season, he told a reporter that James Neal came up with it.

Originally from Quebec, 25-year-old Maxime Lagacé played for four teams in the Quebec Major Junior Hockey League from 2010 to 2014 before moving to the American Hockey League and the Texas Stars; he'd been signed by the Dallas organization a couple years earlier. He played in the ECHL for a couple of years and was acquired by the Vegas Golden Knights as a free agent. He was assigned to the VGK affiliate Chicago Wolves as the Knights' fourth-string goaltender—until he was activated twice in October when Fleury and Subban were injured. He played his first NHL game on October 30 and started his first game the following night.

Lagacé played in 16 games for the VGK and wound up with a record of 6-7-1, quite respectable for a goalie who started the season so far down on the depth chart.

Swede Oscar Lindberg, 27, played hockey in his native country from 2008 to 2013. He was drafted in the 2011 NHL entry draft (57th overall) and moved up to the American Hockey League's Hartford Wolf Pack in 2013, where he spent two seasons. He was traded to the New York Rangers in 2015; he scored his first goal in his first game on opening night.

The Rangers exposed Lindberg to the expansion draft

in 2017 and he was picked up by the Golden Knights. He scored his first goal as a VGK center in the home opener.

In late February, Lindberg was blindsided by Kyle Clifford of the L.A. Kings as he was skating to the bench away from the play; he didn't return for a month. He scored a goal in the last home game of the season against the San Jose Sharks, his first since December 23, then another two games later against the Edmonton Oilers, his ninth of the season.

Yet another VGK player from Quebec, 27-year-old Jonathan Marchessault started playing in the Quebec Major Junior Hockey League as a 16-year-old, drafted in the 12th round. He remained with the Quebec Remparts for four seasons, where he led the league in game-winning goals. Undrafted, he was signed by the New York Rangers and played for their AHL affiliate, the Connecticut Whale. After one season, he signed an entry-level contract with the Columbus Blue Jackets, got traded to the Tampa Bay Lightning where he appeared in two Stanley Cup playoff games, and wound up with the Florida Panthers in 2016-2017, playing for Gerard Gallant; it was his first full season in the NHL.

Marchessault had a breakout year for the Panthers, scoring 30 goals to lead the team. Somehow, that didn't earn him protection in the expansion draft. Did the Panthers believe that his season was a fluke, an anomaly that he couldn't repeat? Florida actually offered up their sixth-leading scorer, Reilly Smith, to Vegas as incentive to take the smallish (five-foot-nine) Marchessault off their hands.

In hindsight, it seems like an inexplicably bad move, but the Panthers had their reasons. They were under new management (the same new management that fired Gallant) and were rebuilding a new system, into which Marchessault apparently didn't fit.

All the better for the Golden Knights, where Marchessault became a top-line forward, along with Reilly Smith. He scored 27 goals and more than doubled his previous year's assist total, giving him a career high point total of 75. "Marchy" also led the team in shots on goal, with 60 shots more than James Neal, who was second. Even untrained eyes could see Jonathan perpetually chasing the puck or working it off the boards—one of the hardest workers on the ice.

The Lucky Lambo

In a promotional arrangement with Lamborghini Las Vegas, Jonathan Marchessault drove a $550,000 Lamborghini Aventador Roadster convertible to home playoff games, starting with Round 2 Game 5 against the San Jose Sharks. The sports car, adorned with the team logo on the hood and the doors, was dropped off at his house in the morning before a game, then picked up the morning after.

After winning the first game Marchessault drove to, the VGK continued the streak in Round 3 Games 3 and 4 versus the Winnipeg Jets, and on to Game 1 in the Stanley Cup Final. The VGK started out at 4-0 when Marchy drove the Lambo—but then the streak ended. ❖

Marchessault is married to former makeup artist Alexandra Gravel, with whom he has three children.

Midway through the VGK's first season, Marchessault signed a six-year contract extension that increased his salary by a factor of five. It was the Quebec native's first major contract, well-deserved as he led the team in post-season goals.

You can't miss 27-year old Brayden McNabb; at six-four and 220 pounds, the defenseman definitely stands out on the ice.

He hails originally from Saskatchewan and played for five seasons with the Kootenay Ice in the World Hockey League. He was drafted in 2009 by the Buffalo Sabres (third round, 66th overall) and bounced between the Sabres and the American Hockey League's Rochester Americans before being traded to the L.A. Kings in 2014.

McNabb was drafted by the Golden Knights and became half of the top defensive pairing with Nate Schmidt. He earned that spot with his physicality as much as his heads-up play; he was known for clearing traffic in front of his own net, manhandling potential scorers out of their position, and jumping on rebounds with surprising quickness.

McNabb is less of an offensive weapon, but he did score a career-high five goals in the Golden Knights' inaugural season, more than doubling his previous high total of two.

In fact, he scored the winning goal in Game 4 against his former team, the L.A. Kings, to clinch the first-round playoff series. On defense, he also shattered his previous career high for blocked shots with a whopping 176 — the only player in the league to surpass 170 blocked shots *and* hits (225).

McNabb was the first player to sign an extension with the Golden Knights after the season began, receiving $10 million for another four years.

One of the few Americans on the team, 26-year-old Jon Merrill grew up in Michigan, where he played with the U.S. National Development Team as a teenager, then attended the University of Michigan, playing for the Wolverines. Drafted by the New Jersey Devils (second round, 38th overall) in 2010, he spent two seasons with the affiliate Albany Devils, then New Jersey for four. Young six-three 200-pound defensemen are a prime asset in the NHL, so he was picked up in the expansion draft. Due to injury and a crowded blue-line group, Merrill played in just 34 VGK games during the regular season.

In Round 1 of the playoffs, the L.A. Kings seemed to target Merrill with some of their physicality — maybe they saw something in him they thought they could exploit. Merrill responded with strong play, perhaps better than he'd played all year. He was taken out of the lineup in the second round against the Sharks, but Vegas knew what they had with Merrill, which is why they signed him to a two-year extension during the season.

Colin Miller comes from Sault Ste. Marie, Ontario, where he also played three seasons for the local Greyhounds in the Ontario Hockey League. A high-scoring defenseman with 20 goals in his third season, Miller was drafted in 2012 by the L.A. Kings (fifth round, 151st overall), then spent two years with the Manchester Monarchs in the American Hockey League.

He was traded to Boston in 2015. When it came time for Vegas to select a Bruins player in the expansion draft, they selected Miller, whose stats had improved in his second season. George McPhee (correctly) believed he could be even better with increased ice time and more responsibility.

Miller is not only fast (he won the fastest-skater competition in the AHL All Star skills competition in 2015), he can outmaneuver even veteran skaters. He also set an event record for the hardest slap shot, at 105.5 mph.

That shot came in handy as he was the leading goal scorer among VGK defensemen with 10. He was also fourth on the team in shots on goal, behind Marchessault, Neal, and Karlsson, respectively. His speed, skating ability, and rocket shot led to Miller finding himself on the ice in power-play situations and other crucial moments in all 82 games during the regular 2017-2018 season.

Miller signed a four-year $15.5 million contract to

remain with the Knights through 2023; the deal included a no-trade clause for seasons three and four.

Also from Ontario and having played for the Ontario Hockey League, 31-year-old James Neal was drafted in 2005 by the Dallas Stars after his rookie season with the OHL's Plymouth Whalers (second round, 33rd overall). He remained with the Whalers for the next couple of seasons, then played with the Dallas-affiliate Iowa Stars in 2007-2008, moving up to the NHL in 2008-2009.

Neal set rookie records, signed a big contract, and continued to improve with Dallas for two more years. He was traded to the Pittsburgh Penguins for the 2010-2011 season, where he saw 38 playoff games in his four seasons. Traded to the Nashville Predators, Neal played in 42 post-season games over his three-year stint in Tennessee.

When the expansion draft was said and done, James Neal was one of the few names on the list with a history of scoring goals. He could be called a journeyman, but even with six team changes in 10 years, he scored at least 20 goals in each season (with the exception of 2010-2011, when he played in only 20 games).

Expected to be the lone bright spot in the Vegas offense, Neal was nonetheless seemingly destined to be traded away before the deadline to help build for the future. In fact, as early as November, Neal altered the no-trade clause in his contract to listing eight teams he wouldn't agree to be traded to. It looked like the team was getting ready to move Neal and he was helping them do so. But the team's Cup drive made it essential to hang onto him for his talent and invaluable playoff experience.

Czech Tomas Nosek played in his country's top league for three years before signing on with the Grand Rapid Griffins in the American Hockey League for two seasons. He bounced between the Griffins and the Detroit Red Wings in 2016-17 and apparently caught the attention of the Vegas Golden Knights by his stellar play in helping lead the Griffins to become the 2017 Calder Cup champions.

Nosek scored the first-ever goal inside T-Mobile Arena in the emotion-packed home opener against the Arizona Coyotes. He also scored an important goal in the post-season against the Winnipeg Jets. The goal came after he'd made a costly mistake and spent time in the penalty box. He also scored two goals in the VGK's Game 1 Stanley Cup Finals victory.

Thirty-year-old David Perron spent a year in the Quebec Juniors and one in the Quebec Major Juniors before being drafted in the first round, 26th overall, by the St. Louis

Blues in 2007; he played in his first NHL game at the age of 19, just three years after playing at the Midget B level in the Quebec town where he grew up.

The first half of his career was spent in St. Louis. Since 2013, he'd been used as trade bait, playing on a different team every year, sometimes two. He played for the Oilers, the Penguins, and the Ducks, before winding up back with the Blues. When Perron found out he was coming to Vegas in the expansion draft, he relished the opportunity to try to fit in somewhere new.

And fit he did. Perron set career-high numbers in both assists and points, joining a slew of other VGK with career highs. Four of his 16 goals were game winners and three came in overtime.

In an article he penned for *The Players Tribune* that ran in December 2017, Perron wrote that he'd texted an old teammate who he knew would also be selected by the expansion team.

The text said, *Vegas?*

Marc-André Fleury replied, *Vegas!!*

David Perron's longtime girlfriend is Vanessa Vandal, one of the co-stars on the three-season Quebecois reality-TV series "Hockey Wives" (*"Mariées au Hockey"*); they have two children.

She says, "The hockey life is intense. My schedule is dictated by David's. They have practice, meetings, physical treatment, travel, games, charities, and events, plus they have to rest their bodies, so there's not much time for anything else."

Brandon Pirri comes from Toronto. He played in the Ontario Juniors before attending Rensselaer Polytechnic Institute in Troy, New York, where he was on the RPI Engineers in the NCAA. He was selected in the second round, 59th overall, by the Chicago Blackhawks in 2009. He bounced between the NHL and AHL for four seasons before being traded to the Florida Panthers; he also played for the Anaheim Ducks and New York Rangers.

Pirri signed a one-year deal as a free agent with the Golden Knights at the start of the inaugural season. He spent most of it playing for the AHL affiliate Chicago Wolves. Called up at the tail end of the season, Pirri showed up big by scoring three goals in two games.

Ryan Reaves, 31, is from Winnipeg, Manitoba. At six-one and 225 pounds, he's a physical force to be reckoned with and is known as an enforcer on the ice. In fact, he was voted toughest in the entire NHL by the players themselves.

He played for a number of years in the Western and American Hockey Leagues and was drafted in 2005 by the St. Louis Blues (fifth round, 156th overall). After seven seasons with the Blues, he was acquired by the Pittsburgh Penguins, brought onboard to ride shotgun for two-time league MVP Sidney Crosby. In the 2016-2017 playoffs during the Penguins run to winning the Cup for the second year in a row, Crosby took a lot of physical abuse and Reaves filled the bill in addressing that.

To give Pittsburgh a fighting, so to speak, chance in their run at a third successive Stanley Cup, the Penguins went after Derrick Brassard, who was playing for the Ottawa Senators. Right before the trade deadline, the Penguins, Senators, and Golden Knights made a three-team deal in which, among other players and draft picks, Brassard made a brief stop with the VGK, which picked up 40% of his salary in order for Pittsburgh to remain under the cap, while Reaves went from the Penguins to the Knights.

Reaves was in a number of skirmishes, but it was more about the intimidation factor; just the presence of a player like Reaves can be a major deterrent when it comes to opposing players getting out of line.

Reaves scored the game-winning and series-clinching goal in the Western Conference Final against the Jets in his hometown of Winnipeg. Before the team traveled to Winnipeg, Reaves was asked about playing in front of his family and friends. He said most of his friends and some of his family would be wearing Jets jerseys, and followed with, "I'm going to have some stuff to take care of when I get back to Winnipeg." That, he did.

Twenty-eight-year-old defenseman Luca Sbisa is perhaps the most international of all the VGK players: born in

Italy; raised in Switzerland where he saw his first hockey game at three and played for the same team as a teenager; played major junior in Canada; spent time in Philadelphia, Anaheim, and Vancouver in the NHL before being picked up in the expansion draft by the VGK; and even climbed Mount Kilimanjaro with his British Columbian wife, Lauren Anaka Sbisa. Oh, and he speaks four languages. If the old joke about all hockey players being bilingual, English and profanity, is true, then make that five languages for Sbisa.

Luca didn't play that much in the VGK's first season after sustaining injuries; he scored two goals and had 12 assists in his 30 appearances during the regular season. He came back for the playoffs and saw action in most of the games.

Nate Schmidt is a 26-year-old American defenseman hailing from St. Cloud, Minnesota. He played high school hockey in St. Cloud, U.S. junior hockey for the U.S. Hockey League in Fargo, North Dakota, and college hockey for the U. of Minnesota Golden Gophers. He was signed as an undrafted free agent by the Washington Capitals in 2013 and spent two seasons in the American Hockey League, then four seasons with the Capitals.

Going undrafted, then unprotected by Washington in the expansion draft, led to Schmidt being greatly under-rated. George McPhee recognized it and snatched him up, though he and the team had to go to arbitration to settle the contract details: two years at $2.23 million each, more than doubling his salary with the Capitals.

Coach Gallant put him in the top pairing of blue-liners for the Golden Knights. Over the course of the season, Schmidt evolved into a reliable and multi-faceted defenseman. He earned 36 points in Vegas' inaugural season, more than double his highest point total in Washington. He also showcased his skating ability on a level that he never had before. His speed and puck-moving skills were another surprise from an expansion player. His end-to-end rushes were regularly praised by analysts when the Knights had national attention during the playoffs.

Along with his partner Brayden McNabb, Schmidt often played against the opposing team's first line, where he consistently shut down scoring chances by some of the top players in the league. When he wasn't outskating the opposition, he was knocking the other team's forwards off the puck; he was among the VGK's top shutdown defensemen, usually assigned to play against the opposing team's top line, making his +19 rating all the more impressive. The post-season solidified Schmidt's position. He appeared in all 20 games, scored three goals, and added four assists.

His fun-loving attitude and charisma shined through in interviews and appearances and made Nate Schmidt one of the faces of the franchise.

Reilly Smith, 27, played in the Greater Toronto and Ontario Junior hockey leagues, then at Miami University for three seasons. He was drafted by the Dallas Stars in 2009 (third round, 69th overall), was traded to the Boston Bruins for two seasons, and wound up back in Florida playing for the Panthers.

After two full seasons with the Panthers, Smith had proven himself to be a reliable forward with good instincts. His availability in the expansion draft hinted at the $3.5 million salary cap over the five years left on his contract. Both Smith and Marchessault, with whom he was traded to the Knights, had played under Coach Gallant with the Panthers.

Smith and Marchessault, along with William Karlsson, quickly became the VGK's top line. Their chemistry and prowess for getting the puck to the net proved to be a recipe for success. Reilly didn't show up on the stat sheet quite as much as his line mates, but many of the scoring chances came from plays he created in the opposing or neutral zones. Early in the season, teammates and analysts cited Smith as the MVP of the team for the completeness of his game and his ability to find and put his teammates in scoring positions.

Perhaps the best example of his complete game was seen in February in Winnipeg. Smith knocked Jets captain Blake Wheeler to the ice in the Jets' zone, took control of the puck, and scored an impressive shorthanded goal. He also exhibited an uncanny ability to find his teammates in scoring positions during the playoffs, leading the team in assists and playing a large part in their post-season success.

Smith also had the bittersweet distinction of scoring the last goal of the Golden Knights' season, against Washington in Game 5 of the Stanley Cup Final.

Yet another Toronto native, six-two, 220-pound, 24-year-old Malcolm Subban grew up in a hockey (and basketball) family and played in the Ontario Major Junior League for four seasons. In 2012, Subban was drafted in the first round, the 24th overall pick, by the Boston Bruins. He remained in the Bruins organization through 2017, though he played in only a few NHL games over the years and bounced back and forth between the Boston and Providence (AHL) Bruins.

Subban was claimed off waivers by the Golden Knights. He replaced Calvin Pickard, the VGK's first pick in the expansion draft from the Colorado Avalanche; Pickard was then waived and wound up with the Toronto Maple Leafs. Subban arrived in Vegas just in time for the season to begin as the backup goalie behind Marc-André Fleury.

Though essentially untested at the NHL level, Subban was thrust into the number-one spot early on after Fleury suffered an injury in the Knights' fourth game. He started the next several games, winning them all, until he himself caught the injury bug.

When he came back, he looked better than ever and kept the team strong until the return of the Flower. He ended the season with a 13-4-2 record in net.

His older brother PK Subban plays for the Nashville Predators; they faced each other in a game on December 8, 2017, where Malcolm made a career-high 41 saves and the VGK beat the Predators 4–3.

Another player with an international resumé, 27-year-old Tomas Tatar comes from Czechoslovakia. He played for junior and senior Slovak teams until he was the 60th draft choice overall of the Detroit Red Wings. He trained for a couple of seasons in the Red Wings AHL affiliate in Grand Rapids, then played in almost every game for four seasons with the Wings.

Tatar signed a four-year $21.2 million contract extension in July 2017 and appeared in 60 Red Wings games through February 2018. Then, in late February, he was watching television when he saw the announcement that he'd been traded to the Vegas Golden Knights.

George McPhee paid a hefty price; the Knights picked up his contract, the second highest salary-cap hit on the team at $5.3 million per year (Fleury's $5.75 million was highest), plus a first-round pick in the 2018 draft, a second-rounder in 2019, and a third-rounder in 2021. He played in 20 regular-season games for the Knights, then half the playoff games.

Shea Theodore is 22, hails from British Columbia, and played four seasons for the Seattle Thunderbirds in the Western Hockey League. A top prospect in 2013, he was drafted (first round, 26th overall) by Anaheim, then spent three years in the American Hockey League. Considered ready to blossom, he was called up by the Ducks in 2016 and scored his NHL first point at age 20.

Theodore came to Vegas in a way that was similar to teammate Alex Tuch; the two became roommates and best friends during their journey to becoming mainstays on the Golden Knights roster. Like Tuch, Theodore was traded to Vegas as an incentive; the Ducks wanted the Knights to stay away from the unprotected Sami Vatanen and Josh Manson. Instead, in a pre-expansion-draft deal, Vegas was steered toward taking Clayton Stoner, with Theodore thrown in. Unfortunately, Stoner was placed on injured reserve prior to the opener and never made an appearance in the Knights' inaugural season.

Shea had to start the season with the AHL's Chicago Wolves, due to a crowded group of blue-liners for Vegas. By the end of the first month of the season, though, injuries presented him with an opportunity to get into the lineup.

The road was rocky at times, but Coach Gallant let the young skater play through and learn from his mistakes. By the time December rolled around, Theodore proved himself a valuable piece of the puzzle with his movement, power-play skills, and ability to disrupt opposing forwards. He scored the game-winning goal against the league-leading Tampa Bay Lightning with 2.3 seconds to go in a game that put Vegas in the national spotlight.

Alex Tuch's story is the classic example of a family bonding around hockey. His father, Carl, started Alex on skates when he was barely three years old. His fated path from upstate New York to the NHL began a year later, even though the minimum age for the beginner's club was five; four-year-old Alex was already big for his age and started competing. When he was seven and playing in a Montreal youth league, he was the biggest player on the team, so the equipment manager gave him the highest number, 89. He's worn it ever since, playing on the U.S. National Development team for two seasons, then starring at Boston College for another two.

Today, Alex Tuch is a six-four, 222-pound forward. He was a first-round pick (18th overall) in the 2014 entry draft for the Minnesota Wild, playing for the AHL's Iowa Wild for half the 2016-2017 season. He was called up to play in the majors, but didn't see too much action. At 20 years old, he was one of the youngest players in the league.

Tuch's journey to Vegas was different than most. He wasn't selected as part of the expansion draft; he was more of a bargaining chip. Minnesota desperately wanted to keep Matt Dumba, but couldn't protect the young defenseman in the draft. Minnesota threw in Tuch, a prospect player, as incentive to take Erik Haula instead of Dumba.

Though Alex was announced as an invitee for the Knights' first development camp, he wasn't expected to show up. But Carl Tuch had two rules for his son: Work hard and have fun. "You're wasting my money if you don't work hard and you're wasting your time if you don't have fun." So there he was, towering over the teenage prospects at the Las Vegas Ice Center, before the Knights' practice facility was finished.

Tuch didn't make the Vegas lineup before the opener. But injuries compelled the Knights to promote him from the affiliate AHL Chicago Wolves after the fourth game of the season. In his first game as a Knight against the Boston Bruins, he seized his opportunity by creating a turnover, rushing the goal alone, then scoring on Tuukka Rask.

He played in every game over the rest of the season, scoring 15 goals with 26 assists and earning 47 points. Not bad for his rookie year.

Tuch turned 22 right after the Knights disposed of the San Jose Sharks in Round 2 of the playoffs. The fans watching practice that day sang "Happy Birthday" to Alex, who smiled and waved his appreciation, before finishing practice. He then organized a dinner party in a private room at Carbone, an Italian restaurant at the Aria casino, to which 20 teammates showed up. On the way in, they took a group photo in front of Aria's Living Wall, displaying the team logo and the chant that enveloped all of Las Vegas: Go Knights Go!

Alex's younger brother Luke plays hockey for Boston University. Like I said, a family affair.

A player considered a bargaining chip evolved into a top-six forward in a single year with the Knights. Forgive a bit of gushing, but this kid is destined for greatness.

Fighting in the NHL

There's an old Rodney Dangerfield joke: "I went to a fight the other night and a hockey game broke out."

Bare-knuckle fisticuffs are part of the game that sometimes cause more heated discussion and mayhem than the fights themselves. They've been an ice-hockey tradition since the early days of the game in Canada. The initial lack of rules, then the introduction of rules that increased the physicality of play and incited fighting, engendered a class of "enforcers" or "goons," essentially bodyguards who protected their teams' stars and primary puck handlers.

Rules about the fights themselves began to be implemented in the early 1920s, when fighting became a five-minute major penalty. In 1977, a new "third-man-in" policy ejected a player who stepped into a one-on-one fight. Later, more rules prohibited leaving the bench to join a fight and instigating a fight in the final five minutes of a game. It all made something of a difference. The seasons between 1982 and 1989 saw a per-season average of 1,175 fights, with an average of one fight every game. Since 1992 when the "instigator rule" was introduced, adding an extra two minutes in the penalty box for anyone deemed to have started a fight, fighting decreased: A fistfight broke out in 30%-40% of NHL games from 2000 to 2012, and in every season since 2013, the average dropped to less than 30%. In the 2017-2018 regular season, there were 406 fights.

But the main reason for the reduction, many believe, is the salary cap. Teams have only so much money to spend on filling their rosters. So paying a player primarily for his pugilistic prowess is counterproductive; teams need skilled hockey players to win the Stanley Cup and finding a skater who combines both skating and fighting skills is becoming harder and harder.

The VGK had only 16 fights in their 82 regular-season games, ranking them 29th out of 31 teams.

Neither GM George McPhee nor Coach Gerard Gallant is a stranger to NHL fights; both were brawlers in their day. They weren't unaware that the playoff run would be tough going and with Vegas being ranked near the bottom for physicality, Ryan Reaves was a perfect fit. He won't be going to the Hockey Hall of Fame, but the stick he used to send a first-year expansion team to the Big Show (he scored the series-clinching Game 5 winner against Winnipeg) is already there.

Opponents of fighting in hockey argue that it leads to concussions and mental-health problems, even death (look up Owen McCourt); it sets a bad example for kids; and it glorifies violence.

Old-time hockey fans believe that fighting is an essential part of the game. Their position is that it makes the sport safer overall by holding players accountable; more stick infractions would occur if players knew they had to answer only to referees and penalty boxes. Fighting also draws fans and increases the game's entertainment value and it's a hockey tradition that exists in the official rules and as an unwritten code among players.

Most NHL players, likewise, believe that fighting is essential and shouldn't be abolished.

As a lifelong fan of hockey, I can add a final thought. In my experience, it's not hockey fans who are opposed to fighting. When a fight breaks out on the ice, 99.9% of those in attendance rise from their seats—not to boo or head for the exits, but to better see the action. This is especially true if it's payback, to settle a score after one of their players was abused by one on the opposing team. Those at home are rewinding their DVR to watch the fight over again, maybe even in slow motion. And everyone checks the "fight card" on HockeyFights.com to see who was voted the winner.

The players, the fans, even the league seem to have little, if any, interest in abolishing fighting. ♣

Chapter 3
The Preseason

The practice arena wasn't ready for the Golden Knights first development camp, so it was held a few miles from the arena site at the Las Vegas Ice Center.

Player development is an intensive four- to five-day camp for prospects who have been selected in an entry-level draft and are under contract, or are invited to attend; either way, the young players participate in preparations of all kinds for hockey at the major-league level. Training their whole lives to make it in professional sports, these guys learn how to be stronger and smarter, more athletic and skilled, laying the foundation in a way that will pay dividends for both the skaters and the team in the future.

All NHL teams develop their draft picks and prospects, but for an expansion team, development is crucial; the Knights were just starting to build their program, right from the ground up, and they had a long road ahead of them.

Forty-four invitees — 24 forwards, 15 defensemen, and 5

goaltenders—participated in the 2017 development camp, broken down into two teams, Gray and White. In addition to the fundamentals, this camp focused on the Golden Knights' culture, evidenced by the presence of owner Bill Foley.

The standouts, reportedly, were Reid Duke, the first player to sign a contract with the Golden Knights; Jake Leschyshyn, whose father Curtis played on the 1996 Colorado Avalanche team that won the Stanley Cup; Keegan Kolesar, acquired in a trade from the Columbus Blue Jackets in exchange for a high draft pick in 2017; Kenny Brooks, born and raised in Las Vegas; and Jake Bischoff, acquired in a trade with the New York Islanders. Entry-draft VGK picks included Jack Dugan, Nick Campoli, Lucas Elvenes, Cody Glass, Nicholas Hague, Ben Jones, Jiri Patera, Jonas Rondbjerg, Nick Suzuki, and Maksim Zhukov, all players whose names might become familiar to Golden Knights fans in the future.

As I mentioned earlier, Alex Tuch was on the list of attendees. Though he'd just turned 21, he'd already played in the NHL and was the only development prospect with major-league experience. He'd never been to Las Vegas, so he wanted to get his bearings in a new city and a new organization; SinBin.com blogger Ken Boehlke wrote, "Alex Tuch looked like a man among boys on the ice"—an early indication of what lay in store for the big forward from Baldwinsville, New York.

Some development-camp attendees, including Tuch of course, would be back for the rookie and training camps in September, so they were preparing for more intensive training. The rest would take what they learned and experienced back to their colleges and semi-pro and minor-league teams with a better idea of what to expect when the time came for their next step.

City National Arena held its soft opening in late August, in time for the VGK's first rookie camp that convened on September 7. Twenty-three rookies gathered for this camp, including featured players Alex Tuch, Tomas Hyka, Reid Duke, and Jake Bischoff, along with the draft picks and trades, including Dylan Ferguson who had no idea then what fate held in store for him. At the end of the five-day camp, these players traveled to Los Angeles to take on their counterparts on the L.A. Kings for two rookie games at the Toyota Sports Center in El Segundo.

The VGK rookies lost the first one to the Kings' 6-2 — but for the first time in history, hockey players were wearing Vegas Golden Knights uniforms and playing against the team that would become their arch-rival. Rocky Thompson, head coach of the Chicago Wolves, Vegas' minor-league affiliate, was in charge of the new kids on the block in L.A.

The VGK redeemed themselves in the second game, shutting out L.A. 4-0; 18-year-old Cody Glass, Vegas' top draft pick and the sixth overall in the entry draft, scored a goal and had two assists. He and Nick Suzuki, who was also drafted by the Knights in the first round, proceeded to training camp with 58 other players.

Though training camp officially began on September 14, "the guys" (how they refer to one another) began to drift in a week or so beforehand. A couple dozen early-birds took a spin around City National, on and off the ice. They skated together, passed the puck around, and started to form friendships.

Meanwhile, George McPhee and Coach Gallant still had a blank slate, with a week or so before the veteran players were scheduled to arrive, a couple weeks before the first preseason game in Vancouver against the Canucks, and a little less than a month before the season opener in Dallas against the Stars.

Concurrently, real life went on, as all the new Las Vegans rented, bought, or built houses near City National, learned their way around Summerlin and the city, and no doubt partied a little in the casinos and clubs.

And the fans began the parade to practices, hundreds of them arriving hours early to get seats in the bleachers where they could become part of this new phenomenon that was starting to create a buzz in the neon desert.

For the first preseason game on September 17, 2017, the Knights fielded a team of entry-draft picks, rookies, young traded players, and a couple of veterans fighting for a spot on the roster. In the lopsided 9-4 victory over the Vancouver Canucks, 21-year-old Tyler Wong, a forward from Alberta, scored a hat trick and 25-year-old Czech Tomas Hyka scored two goals of his own. Both returned to the Chicago Wolves for the season, though Hyka was called up toward the end of the season and played in 10 games for the Knights.

A couple nights later, the VGK were in Denver to play the Colorado Avalanche. This game looked a little more like a team was taking shape: Deryk Engelland, Jonathan Marchessault, Luca Sbisa, Reilly Smith, Alex Tuch, Pierre-Édouard Bellamare, Erik Haula, David Perron, and Colin Miller all saw ice time. Tomas Hyka registered another goal, his third in two games. Oscar Dansk in net was a perfect 18 for 18, while Max Lagacé saved 10 of the 11 shots that came at him, giving up the only goal in a 4-1 win.

Some veterans, including William Karlsson, David Perron, Nate Schmidt, and Brayden McNabb, along with some prospects—Cody Glass, Keegan Kolesar, Tyler Wong—took the ice against the Sharks in San Jose and sustained the Vegas Golden Knights' first loss, 5-2.

And that was the way the preseason continued, as Coach Gallant tinkered with the VGK DNA. In the fourth road game in a row, the VGK beat the Ducks in Anaheim 4-2, then took a 3-2 loss to the L.A. Kings in the Knights' first home game at T-Mobile Arena and a 4-2 loss to the Colorado Avalanche on September 28 in the penultimate preseason game.

Even though the roster looked very much like the team that would play in the first game of the regular season a few nights later, the VGK lost 5-3 to the San Jose Sharks at home on October 1, winding up with a 3-3 preseason record. The players changed into street clothes, walked to their cars, drove home—and that was when the texts and calls started flooding in, asking if they, and everyone they knew in Las Vegas, were still alive.

That night, October 1, a major country-music festival was taking place at Las Vegas Village, a concert site built on a 15-acre parking lot across from Luxor, which sits next door to Mandalay Bay. The Village's biggest event was the Route 91 Harvest Festival, named for the original U.S. highway that ran between Las Vegas and Los Angeles. This country-music extravaganza launched on October 3-5, 2014, featuring Jason Aldean, Miranda Lambert, Blake Shelton, Dierks Bentley, and another 35 country acts, and drew 15,000 attendees per day. In 2015 and 2016, the festival sold out its capacity of 25,000 per night. In 2017, as everyone in the world knows, more than 22,000 country fans, 85% from out of town, came out for the fourth festival.

Roughly a quarter-mile across the Strip, 58-year-old loner Stephen Paddock knocked out two windows in an east- and north-facing suite on the 32nd floor of Mandalay Bay and proceeded to rain more than 1,100 rounds down on the crowd at the festival. Paddock killed 58 people and wounded more than 500 more in the deadliest mass shooting in U.S. history before he shot himself to death moments before Las Vegas Metropolitan police burst through the door to the suite.

T-Mobile Arena is a long block north on the Las Vegas Strip from Mandalay Bay. Even though the Route 91 Harvest Music Festival and the Vegas Golden Knights' final preseason game were going on less than a mile from each other, the hockey fans didn't come under fire; the game ended a little more than an hour before the shooting began.

Immediately after the game, I went to dinner with a couple of friends in the steakhouse at the Gold Coast casino, about two miles west of the Strip. Afterward, my friends left for home, while I stayed at the Gold Coast to play some video poker. A short time later when my phone started to blow up, I found out that a major disaster was in progress nearby, but I had no clue what it was.

I saw a panic building among the people around me, who were also trying to process a lot of conflicting information about what was going on, all of it bad. Was it safe to go home or even go outside? One friend texted that gunfire was reported at MGM; another heard it was happening at the Tropicana. Then we learned that the Strip was completely closed and all the casinos in the area were locked down tight. We were trapped at the Gold Coast.

It had been many years since I was a police officer in New York City, but instincts kicked in and I started planning an emergency exit if, in fact, this was a moving situation.

It wasn't until the sun came up and the lockdown was lifted that I made the decision to go to my car and head home. I'd lived in Las Vegas for 18 years and had driven home at every imaginable hour after leaving a poker or blackjack table or video poker machine. This is a 24-hour town and there's always activity, with people on the streets and the highways. In the early-morning hours of October 2, however, it seemed like I was the only one out on the road. Other than emergency vehicles, I had 10 lanes of Interstate 15 to myself. After all the agitation and confusion, I felt like I was in a soundproof booth.

Las Vegas awoke to the full horror of what this lunatic had wrought.

Slowly, slowly, slowly, the real story started to surface.

The 911 calls. Jason Aldean's performance suddenly stopping and the lights going out. Heroics from concert-goers and first responders. The initial number of casualties. The hospitals overwhelmed. The calls for donated blood and lines of volunteers stretching for blocks. Flowers multiplying as if by magic at the Welcome To Fabulous Las Vegas sign.

As for the VGK, after the last preseason game the night before, most players had headed to the places they called home since arriving in this suddenly shell-shocked city only a few weeks earlier; some already had apartments or houses, while others were still living in hotel rooms. A few stayed out; if they were far enough away from the Strip, they were tracked down by team security and eventually escorted home. If they were on the Strip, they waited through the night with the rest of the stranded visitors for the all-clear.

The Vegas Golden Knights had yet to play in a home game. Their names and faces were still unfamiliar when they showed up to donate blood, visit victims in the hospitals, and meet with first responders and sign autographs at the command center, but the gesture made a lasting impression on a city desperate for a remedy to the madness, for some semblance of returned sanity.

The first game of the first season took place four days later, on October 6, in Dallas. The Stars organization showed a tremendous amount of class, and respect for the visiting Knights, who all wore Vegas Strong T-shirts before dressing for the game. When they glided out onto the ice, they were a first-year team representing a deeply damaged city, wearing their jerseys with dignity and pride.

During introductions and the national anthem, Star players lined up behind, instead of across from, the Knights. This simple yet profound gesture expressed unity and solidarity in the face of tragedy, that even though they were opponents that night, everyone was on the same team off the ice.

Mostly forgotten in the midst of everything that had just happened and all that came after, the Stars scored first, its first goal of the season, on a power play with 2:59 left in the second period on a lucky bounce off the post. At 9:33 in the third, James Neal tied the game with the first goal in Golden Knights' history. McPhee had acquired Neal to score goals and that was exactly what he did when he scored his second and winning goal with 2:44 left in the game. Neal took a pass at an odd angle, went down on both knees, managed to control the puck, and chipped a shot right over the left shoulder of Stars' backup goalie Kari Lehtonen. At the other net, Marc-André Fleury blocked 45 of the 46 shots he faced for a .978 save percentage.

In the Knights' second game, also on the road, the Arizona Coyotes opened up the scoring early in the first on a deflection and led most of the way by one. With a little more than a minute left in the third period, Nate Schmidt picked up a loose puck near the net and kind of eased it past Coyotes' netminder Antti Raanta, sending the game into overtime. Again, with about a minute left in OT, James Neal scored his third and the team's fourth goal of the season to make it two in a row, on the road, for the Golden Knights. The next game would be their first at home in T-Mobile Arena—where the team's inaugural season would really begin.

It was supposed to be a spectacular opening-night ceremony, worthy of a team that played in an arena on the famed Las Vegas Strip. It should have been full of the flash, glitz, and spectacle befitting the Entertainment Capital of the World.

But Bill Foley and the entire Golden Knights organization had a situation on their hands. Though they'd planned the opening extravaganza for months, just nine days after 58 innocent concert-goers were brutally gunned down a short walk from T-Mobile Arena and with the entire city still nearly paralyzed, introducing the team and their vision for NHL hockey in Las Vegas became a distant consideration.

In eight days, they came up with an alternate plan, not only to help the city heal, but also to celebrate the selfless emergency personnel who stood shoulder to shoulder while the bullets were still flying.

For the lead-up to the game against the Arizona Coyotes, the Golden Knights' executives, coaches, and players walked down a gold carpet from the plaza outside T-Mobile into the arena, stopping to shake hands with, speak to, and sign autographs for hundreds of fans strung along the stanchions. An hour later, those and other fans marched across nearby New York-New York Hotel-Casino's replica Brooklyn Bridge to the front doors of T-Mobile, which opened at 5 p.m.

The emotion of the opening ceremony was carrying over from the day before, when the VGK players discussed the plans for the ceremony in the locker room. According to Coach Gallant, "It was pretty tough. And that was just us talking about it."

Opening-night ceremonies always introduce the members of the team, coaches, and managers to the fans, but on the long-awaited home premiere of Las Vegas' first major-league sports team, 25 first-responders, nurses, doctors, EMTs, firefighters, and police officers were introduced before the team.

One by one, followed by spotlights, each walked onto the ice and was met by a VGK player, who was also introduced; together, the two crossed the blue line. Then, the names of the 58 victims were illuminated in gold on the ice during 58 seconds of silence.

The silence of 18,000 people in a sports arena is overpowering beyond description. Never, in all the sporting events in all the countries of the world, has there been a silence so profound or poignant. It was one of the most emotionally galvanizing moments in history and it was shared by millions of people watching the game on national TV.

Finally, Deryk Engelland, the long-time Las Vegas resident and the Knights' elder statesman, addressed the crowd. Holding a microphone in one hand and a hockey stick in the other, he praised the first responders who worked tirelessly and courageously. He told the fans that he'd met his wife in Las Vegas, his kids were born in Las Vegas, he was proud to call Las Vegas home, and he and his teammates would do everything in their power to help the city, and the country, overcome what had happened. Engelland did himself and his team proud with a steady and superbly delivered two-minute speech in front of 18,000 mesmerized fans.

It was clear that the entire Vegas Golden Knights organization, all the fans, and everyone watching on television knew that the team's first home game, its third of the season, would be the most important one they would ever play.

This season had begun.

The Heart of Hockey in Las Vegas

The Golden Knights practices, at the team's City National Arena facility, turned into a phenomenon.

Early in the season, two of the five rows of bleacher seats were filled with locals getting a free taste of their new team. On the opposite side of the rink, a small group of fans gathered, hoping for autographs from players who were nice enough to stop by on their way off the ice. By mid-season, practices were standing room only and the team brass learned that kids were sometimes being pushed aside on the autograph line by adults—overzealous fans acting like children or would-be profiteers selling signed memorabilia on eBay. The fix: Autographs were restricted to children under 14 in a controlled line.

By the time the playoffs rolled around, lines of fans wanting to attend open practices wrapped around the building. The team implemented a wristband policy to avoid exceeding fire-code limits. Many people were turned away.

City National Arena houses two full-size NHL ice rinks, one for the team and one for the public, with bleacher seating for 600 at each; the team takes its ice time from 9 a.m. to 1 p.m. on the west rink. The building also contains the team offices, a weight room, medical facility, players' lounge (among the world's most luxurious for a hockey team), retail store, skate rental, snack bar, and restaurant. Montana-based MacKenzie River Pizza, Grill and Pub is part of the Glacier Restaurant Group owned by Bill Foley; it's open to the public and is located between the two rinks with views over both.

It's a cool place to grab a craft beer and take in a VGK practice or local league game. But what about the pizza?

Mackenzie River is a chain out of Montana a state not exactly known for its Italian cuisine. But they can make pizza in the Northwest too. Smalls start at $12.50, and larges top out at $24.50. There's BBQ, Hot Hawaiian, Buffalo Wing, and the Stockman that comes with pepperoni, bacon, sausage, and steak. And the chicken chili ain't half-bad.

When the Knights aren't practicing, the two ice sheets are used for a multitude of youth and adult hockey programs.

The Knights have generated enormous enthusiasm for hockey in the Las Vegas Valley. Its first series of Sticks for Kids programs attracted 2,500 children. Many of them went on to Learn To Skate and NHL-sponsored Learn To Play classes. The Skating Academy grew from a few dozen kids to nearly 1,000 after being open for only seven months.

Las Vegas' existing youth-hockey program, the Nevada Storm, joined forces with the Golden Knights outreach efforts under the new name, Junior Golden Knights. It all culminates with the travel teams that see more ice time, receive professional-level coaching, and participate in a higher level of youth-hockey competition, playing against other travel programs and attending tournaments in nearby states. And who knows? Some of the Junior Golden Knights might be destined for the NHL. The Nevada Storm turned out Jason Zucker, who now plays for the Minnesota Wild.

The arena also put on watch parties for Golden Knights games. Fans could see the games on a large projector screen while they skated or from inside McKenzie River on one of the many TVs.

The games take place at T-Mobile Arena, but the heart of hockey in Las Vegas beats in the suburbs, at City National Arena. ♣

Chapter 4
The Season

Coach Gallant had some trepidation that after the emotion of the ceremony before the Vegas Golden Knights' first-ever appearance at home, the team would experience a letdown when the game started. But it was just the opposite. If anything, it revved them up so high that it was as if they'd been shot out of a cannon.

For the first 10 minutes, Arizona looked like stationary cones on the ice. The VGK's hyperspeed not only stunned the Coyotes, it aroused the crowd to a fever pitch, allowing all the pent-up turmoil and tension to erupt. When Tomas Nosek scored the first goal barely three minutes into the game, the response nearly blew the roof off the arena. I was there and I'd never, in nearly 60 years of attending hockey games, heard anything like it.

Before the response could die down, Deryk Engelland fired a shot from such a distance that it passed two Knights, two Coyotes, and one goaltender, all of whom could barely turn their heads fast enough to see it hit the back of the net.

Less than a minute later, James Neal scored, then ripped in a second goal, his fifth in three games, and before the Coyotes and the world knew what had hit them, the Golden Knights were ahead 4-0 with nine minutes left in the *first period*.

It was an otherworldly 11 minutes of hockey that even veteran observers said made their hair stand on end.

Between the first and second periods, I looked around at the sellout crowd. I don't know its exact size, but I'm sure it was more than 18,000. Ten years from now when this story is told, no doubt an excess of 200,000 will claim to have been there! But you know what? They really *were* there, because the entire city was as one that night.

I was especially gratified to see how many children were in attendance. At first I thought, this is a school night. Shouldn't they be home asleep already? Then I remembered what they were part of—and what they were witnessing wasn't something you can learn in school.

In the second period, Oscar Lindberg smashed one home and after two meaningless goals by Arizona, the Vegas Golden Knights won by a score of 5-2. After beating the Dallas Stars 2-1 on October 6 in Dallas and the Arizona Coyotes 2-1 on October 7 in Phoenix, the Vegas Golden Knights became the only expansion team in NHL history to win their first three games.

In a post-game interview, I asked Deryk Engelland if his goal stood out as one that he will always remember. "It will go down," he responded, "as the biggest goal of my career."

After his gripping pre-game address, to go out and score a goal left his mark not only on the game, but on the city.

In so many ways that first night at T-Mobile, the team captured the hearts of a citizenry desperate for something positive, something life-affirming, to hold onto. Neither the Vegas Golden Knights nor Vegas itself ever looked back.

Game 4, Detroit Red Wings at T-Mobile Arena, 10/13/17

In the second home game of the season, though, everyone might have looked over their shoulders, just a bit.

The Golden Knights were 3-0, but the Detroit Red Wings were 3-1, coming off a road win in Arizona. The Red Wings scored first in less than two minutes. But Vegas responded in the second period on a goal by Jonathan Marchessault, his first as a Golden Knight. Detroit came back to take the lead with five minutes left in the second period. But again, the VGK responded; James Neal scored his sixth goal in four games to tie the score at 2-2. When Erik Haula scored next, the Knights led for the first time in the game, with 3:15 left in the second.

Ah, but then came the third. The Red Wings tied the score again early in the period, then came back with another on a save-rebound-goal, and after another goal, the final score wound up at 6-3. The Vegas Golden Knights had lost their first game, and the first at home. There'd be more losses in the next 78 games, but this one felt monumental.

The Knights had entered the third period with a 3-2 lead and gave up four unanswered goals on turnovers, ending the three-game winning streak.

Later, we learned that Marc-André Fleury had suffered a concussion when he was run over by Anthony Mantha during a Red Wing rush to the goal. After that, he wasn't the same; he saved only 21 of the 27 shots on goal by the time of the final merciful buzzer. Fleury didn't return to action for more than six weeks.

Record: 3-1-0

Game 5, Boston Bruins at T-Mobile Arena, 10/15/17

Two expressions often heard here in Las Vegas, especially in casinos, are "ship it," in reference to winning a pot at a poker table, and "tuck it," the procedure when you hold what you believe to be a winning blackjack hand.

Well, T-Mobile Arena doesn't have any gaming tables, but in the VGK's third home game, there was still a good deal of shipping and tucking as the Vegas Golden Knights defeated the Boston Bruins, an original-six NHL team, by a score of 3-1.

This game was a definite test for the young team, coming off its total collapse against the Red Wings. Vadim Shipachyov and Alex Tuch were called up for this game to replace injured starters. The "ship-it" part came from Shipachyov, who was playing in his first-ever NHL game. No problem for Ship, as he scored his first NHL goal! (The

30-year-old Shipachyov, a standout in Russia's Kontinental Hockey League who was signed to a two-year $9 million contract, never made the grade. He was sent down to the AHL Chicago Wolves, called back up, sent back down, disappeared, returned, then "retired" from the NHL and returned to Russia.)

The "tuck-it" part came when Alex Tuch executed a slick takeaway from a Bruin, then slid the puck between the opposing player's legs, and swooped in on Tuukka Rask, the Boston netminder. Rask had played in more than 300 NHL games and won a Stanley Cup in 2011 with the Bruins; in 2014, he was awarded the Vezina Trophy, given to the top goaltender of the year. Tuck was coming in on a world-class goalie with a semi-breakaway, but he nailed it with a wicked snap shot over Rask's shoulder—for his own first NHL goal in just his seventh pro game.

Malcolm Subban, the VGK's backup goaltender, didn't face a lot of direct shots, as his team kept Boston and the puck on the outside of the faceoff dots. The Bruin's single goal came on a fluke, when an intended pass to the front of the net found its mark off a VGK defenseman's leg with just 30 seconds left in the game. Slipping past Subban, it ruined what should have been not only his first NHL win, but his first NHL shutout, which would have come against the team for which he last played.

With the VGK's fourth win in five games out of an 82-game schedule, all indications were already pointing to a group of players that, like most good teams, could rebound from a tough loss, including the sidelining of its star goaltender, in an impressive fashion, even against a team that had been playing in the NHL for the last 93 years. That long history was clearly evident in the large contingent of Boston Bruins fans at T-Mobile, wearing black-and-gold sweaters with pride. But the rest of the almost sold-out crowd consisted of VGK fans, also proudly wearing their team colors. The Golden Knights had clearly started to develop a fan base.

I know, as a lifelong New York Rangers fan, that once you identify with a team, it becomes *your* team. You speak about them like you play for them, like the coach and GM call you for advice. You live and breathe with them. You suffer with them and rejoice with them. Seeing all the young people at T-Mobile, many of whom were attending their first-ever hockey game, was a special sensation. For some, it was the beginning of a bond that would last *forever*.

Record: 4-1-0

Game 6, Buffalo Sabres at T-Mobile Arena, 10/17/17

In the long run-up to the creation of a Las Vegas NHL team, the question on my mind and many others' was: Could Sin City actually support major-league sports, particularly hockey?

I anticipated a honeymoon stage for Las Vegas accepting the Golden Knights. As Jason Gay of the *Wall Street Journal* put it, "We all knew the Golden Knights would stink in their opening year. Stinkage was just assumed. It's the rule for expansion teams. You suffer for a bunch of years, come up with a plan, and pray it eventually works out, or they shut you down and move you someplace else."

Well, they won their first two games on the road. They won their first and third home games, in spite of losing their All Star goalie to a concussion in their only loss. And they played to sold-out crowds.

On October 16, the VGK took off on a two-game road trip. When they managed to squeak by the Buffalo Sabres 5-4 in overtime, they'd won their fifth of six games, three of them on the road. When you're winning, it's easy to overlook potential problems, but the VGK had a problem: They were having a hard time playing for 60 minutes.

Similar to the Detroit game, where they gave up four goals in the last 15 minutes, they let Buffalo back into the game when they surrendered a three-goal lead with only 10 minutes remaining, pushing the game into overtime. But they dodged a bullet when David Perron scored his second goal of the game to avoid a complete disaster.

Meanwhile, 21-year-old Alex Tuch was making it very difficult for Coach Gallant to keep him out of the lineup. He scored the second goal of his career on a well-directed tip off a shot from the point by Deryk Engelland and caused havoc near the net as he continually placed himself right in front of the opposing goaltender, limiting his view of impending shots.

Though the VGK nearly blew it in Buffalo, one thing was becoming clear. They knew how to win.

Record: 5-1-0

Game 7, St. Louis Blues at T-Mobile Arena, 10/21/17

Four nights later, on October 21, the Knights were out-played, outshot, and forced to field their third-string goalie. But no need to worry!

Right from the start, this team knew what it had to do. It was almost like the rope-a-dope made famous by Muhammad Ali—he just leaned back on the ropes and let his opponents punch away until they exhausted themselves. Then

Watching Hockey

Part of the problem with mainstream acceptance of hockey is that new fans don't know how to watch it, especially on TV. Aside from being unfamiliar with the rules, the game is very fast and the puck is very small. Hence, many have trouble following the puck's movement. A laser-tracker with a trailer was tried to aid in following the action on TV, but that was abandoned. In the end, watching hockey is an acquired skill.

It gets easier as you watch more games and begin to understand the way the puck moves in relation to the positioning of the players and the geometry involved in the way it caroms off, or slides around, the boards. Much can be inferred from the movements of the players. For example, usually the quickest way to determine that a goal has been scored is by the scoring team's reactions—raised sticks, fists pumping, elation all around, and a stoppage of play. ♣

The Greatest moved in for the knockout.

In game seven, the VGK let the St. Louis Blues shoot themselves out: 49 shots to Vegas' 22. More than 30 minutes into this contest, the Knights had only six shots on goal— less than one shot every five minutes. The Blues' goalie, Jake Allen, could have been at the concession stand, having a hot dog and beer, given the number of shots coming his way.

On the other side, Malcolm Subban, the second-string goalie, was standing on his head. In the hockey world, that means he stopped everything thrown at him. In a veritable shooting gallery, the St. Louis Blues kept loading the gun and firing puck after puck at Subban who, wearing a bullet-proof vest, was up to the task.

After a hard-fought two periods, the third period began with the VGK leading 2-1 on goals by Reilly Smith and Colin Miller.

Early in the third, Subban stretched out his right leg to make a save and immediately crumbled to the ice. Though play continued and he slowly got back up on his skates, it was clear that he'd injured himself. No worries! Oscar Dansk, the third-string goalie, had been called up a few days earlier. Though he'd never played a single minute in an NHL game, Dansk was now tasked with protecting a one-goal lead.

Subban's injury came just before a TV timeout, so Oscar had a little extra time to loosen up and get some of the but-terflies out of his system. Or not—the first shot he faced found home, the score was tied 2-2, and the VGK were heading into back-to-back overtimes.

That was the first and only shot that got by the new

starting goaltender, however, as he also stood on his head from then out. This was especially true in overtime, during which the teams skate 3-on-3. This creates lots of space and scoring opportunities, but Oscar handled it like Las Vegas' former mayor Oscar Goodman handles a martini.

With just a little more than 30 seconds left in overtime, it appeared the game was headed to a shootout. In that case, St. Louis would have been a huge favorite, given the advantage of a seasoned goalie in the net and the Blues' potent roster of "snipers," hockey lingo for players with incredibly accurate shots. The Blues snipers would be firing on Oscar playing in his first-ever NHL game.

No worries!

With just 23.8 seconds left, Reilly Smith made a sweet cross-ice pass to William Karlsson, who one-timed it on a beautiful snap shot past the goaltender, who was still facing Smith.

With the win, the VGK broke another NHL record, being the first expansion team in the history of the game to win six of their first seven games.

We used to say that what happens in Vegas stays in Vegas, but everyone around the NHL and hockey fans the world over were starting to get an inkling of something out of the ordinary happening. This was no David Copperfield smoke-and-mirrors act. This was the Vegas Golden Knights, giving their fans nothing to worry about.

Record: 6-1-0

Expansion-Team Records for the First Seven Games

L.A. Kings (1967-1968): 3-2-2
Philadelphia Flyers (1967-1968): 2-2-3
Tampa Bay Lightning (1992-1993): 3-3-1
Florida Panthers (1993-1994): 2-2-3
Vegas Golden Knights (2017-2018): 6-1-0

Game 8, Chicago Blackhawks at T-Mobile Arena, 10/24/17

In the now-famous movie *Hangover,* a group of guys venture to Vegas and after a night of debauchery and mayhem, they wake up to find a tiger in their room.

Well, the Chicago Blackhawks spent three days in Las Vegas before their game on October 24 and though they didn't find a tiger, they did find the Knights. Over the last eight years, the Blackhawks had won three Stanley Cups. They also had a core of team members who'd played together for 8 to 13 years—an astonishing 3,717 games combined!

The VGK had played seven games together.

Everyone, including the Vegas oddsmakers who are pretty good at setting a betting line, made Chicago the strong favorite, despite the VGK's impressive start, especially at home.

T-Mobile Arena was once again full and the energy was

evident even before the game started. A large contingent of Chicago Blackhawk fans were in attendance and their red home sweaters were all over the arena.

A few teams travel well in the NHL, which means their fans show up at away games in large numbers. Chicago is one of them, along with the other original NHL teams: New York, Toronto, Boston, Detroit, and Montreal. And can you blame them? They have a choice of games to travel to, including Saint Paul, Winnipeg, and Edmonton. Don't get me wrong; I have nothing against going to any destination, especially to see a hockey game. But add Las Vegas into the mix and which city would *you* rather choose?

I have a number of friends here in town from Chicago and when they heard I had season tickets, they were blowing up my phone to be first in line to remove them from me.

As it turned out, Chicago fans had a limited amount of time to cheer. The Blackhawks scored within the first 3 minutes and 30 seconds and that was that. The VGK scored the next four goals, before Patrick Kane's meaningless goal with just over a minute left in the game.

Third-string goalie Oscar Dansk saved 29 of 31 shots. Three different goaltenders had recorded the VGK's first seven wins. And coming into this game, 20 of the 21 VGK players had registered one point or more. Coach Gerard Gallant was engineering a complete team effort.

Record: 7-1-0

Game 9, Colorado Avalanche at T-Mobile Arena, 10/27/17

Speaking of a complete team effort, on October 27, in a game in which the VGK thrashed the Colorado Avalanche 7-0, all seven goals were scored by different players. Plus, 11 players earned at least one point.

The VKG didn't have any superstars, but it did have 20 players and a coach all left on the proverbial curb by their previous teams.

James Neal was the only exception. In the 2016-2017 season, he was a top-six forward for Nashville. However, with only one year left before he became an unrestricted free agent, the Predators made a salary-cap decision to expose him to the expansion draft. He could have mailed it in, but if anyone had any questions regarding Neal's commitment to his new team, this game laid them to rest.

In the first period, he was smacked in the face by a Colorado stick, resulting in a busted lip that required stitches; some teeth seemed to go missing as well. He spent the remainder of the first period undergoing facial repairs, but was on the ice for the beginning of the second! If this had happened to a baseball player, he'd be out for two weeks.

Fast forward to the final two minutes of the game, with the VGK up 7-0. An Avalanche player unleashed a blistering shot from which many players on a team with a 7-0 lead would just step aside. But Neal wanted to help preserve 23-year-old Oscar Dansk's shutout, the VGK's first, and he hurled himself in front of the shot. The puck shattered his stick! Play continued and Neal, without a stick, a few teeth missing, and a busted lip, dove in front of another shot that was headed to the goal.

No doubt about it, hockey players are the toughest SOBs who play professional sports. In game nine, James Neal showed the other 19 castoffs that even though he was a top player for Nashville and came within two games of winning a Stanley Cup, he was willing to lead with his face in a 7-0 rout.

Though it was still early in the season, with a record of 8-1, fans like me couldn't help but start to wonder if this team could make the playoffs. Only two teams in the NHL's entire 100-year history had rolled 16 points in their first nine games and missed that year's playoffs — the 1986-1987 Pittsburgh Penguins and the 2015-2016 Montreal Canadiens. And with the big win over Colorado, the VGK owned the highest winning percentage among the 31 teams: .889%.

Perhaps most tellingly, the atmosphere at T-Mobile was already playoff-like. There was that kind of buzz in the arena, all over Las Vegas, and even around the country, which was where the team was headed — on a tough six-game road trip, their longest of the season.

Record: 8-1-0

Game 10, Islanders in New York, 10/30/17

Late in the second period of the first road game, against the New York Islanders, and after giving up two goals on

19 shots, third-string net minder Oscar Dansk went down with a leg injury.

In their entire system, the VGK had only five goaltenders signed to a contract. Established teams have years, if not decades, to build their organizations and develop players beneath NHL level. The VGK didn't have that luxury; hell, prior to June 2017, they didn't have a single player under contract or in development status in the team's minor-league system.

Like baseball (pitcher) and football (quarterback), hockey's key position is the goaltender. Neither Marc-André Fleury (number one) nor Malcolm Subban (number two) were close to returning to the lineup; with Dansk injured, the Knights were reduced to playing the fourth goaltender, Max Lagacé, who gave up four goals on 11 shots, sealing the fate of the game. It was the VGK's second loss.

The VGK now had a *major* problem. The last goaltender under contract was 19-year-old Dylan Ferguson, who had a record of 4-9-0, a 4.05 goals against average, and an .878 save percentage with Kamloops of the Western Hockey League. These weren't exactly outstanding numbers. And throwing a teenage goalie into the lion's den of the NHL could be devastating for his future. Even the strongest prospects, when first drafted and signed in the NHL, develop slowly and rarely see time with the big club. But the VGK didn't have that luxury. They were a first-year team with the depth of a puddle in the desert—and the top three goaltenders in their system were wearing hospital gowns.

The famous saying "next man up" clearly applied to the

Knights just then. Good teams rise to the occasion, but this occasion was dire.

Record: 8-2-0

Game 11, Rangers in New York, 10/31/17

Against the New York Rangers in their 11th game, the Knights' fourth-string goalie was in the net against the Rangers' world-class Henrik Lundqvist. Lundqvist was only one win away from becoming the goaltender with the ninth most wins in the 100-year history of the NHL. On the other side of the ice, Max Lagacé was making his first-ever NHL start.

One would think, with 10 goals scored in the game, that both goalies had an off night. Just the opposite was the case. Each was outstanding, making one save after another.

Lagacé, in fact, couldn't be blamed for any of the goals scored against him. They were all breakdowns of his defensemen and forwards. Some shots were uncontested from the point, with a Ranger standing directly in front of him and limiting his vision. At least one other was an errant pass that wound up right in front of Lagacé, where a Ranger forward promptly poked it in.

In the NHL where the parity among teams is strong, you can't play 40 minutes of a 60-minute game. You can't sit back or go into a shell for the third period. You can't muster a mere five shots on net and expect your rookie goaltender to save your sorry butt. Henrik Lundqvist might be able to do this, but not a player starting his first-ever NHL game.

At the start of the road trip, the VGK were the number-one team in fewest goals allowed, but in the two games in New York, they surrendered 12. With the 6-4 loss to the Rangers, they also recorded their first two-game losing streak.

Record: 8-3-0

Game 12, Bruins in Boston, 10/31/17

Sometimes losing a game can restore a team's confidence. In the VGK's 12th game against the Boston Bruins, they finally played 60 full minutes of hockey. In addition, there was no parade of players going to the penalty box, as was the case in New York.

A team is only as good as its goaltender and a goaltender is only as well as the players in front of him can limit the other team's offense.

The VGK played a sound defensive game against the Bruins, with no scoring in the first period and only 13 shots total. The second period was much more energetic, somewhat to be expected from a team playing three road games in four days and needing the first period to get the competitive juices flowing. The second period ended, after 20 shots each making it to the goaltender, all tied at 1-1.

In the third period, Lagacé seemed comfortable as he was finally getting the support he needed. He made an outstanding save against Patrice Bergeron, who seemed to have an open net until Max slid across to rob him of a sure goal.

On the game-winner, the initial shot was once again saved by Lagacé, but the rebound lay in the crease, was pushed in, and the Knights lost a heart-breaker, 2-1. They were also looking to end the losing streak, which now stood at three games.

Record: 8-4-0

Game 13, Senators in Ottawa, 11/4/17

Against the Ottawa Senators, the Vegas Golden Knights worked hard, played the entire 60 minutes, and won their first game of the long road trip, 5-4.

They scored the first goal of the game, then protected a third-period lead, and never trailed. They rendered Erik Karlsson, one of the league's best players, nearly a non-factor. Max Lagacé never saw Karlsson's goal late in the game, due to a number of players from both teams directly in front of the net; he didn't even look as the puck went top shelf over his right shoulder. That goal closed the VGK lead to 5-4, though it only made it somewhat interesting.

This was another complete team effort for which the VGK were starting to become known, with four different players scoring the five goals: Alex Tuch and William Karlsson recorded their fourth goals of the season; Jonathan Marchessault also had his fourth, along with two assists; and Erik Haula logged his third and fourth goals of the year. The VGK scored a season-high three power-play goals and four different goaltenders had now won at least one game in the young season. Most teams have only two goalies record their total wins.

Record: 9-4-0

Game 14, Maple Leafs in Toronto, 11/6/17

In the next game against the Toronto Maple Leafs, unlike against Ottawa, Toronto's best player, Auston Matthews, was a big factor in the result. You won't find his name among the goal scorers and prior to the drop of the puck, he was questionable to start. If that demonstrated how good he can be at less than 100%, it's scary to think just how much talent one of the best young players in the NHL is really blessed with.

These days, it's not often that you see a player take the puck from his own end and skate the length of the ice. Rather, tape-to-tape passes get the puck into the offensive zone. In his game against the VGK, Matthews took a pass in his skates, kicked it up to his stick, flew up the center of the ice through the neutral zone, slid over along the right-wing boards, accelerated around defenseman Luca Sbisa, and wound up in front of Max Lagacé untouched, who nonetheless stopped Auston's initial shot, but let the loose puck get past him for an early lead. Pure talent on display.

James Neal tied the game 58 seconds later to slow down the Maple Leaf's onslaught, somewhat, but the Leafs added two more before the period ended at 3-1.

Vegas got a handle on the game and shut down Toronto for the entire second and third. Reilly Smith added a power-play goal to close Toronto's lead to 3-2 after two periods and Deryk Engelland tied the game again at 3-3 late in the third period. The game ended in a tie, as did overtime, forcing the first shootout in the VGK's short history.

In a shootout, each team gets to choose three players to take on the goalkeeper (in turn) uncontested. The team that scores the most wins. In my humble opinion, this isn't the optimal way to decide a fast-skating hard-hitting momentum-swinging 60-minute game of skill. Overtime and shootouts are like a coin toss; the best team doesn't always win. The three VGK shooters couldn't dent the net, while Toronto scored one to register a win and the two points. The VGK picked up one point in the OT loss, giving them three out of a possible 10 points in the first five games of the six-game road trip.

When Toronto forward Zach Hyman crashed into Max Lagacé, the VGK goaltender appeared to be shaken up. Had he not been able to continue, the team would have been down to its last goaltender, Dylan Ferguson, who'd turned 19 a couple months earlier. But Max remained in the game and started the next, against the Montreal Canadiens.

Record: 9-4-1

Game 15, Canadiens in Montreal, 11/7/17

In the sixth game of the nine-day road trip, with four of

the six played on back-to-back nights, the VGK looked worn out and their forecheck was nowhere to be found. They were outshot 13-2 in the first period. In the second period, it rose to 18-4. The Canadiens dominated, with constant

Forecheck and Back-check

The forecheck is a defensive play made in the offensive zone in an attempt to regain control of the puck. Generally speaking, the more skilled the skater, the more aggressive the forecheck.

Though every skater in the NHL is among the best of the best, the fourth line of a team has usually been judged by the coaching staff to be the lowest on the offensive-skills totem pole. That said, the fourth-line players are usually the ones who thrive on the forecheck. It creates offensive chances, giving a boost to their team, and it saps the energy of the opposing team's defensive players, which helps when fresh first and second lines come back against tired defensemen.

Back-checking occurs when offensive players rush back to their defensive zone in response to an opposing team's offensive push. They harass the player with the puck and try to poke it away with their sticks without incurring a penalty.

It takes a lot of energy to play all 200 feet of the ice and a player who back-checks is a coach's dream. Everyone wants to score goals, but a back-checking player is equally focused on preventing the other team from scoring.

Game after game, the VGK's number-one line of Karlsson, Marchessault, and Smith played all 200 feet of the ice. Their scoring and back-checking skills yielded a combined rating of +116. The line also scored 92 goals in 82 games. ✤

waves from one end of the ice to the other, and the final score, 3-2, was deceiving; the VGK were never in this game. Even though Max Lagacé played well, when your team gets six shots on the opposing goalie in the first 33 minutes, your chances of success are slim to none—and Slim was headed west like the rest of the team.

The Golden Knights ultimately secured only three points out of a possible 12 on the road trip. They returned home with a disappointing 1-4-1 result. In their final two games on the road, in all 125 minutes of play, they never held the lead. After leaving Las Vegas with a record-setting eight wins and one loss, they closed out the road trip with five losses total.

Record: 9-5-1

Game 16, Winnipeg Jets at T-Mobile Arena, 11/ 10/17

The first home game for a team following a long road trip is much more difficult than any on the road. The players have to travel from that last city, settle in to home life, and deal with matters that occurred while they were gone. Before they know it, they have to head out to the arena and play a game when they're jet-lagged and road weary and might not be entirely focused.

On the other side of the coin is the team that travels to play the new Vegas franchise and has too many days off before the game. Even though my friend Eddie Rivkin didn't provide the waiting Winnipeg Jets with his outstanding bottle service and Las Vegas VIP treatment (of course, this is only a joke; Eddie would never consider trying to alter the outcome of a game he could wager on), with this game, the two of us started to identify a possible trend: the effects on a visiting team arriving in Las Vegas with a few free days.

Everyone knows that Las Vegas has a ton of distractions. For example, slot machines are everywhere — except in the bathrooms, the only place here where you have a small chance of recovering your common sense. And professional athletes are, after all, human. They're young men full of testosterone and strong appetites and emotions, especially when they're on some kind of quest in an adult fantasy world. I should add that most teams arrive the night before a road game, checking into their hotel sometimes as late as 3 a.m. after coming in from a game they played the night before. They have very little free time. Most take a morning skate around 10 to 11, then return to their rooms for a pre-game nap and arrive at the rink a couple hours before game time. But the VGK's home-ice advantage was starting to look like the best in the league, especially if the team arrived two to three days before the game.

Coming into this game, the Winnipeg Jets were on a roll, winning eight of their previous 12 games. On the other hand, the VGK had outscored the opposition 35-19 in games at T-Mobile Arena. The Knights were scoring an average of 4.29 goals per game at home and they added to that by putting a whopping five past Connor Hellebuyck, the Jets' undefeated goaltender, who was 8-0-3 until this game, where he was replaced after the second period.

With the VGK's 5-2 win, the team now had four play-ers who'd scored two goals in one game: James Neal, Reilly Smith, David Perron, and William Karlsson. In just 16 games, Karlsson had scored six goals—the same num-ber over his entire previous season with the Columbus Blue Jackets.

Of the VGK's eight home games thus far, they'd won seven. In three of their wins, they faced the Chicago Black-hawks, the Colorado Avalanche, and the Winnipeg Jets, all of which had two free nights and three free days in Las Vegas; they outscored these opponents 16-4. Sure, it was a small sample, but a trend has to start somewhere and this one looked potentially juicy.

Record: 10-5-1

Game 17, Oilers in Edmonton, 11/14/17

Game 17, against the Oilers in Edmonton, was the kind of contest after which a coach would just prefer to "burn the tape," meaning not even bothering to review. Nothing Coach Gallant could do or say would sugarcoat or somehow, some way, pull something positive out of the 8-2 loss. Six different Oilers scored, with the 21-year-old superstar Connor McDa-vid and Ryan Nugent-Hopkins, both first-round picks, scor-ing two each. It was, in my opinion, the first game of the season in which the Knights never had a chance.

The only possible positive was that the VGK's fifth-string goaltender, Dylan Ferguson, on loan to Vegas from

Kamloops of the WHL, got to experience playing in the NHL as a 19-year-old. Very few players of his age ever see the ice in a regular-season game. But because Max Lagacé gave up seven goals on just 29 shots, Dylan got the call from the bench. He gave up only one goal, though the Edmonton Oilers might have dialed it back a bit, being ahead by five.

The opening periods on the road for the VGK continued to stink up the arenas, forcing the team to chase the Oilers' three-goal lead in the first period. Pressing when behind burns up a lot of energy and creates more odd-man rushes back into your defensive zone, which generate scoring chances. Those, in turn, create power plays for the opposition; attempts to slow down or catch up to the offensive players often cause infractions.

After opening the season with two straight wins on the road, Vegas went 1-5-1 in away games. This was a big contrast to 7-1-0 at home.

Record: 10-6-1

Game 18, Canucks in Vancouver, 11/16/17

In hockey, the word "rebound" is rarely positive, especially if it happens in your defensive zone after your goaltender blocks a shot. Almost every NHL-caliber goaltender will make saves on almost all of the original shots he can see. But when the puck ricochets in front of or to either side of the goalie, who is now out of position from making the original save, forwards love it, coaches lose their hair, and goaltenders lose their starting jobs.

In the next game against the Vancouver Canucks, there were plenty of rebounds, but they weren't the dangerous kind. Rather, the VGK, and Max Lagacé specifically, had the kind of rebounds that are remembered long after the game, which the VGK won 5-2.

In Lagacé's case, he was coming off the horrible result in Edmonton. And with second-string goalie Malcolm Subban accompanying the team on the current road trip and close to returning, the pressure was really on Max to rebound from the Oilers disaster, and he did.

The team as a whole also had to rebound and they dominated the entire first period, as well as a good portion of the second. A defensive breakdown and some sloppy play in clearing the puck out of the zone late in the second period allowed Vancouver to tie the game at 2-2. This could have been devastating to the team's mindset, especially after the Edmonton massacre. To their credit, the Knights got back to playing solid two-way hockey and regained control of the game. Scoring three third-period goals didn't hurt. And all five goals in this game were scored by different players: William Karlsson (his 7th), David Perron (6), Erik Haula (6), Reilly Smith (6), and Jonathan Marchessault (5).

I credited the coaching staff; even this early in the season, it didn't take long for corrections after bumps in the road. With the win, the VGK were in second place in the Pacific Division, only one point behind the L.A. Kings — all without their number-one goaltender, who hadn't played for more than a month.

Record: 11-6-1

Game 19, L.A. Kings at T-Mobile Arena, 11/19/17

Speaking of the Kings, in the Knights' next game, the Kings walked into a nightmare, especially their goaltender Jonathan Quick, who was pulled after giving up three goals on nine shots, highly unusual for him.

Before the Kings even broke a sweat, William Karlsson put a goal between Quick's pads and the onslaught was under way. Karlsson's second goal, his ninth in the last 13 games, turned out to be the winner in the 4-2 final score. Both goals were off passes from Reilly Smith. A Cody Eakin goal was sandwiched between Karlsson's two and Alex Tuch added an empty-net goal to stretch the VGK lead back to two goals after L.A. closed to within one.

Interestingly, Malcolm Subban was activated for the game, but Coach Gallant stayed with Max Lagacé, who'd been playing well. Lagacé made 27 saves on the 29 shots

---

Empty Net

An empty-net goal occurs at the end of a game, usually in the last couple of minutes, when a team trailing by one or two goals "pulls" its goaltender and leaves its net defenseless in order to add an extra skater on offense.

It's a strategy that drives sports bettors crazy, as an empty-netter can affect both game and totals wagers. If you've bet under 5.5 and the score is 3-2, an empty-net goal turns a winner into a loser—and vice versa for the over bettors. ♣

he faced and was especially potent late in the third period, when the Kings were throwing shots at him from all angles.

The win brought the VGK's home record to an impressive 8-1-0 and they trailed the division-leading L.A. Kings by one point.

Record: 12-6-1

Game 20, Ducks in Anaheim, 11/22/17

The VGK's 20th game, against the Anaheim Ducks, reminded me of why counting cards can be frustrating and playing poker can drive you completely out of your mind. In blackjack, card counters have an edge over the house, which is why they're often backed off or barred. Yet even with this edge, they don't always win. In poker, you can outplay your opponents, getting them to put their money into the pot with inferior hands, only to see them catch a miracle turn or river card to squash your superior play.

In this game, the VGK were the superior team, but the scoreboard hardly reflected that for the first 39 minutes of the game. John Gibson, the Anaheim Ducks' goaltender, was the number-one, number-two, and number-three star of the game for those 39 minutes. Indeed, the VGK set a team record with 49 shots on Gibson and didn't score their first goal until he'd already saved 30 shots. That brought the score at the end of the second period to 2-1, Ducks.

The Knights scored another three goals in the third period and on defense they held the Ducks to zero shots on net for more than 10 minutes.

The VGK completely shut down Anaheim and the game ended with a Knights victory, 4-2. It was frustrating to watch them outplay, outskate, and outshoot the Ducks and have nothing to show for it—until, that is, they refused to accept that Gibson was unbeatable. Then they beat him.

A day before the Ducks' game, Anaheim coach Randy Carlyle was asked what he'd like to see different about his team. He responded, "I wish my team played like a team, like the VGK do."

This came from a man who played in 1,055 NHL games and was in his 13th year as an NHL coach, with 806 regular-season games and 86 playoff games. He knows what a team effort looks like.

With the comeback win and the L.A. Kings' loss, the VGK moved into first place in the Pacific Division. Imagine—a first year expansion team leading its division after 20 games, a quarter of the season.

Record: 13-6-1

Game 21, San Jose Sharks at T-Mobile Arena, 11/24/17

No comeback was necessary in the next game against the San Jose Sharks. Once again, the team came out flying. San Jose's first shot at goaltender Max Lagacé came at the 1 minute 35 second mark; Max made a great save on the clean breakaway. That was also the Sharks' last shot for the next

15 minutes. The VGK scored two power-play goals against the number-one-ranked penalty-killing team in the entire league coming into the game.

They led 4-1 in the second period.

But then they surrendered three unanswered goals by the Sharks and were lucky that the second period ended with the game tied. The break allowed them to compose themselves and regroup for the last period.

It's rare to see four goaltenders play in the same game, but both Max Lagacé and San Jose's Martin Jones were replaced. It was the third time in the past four games the Golden Knights chased the opposing team's starting goaltender. Malcolm Subban, the reactivated second-string goalie, was on the ice for the third period and stopped all shots that he faced; neither team scored in the third, sending the game into overtime. Before San Jose could even register a shot, Jonathan Marchessault scored 1 minute and 21 seconds in.

Malcolm Subban hadn't played since October 21, but he didn't seem rusty. He got credit for the win and his record for the season remained a perfect 3-0-0.

The VGK were now an amazing 9-1-0 at T-Mobile. They remained in first place in the Pacific Division.

Record: 14-6-1

Game 22, Coyotes in Arizona, 11/25/17

The Arizona Coyotes dominated the entire first period and the beginning of the second in the VGK's next game, its

22nd. Then Tomas Nosek, William Karlsson, and Erik Haula scored in a span of 1:42 during the second period to lead 3-0. But just like the previous game against the Sharks, the VGK let the Coyotes back into the game with two goals in the third period to close the gap and force the players, coaches, and fans to hang on for a 4-2 win, which kept Malcolm Subban's NHL record undefeated at 4-0-0.

William Karlsson continued his incredible scoring pace with his team-leading 13th goal. In his previous two seasons in the NHL, Karlsson scored a total of 15 goals combined.

Record: 15-6-1

Game 23, Dallas Stars at T-Mobile Arena, 11/28/17

In their 23rd game, the Dallas Stars not only broke the VGK's second five-game winning streak of the season, but handed the Knights their first home loss in six weeks. It was also the first time they were shut out (3-0) and it was Malcolm Subban's first loss as the VGK goaltender. Subban had given up only eight goals in his four previous games; against the Stars, three goals were scored against him.

On the other side, the VGK faced the tallest goalie in the league. Ben Bishop is six-seven and could easily play in the NBA. In front of the net, he's a veritable wall. He stopped all 34 of the Knights' shots.

You don't often see a hat trick (when one player scores three goals in a game) in the NHL. In the 1,230 games played in the 2016-2017 season, only 70 produced a hat trick, a tad over 5%. But you see a natural hat trick (when the player scores three goals in a row) even more rarely. Dallas Stars' forward Radek Faksa scored the natural hat trick in the second period in 6 minutes and 46 seconds. Wow.

Record: 15-7-1

Game 24, Wild in Minnesota, 11/30/17

The VGK had three glorious scoring chances in the first two periods of their next game against the Minnesota Wild on the last night of November. Shots by Brendan Leipsic, James Neal, and Jonathan Marchessault all ricocheted off the posts or crossbar back onto the ice. Sometimes the hockey gods can be cruel that way, because the Wild's first two goals hit the posts and went in. The Wild's third goal took another crazy bounce that went off Deryk Engelland's glove and landed right at the skates of Eric Staal, alone in front of the net; with the easy put-in, Staal became the only player in the NHL to score a goal against all 31 teams in his career.

Malcolm Subban played great after having a subpar performance in his previous outing versus Dallas; unfortunately, the 4-2 loss was his second loss in a row. It was also only the second consecutive loss for the VGK; they'd lost back-to-back games against Toronto in a shootout on November 6 and at Montreal the following night.

In the game, Brayden McNabb scored his first goal of the season. Just two days earlier, even though he'd yet to score a goal, he was awarded a four-year $2.5 million contract. You might think $10 million is a lot to pay a player who doesn't score many goals, but defensemen are paid to prevent goals and Brayden was ranked third overall in the league in the so-called 50/50 Club. This statistic records a player's number of hits and blocked shots. Before this game, Brayden had 56 hits on opposing players and 53 blocked shots. Not just anyone can block slap shots resulting in pucks coming at you in excess of 100 mph. Putting your body in front of one of these projectiles isn't for the faint of heart. One thing's for sure: Brayden will have enough money to keep a good supply of ice packs at home—recovering from all the bruises that those shots cause.

Record: 15-8-1

Game 25, Jets in Winnipeg, 12/1/17

The Knights were at it again in a back-to-back game against the Winnipeg Jets on December 1 that again revealed the team's Achilles heel: the third-period meltdown. Going into the third, the score was tied up 2-2, but once again the Knights lost control of the game and allowed the Jets to score five goals and win the game 7-4.

Coach Gallant had mostly made the necessary adjustments over the course of the season, but his goaltending choice in this game, playing Max Lagacé over Malcolm Subban on the road against one of the hottest team in the Western Conference, was a surprise. Why play your fourth-string goalie when your team is already thin in net and your second-string goalie is healthy and available? Of course, it's easy to second guess a coach and his decisions, especially in hindsight, but with Subban playing only six games so far in the season, fatigue wasn't the issue that kept him out the lineup. I believe Coach Gallant was trying to steal a victory and give his number-two goaltender a night off. After that plan went awry, the Knights were now looking at a critical situation in their next game on December 3 at T-Mobile against the Arizona Coyotes.

Record: 15-9-1

Game 26, Arizona Coyotes at T-Mobile Arena, 12/3/17

Not too many visitors realize it, but due to the constant development of new and ever-expanding residential areas previously occupied only by non-humans, Las Vegas has a coyote problem. They don't pose a threat to humans, but they do feast on small dogs and cats. When I walk my dogs, I carry one of my hockey sticks, just in case. Hockey sticks can be useful off the ice.

But on the ice, Vegas has no Coyote problem. They won their 26th game 3-2 in overtime to remain undefeated in their series with Arizona. Coming into the game, Vegas was 4-0 in overtime, not including shootouts. With this OT win, they'd come up perfect at 5-0 during the five-minute OTs.

In addition, the Golden Knights' record rose to 8-1-0 versus teams in their own division. They averaged 3.88 goals per game. They were 10-1-0 when scoring the first goal and had an amazing 10-2-0 record at home. The defensive core registered 51 points, which tied them with Toronto for the league lead.

Best of all, the list of injured players that began plaguing the VGK in game four all but evaporated. First-string goalie Marc-André Fleury was cleared to resume practice and both David Perron and William Carrier were taken off Injured Reserve.

Record: 16-9-1

Game 27, Anaheim Ducks at T-Mobile Arena, 12/5/17

The Knights' next opponent, the Anaheim Ducks, were missing four key players in their lineup. As such, they managed to play only 20 minutes of a 60-minute game, all in the second period, during which the Knights seemed to be absent. John Gibson, the Ducks' netminder, played the entire first period by himself, stopping everything the VGK shot at him for the first 18½ minutes.

The two goals Vegas scored at the end of the first are rarely seen in a hockey game. These "alley-oop" goals came 16 seconds apart, slowly flipping over Gibson as he was lying on his back after saving the initial shots, reaching up with his glove hand to try to catch the puck before it landed behind him in the net.

On the other end of the ice, Malcolm Subban spent most of the first period relaxing. But for the rest of the game, Subban was like an octopus, multiple arms and legs stopping just about everything shot at him; he did give up three straight goals in the second period. But Erik Haula redeemed a bad play by scoring the tying goal late in the third.

The five-minute overtimes in NHL hockey are both heart-stopping and entertaining. Most fans stand the whole time. This game's OT session was especially enthralling, as the Ducks had a full two-minute power play that added more drama. The VGK were awarded their own PP with just under 30 seconds left. Finally, young Alex Tuch scored the only goal in the shootout, to give the Knights the 4-3 win.

Record: 17-9-1

Game 28, Predators in Nashville, 12/8/17

The Knights' road game against the Nashville Predators was a lot like what often happens around the holidays when families get together. You just never know what the night will bring.

The Knights were taking part in a new tradition that most teams have adopted over the last few years in the NHL. The Dad Trip encourages fathers of the players to accompany their sons' teams on short road trips. It's an overdue reward for the parents who were instrumental in the development of their sons' hockey aspirations from the first day they laced up the skates for them — most little boys can't properly lace up their skates. A Mom Trip was scheduled for later in the season.

This was a true family reunion for the Subban family,

as Vegas Golden Knights' goaltender Malcolm Subban was playing for the first time against his older brother PK, with their dad on the trip with the VGK. In fact, the elder Subban raised three hockey sons; the Subbans' youngest brother Jordan was in the L.A. Kings' system.

Mr. Subban left no question about who he was rooting for that night—he attended the game wearing a VGK jersey.

Unlike his younger brother Malcolm, who's unassuming and just goes about his business, PK is flamboyant. Not only is he entertaining to watch during the game, but his pre-game ritual is always a treat—dancing on the ice to the ambient music, flipping up the pucks and catching them on the blade of his stick. PK is never at a loss for words and his style pretty much sealed his fate in Montreal. He was loved there by the fans and his charitable work was of epic proportions. But in Montreal, they don't believe in a player being bigger than the coach or the team and with PK, that was the case. He was traded to Nashville, which came within two games of winning the Stanley Cup after PK arrived there.

This was a strange game. At first, the VGK looked like they'd coast to two points holding a 2-0 lead with just 5 minutes and 23 seconds left in the second period. Nashville scored late in the second to close the gap and once again, the third period proved to be the team's nemesis when the Predators tied it up. Late in the third with the score still tied, two points looked like one point. But when Nashville scored a second unanswered goal to take the lead, the two points that became one point now looked like no points. These family gatherings aren't good for the heart!

Malcolm Subban was pulled for an extra skater and

time was running out. But with a mere 39.5 seconds left, Erik Haula tied the game and the one point was again a good possibility.

In the shootout, Malcolm Subban was not to be denied. He efficiently (and quietly) outplayed all six Nashville shooters who skated at him in one-on-one confrontations. At the other end of the ice, Nashville's Pekka Rinne also stopped the first five VGK shooters. But the last one, Reilly Smith, beat Rinne under his right arm, which ended the game and gave Vegas the two points they had and lost, then hoped to salvage one, and finally reclaimed both in the standings. Vegas was now 7-1 in games that required more than 60 minutes.

In total, the Predators had 44 shots in regulation and overtime. Subban stopped 41 of them. He was perfect in OT and the shootout. At the end of the game, there was one proud papa with the last name of Subban.

In another type of reunion, James Neal was playing against the team that gave him up to the expansion draft. Neal, who'd logged 252 goals in his career, scored one in this game. He almost certainly wouldn't admit to this, but you've got to figure he wanted that one badly.

Record: 18-9-1

Game 29, Stars in Dallas, 12/9/17
Just as the game at Nashville offered James Neal a chance at redemption of sorts, so too did Max Lagacé return

to goalie duty in the VGK's 29th game against the Dallas Stars. Before signing with the Golden Knights, Lagacé spent three years in the Dallas system. Coach Gallant employed this former-team factor in starting Max over Malcolm. Professional athletes take a lot of pride in what they do and Lagacé was handed the opportunity to show Dallas, and the Knights, and the nation that was now following the team, that he could play.

His playing time limited—with Subban healthy and first-string goalie Marc-André Fleury now skating with the team—Lagacé took full advantage, stopping 35 of the 38 shots he faced and making 15 much-needed saves in the third period. Third periods had continued to be unkind to Vegas. At the time, they ranked 28 out of 31 teams in goals surrendered in the third. In this game, they took a two-goal lead into the last period, but the Stars scored a goal to make the game a lot tighter than the 5-3 final score indicated.

The game was like a tennis match, with goals scored one after another, but the VGK never trailed. Alex Tuch opened the scoring, only to see Dallas tie it up 2 minutes and 15 seconds later, ending the first period tied at 1-1. When David Perron scored a power-play goal in the second to take a 2-1 lead, Dallas answered only 27 seconds later to tie it again. Vegas scored two quickies—four goals in 3 minutes and 37 seconds! If you got up to grab a drink after a goal, you probably missed the next one or maybe even two.

Record: 19-9-1

Game 30, Carolina Hurricanes at T-Mobile Arena, 12/12/17

In the game against the Carolina Hurricanes on December 12, the Knights' 30th, Marc-André Fleury finally returned to the net for the first time since he was injured on October 31. It didn't appear that he was at all rusty from missing 25 games over six weeks. He was his old self as he was tested early by Carolina, who outskated, outplayed, and out-scored the VGK in the first period. The Hurricanes scored again in the second, but the Knights tied it up 2-2 on goals by Deryk Engelland and Reilly Smith. The third period was scoreless thanks to Fleury, which sent the game into OT, also scoreless. In the shootout, each team scored one goal among the first three shooters. Both shooters going fourth failed to score. The fifth shooter for the VGK missed, after which Carolina's Phillip Di Giuseppe finally beat Fleury for the Carolina win. Even so, Fleury was back on top of his game with 35 saves on 37 shots, 15 in the third period.

The loss was the first in five games. The previous three home games went into overtime—a treat for the thousands of new hockey fans in attendance. Even if you're a long-time hockey fan, OT is always special and now that the league has gone to three-against-three skaters, there's usually non-stop action for the entire five minutes.

Record: 19-9-2

Game 31, Pittsburgh Penguins at T-Mobile Arena, 12/14/17

Next up was Pittsburgh, back-to-back Stanley Cup champions, arriving to play at T-Mobile.

James Neal played 199 games as a Penguin between 2011 and 2014. Marc-André Fleury spent 13 seasons with Pittsburgh; he was the number-one overall pick in the 2003 draft, recorded 375 wins with 44 shutouts, and won three Stanley Cups: 2009, 2116, and 2017.

Neal scored on the VGK's very first shot of the game to notch a 1-0 lead. And Fleury was a force in the net, stopping 24 of the 25 shots he faced. Jon Merrill, who hadn't played since December 1 and was in only his sixth game for Vegas, scored the winning goal in the 2-1 contest. With it, the VGK now had 19 players who'd scored at least one goal in the inaugural season.

It was Fleury's first win since October 10, the team's home opener. When he was asked about the win versus his former team, he said, "For a little while, I can be relieved. I'm glad it's over and we got the win."

Record: 20-9-2

Game 32, Florida Panthers at T-Mobile Arena, 12/17/17

Getting a 21 is what everyone who comes to Vegas to play blackjack strives for. But for Coach Gallant, the VGK's 21st win was extra special: It came at the expense of the Florida Panthers, who fired Gallant from his head-coaching duties almost exactly a year earlier—and rather ignominiously to boot. They literally dumped him on the side of the road, abandoning him after a road game and leaving him to find his own way home.

In the post-game press conference, Gallant was deadpan, claiming it didn't have any special significance. But trust me when I tell you that behind closed doors, Gallant was tickled pink. Coaches are no different than players; they all love to win. And when it comes at the expense of a team for which they once coached or played, it raises that bar.

It wasn't an easy win, as the Knights trailed 2-0 after Florida scored two quick goals just 5 minutes and 13 seconds into the game.

Leads of 2-0 in the NHL are critical, because the next goal scored often determines the momentum of the game. Scoring the third goal for a 3-0 lead will, for all intents and purposes, demoralize a team and make for a long evening of hockey. On the flip side, scoring the next goal to eliminate the shutout and cut the lead in half provides much-needed confidence and determination for the trailing team.

Exactly that happened when the VGK made it 2-1. They scored the tying goal late in the first, all but taking control of the game. Then they buried another three unanswered to win 5-2.

You could tell that the players really wanted this win for their coach and they made it happen. It carried the VGK record in December to 6-1-1. It was also Deryk Engelland's 500th NHL game.

Also, the hangover effect on teams spending a few days

off before playing in Las Vegas remained perfect; Florida spent two days off before the game.

Best of all, the Knights looked primed to take on the league-leading Tampa Bay Lightning two days later.

Record: 21-9-2

Game 33, Tampa Bay Lightning at T-Mobile Arena, 12/19/17

The Lightning were riding a seven-game winning streak into this game. Would the VGK skate stride for stride with a team that had the most points (50), a plus-44 goal differential, an impressive 11-3-1 record on the road, and was the favorite to win the Stanley Cup?

The fans were psyched. The atmosphere at T-Mobile was again playoff-like, with the crowd up on its feet numerous times throughout the game to cheer their team through the biggest test they'd yet faced.

That night, every hockey fan outside of Las Vegas found out that what happens at T-Mobile Arena doesn't stay in T-Mobile or even Vegas. Our dream was now your team's nightmare.

Jump out to a 2-0 lead with two power-play goals in the first period? Big deal! We'll just score two PP goals of our own to tie the game.

Given up only 80 goals in 32 games, an average of 2.5 per? No problem! We'll score four goals on you.

Highest scoring team in the league with 123 goals? So

what! We'll score one more goal than you — *and with just 2.3 seconds left in the game*.

After posting a 4-3 victory, the VGK were 7-1-1 in December and the number-one team in the Western Conference.

Again, the Vegas flu did its dirty work: Tampa Bay arrived on December 17 for the game on the 19th.

Record: 22-9-2

Game 34, Washington Capitals at T-Mobile Arena, 12/23/17

Who knew then that the Tampa Bay Lightning would ultimately play the next team up at T-Mobile, the Washington Capitals, in the Eastern Conference Championship? Not the Golden Knights, not that they'd have cared. So the Capitals earned the Presidents Trophy, awarded to the team that accumulates the most points, two seasons in a row. Ho hum. We'll just shut you out, 3-0.

Back-to-back Stanley Cup champions Pittsburgh Penguins come to town and are sent packing with a loss. League-leading Tampa Bay Lightning step up and get shot down. Then, back-to-back Presidents Trophy-winning Washington Capitals try their luck and Marc-André Fleury records his first-ever shutout with the VGK, making 26 saves.

The VGK were now on a four-game winning streak; they'd also won eight of their last nine games. The experts, however, still wouldn't let up. "They're playing way over their heads." And, "The writing is on the wall." And, "The collapse is imminent." Oh yeah? Slightly less than halfway through the 82-game season, when, exactly, was this can't-be-happening campaign supposed to end?

Record: 23-9-2

Game 35, Ducks in Anaheim, 12/27/17

In the first 20 minutes of the VGK's 34th game against the Anaheim Ducks, the Knights looked sluggish and were dominated. If it hadn't been for Malcolm Subban, it could have gotten ugly real quick. But the coma didn't last the entire first period. With two minutes and 10 seconds left, former Duck Shea Theodore ripped a shot over Anaheim goaltender John Gibson's right shoulder. The VGK then proceeded to score the next four goals, monopolizing the remainder of the game, sealing the 4-1 win.

Malcolm Subban made 27 saves and recorded his ninth win in 12 starts. Cody Eakin recorded his fifth goal of the season; in the last 60 games he played with the Dallas Stars, Eakin scored a total of three goals. Eakin was just one of the many examples of how the players bought into Coach Gallant's whole-team system and could compete every night against any team in the league.

The Golden Knights were unquestionably on a mission.

Record: 24-9-2

Game 36, Kings in L.A., 12/28/17

The following night, December 28, the Western Conference-leading VGK dispatched their Pacific Division rivals, the L.A. Kings, who were chasing Vegas for a superior playoff position. Yes, as early as December, we were talking about playoff seeding. Believe me, only the most stubborn old-school experts were thinking this was just an anomaly.

Frankly, though the final score was 3-2 and won in overtime, the Kings didn't deserve even to be in this game with Vegas. Not only were they completely overshadowed, but they went without a shot on net for more than 11 minutes for one stretch and 12 minutes for another—in all, more than an entire period of play. In the third period, the chances at net were 47-22 in favor of the Knights.

Fleury stopped 26 of the 28 shots he faced and the first goal was no fault of his own, as a slap shot from the point was deflected off Jonathan Marchessault's stick when he was attempting to get in front of it. The goal was credited to Marion Gaborik, but I watched the replay six times in slow motion and never saw the puck hit him. I suspected that in an attempt to get Marion going, as his normal goal production was way down, Derek Forbort, who took the shot, might have claimed that he saw it go off of Gaborik. Hockey players are unselfish like that; they'd rather see a goal scorer get out of a slump and help their team than take credit for the goal. This is especially true for defensemen, who aren't paid to score goals.

The Kings stayed in the game by the grace of Knights' forward Pierre-Édouard Bellemare's mental blunder in skating to retrieve a new stick after his was broken. (He should've stayed in play without a stick or taken one from a teammate.) Bellemare's brain fart led to Drew Doughty's late goal, which sent the game into overtime and allowed L.A. to steal a point.

After the game, NHL veteran Doughty contravened the well-known convention of not giving an opposing team a statement to hang up on the locker-room wall for extra incentive. He said, "There's no way they'll be a better team than us by the end of the season." He had no idea how those words would come back to haunt him.

Record: 25-9-2

Game 37, Toronto Maple Leafs at T-Mobile Arena, 12/31/17

The VGK closed out an amazing 2017 with a game against the Toronto Maple Leafs at T-Mobile that started at 12:30 p.m. to make room for the Strip's 300,000 New Year's Eve revelers.

In the game, which the VGK won 6-3, William Karlsson tallied the first hat trick of his career and the first-ever for the Golden Knights. The New Year's Eve party hats rained down on the ice after the game in celebration.

Karlsson's third goal in the game was amazing to watch: Even though it was shot into an empty net, Karlsson was

Broken Stick

According to NHL rules, playing with a broken stick receives a minor two-minute penalty. A replacement stick may be obtained only from the bench or a teammate on the ice. A goalie can continue to play with a broken stick or no stick, but he can't leave the ice during play to retrieve a new one, only when the action is stopped. A teammate can hand a goalie his stick; if it's slid or thrown to him, he receives a two-minute penalty.

The closest player to the goalie is most likely a defenseman, who'll give him his stick or try to retrieve one from the bench. But it's the same drill for a forward.

When a defenseman breaks his stick, the closest forward will give him his stick, even if it has the wrong curve to it. All NHL players use a stick with a slight curve based on if they shoot right-handed or left-handed. It's actually more important for a defenseman to have a stick than a forward. The defenseman uses it to pass the puck out of his zone, shoot it toward the net while his team is in the offensive zone, block or deflect shots, and limit cross-ice passes. The forward who gives his stick to a defenseman will go to the bench when he can to retrieve one for himself. ♣

diving, sliding on the ice, stretched out to beat a defenseman, and just sweeping the puck with his outstretched stick. It was his 20th of the season, which led the team. By comparison, Karlsson had a total of 15 goals over his last two seasons with the Columbus Blue Jackets.

With the win, the Knights added to their record of 16-1-0 when scoring first.

They also increased their winning streak to seven games and set yet another 100-year-old NHL record for the most wins by a first-year team in December: 11. Just how many records would this team break?

The only person who might have had mixed emotions was none other than Marc-André Fleury; in winning the game, Malcolm Subban had his own six-game winning streak going. Both goalies were playing so well that Coach Gallant had to choose between them. Who would have thought in October and November that having too many goalie options would be a problem—when the VGK were playing their third-, fourth-, and even fifth-string goaltenders?

Record: 26-9-2

Game 38, Nashville Predators at T-Mobile Arena, 1/2/18

Starting the new year, the Vegas Golden Knights were the number-one team in the Western Conference and the number-two team in the entire league. They were in the midst of an eight-game winning streak and they owned the best home record in the NHL at 17-2-1. They'd accumulated points in 13 straight games with a record of 12-0-1. They hadn't lost in regulation since December 1 and they'd beaten all of the league's top teams.

The playoff buzz started to spread in earnest.

In their 37th game against the Nashville Predators, the VGK shut them out 3-0. They jumped out to a 2-0 lead and with this win, they were 10-0 when they had a lead of two-zip. They were now 17-1 when scoring first and 15-2 when entering the third period with the lead.

Marc-André Fleury played for the VGK and play he did, stopping all 29 shots he faced and recording his second shutout in his last three starts. It was his fifth win against no regulation losses and one shootout loss since returning from his injury; his overall record as a VGK now stood at 8-1-1. He hadn't lost in regulation since October 13.

Brayden McNabb was a wrecking ball on the ice, crushing any Nashville player who dared to attempt to carry the puck across the blue line. McNabb is the only player in the NHL who had combined (at the time) for 90+ hits, 90+ blocked shots, and a +10 rating. Yes, fighting is part of the physicality of the game, but you can accomplish the same effect without having to go to the penalty box for five minutes. McNabb proved that in spades during the first half of the season.

Record: 27-9-2

Game 39, Blues in St. Louis, 1/4/18

The speed of the St. Louis Blues, especially in the first period, not only matched that of the Knights, but for the most part, they were the quicker team and used the VGK's normal game plan to beat them 2-1 and stop Vegas' latest win streak at eight in a row. Even though the win streak was over, there was no finger-pointing among the VGK; in games where you score only one goal, you can't expect to win many.

Fleury gave up only two and stopped the other 37 shots he faced, but the Blues still managed to outscore the VGK by that one goal. St. Louis won 61% of the faceoffs, which becomes a puck-control factor and affects the pace of the game. This game, three full months into the six-month regular season, also finally nudged the VGK's overall losses into double digits.

Record: 27-10-2.

Game 40, Blackhawks in Chicago, 1/5/18

Against the Chicago Blackhawks in a back-to-backer, the game was a roller coaster of momentum swings. Vegas returned to its first-period dominance, jumping out to a 2-0 lead. The Blackhawks scored their first goal with 1:59 left in the first period to make it 2-1. Vegas made it 3-1 and it seemed like that would stem the Chicago tide, but the Blackhawks closed the gap at 3-2.

When Chicago scored the next goal to tie it 3-3, it appeared that the VGK's back-to-back games might be taking an energy toll. Blowing two two-goal leads is never a good thing, especially on the road, where it gets the crowd back into the game and gives the home team a spark. When the Blackhawks scored 30 seconds into the third period, giving them the lead for the first time in the game, the wheels seemed to be coming off of the Vegas bus. But the Knights regrouped and scored and it was anyone's 4-4 game.

On a play that Chicago defenseman Connor Murphy most likely wanted back, he pinched in on the blue line, only to see Reilly Smith chip the puck past him and break in all alone to score the winning goal.

It was the first game that Vegas had given up more than three goals since the miserable 7-4 loss to Winnipeg way back on December 1. Malcolm Subban registered 28 saves, recorded his seventh consecutive win in net, and increased his record to 11-2-0. The Chicago game was also the fifth win out of the last six road games for Vegas. Scoring the game's first goal, the VGK increased their record to 18-1-0 when they scored first.

Ryan Carpenter made his VGK debut after being claimed from San Jose on Dec. 13.

Record: 27-10-2

Game 41, New York Rangers at T-Mobile Arena, 1/7/18

Two nights later, the VGK's home game against the New York Rangers featured two of the fastest teams in the league. The VGK had grown accustomed to being the faster team on the ice, but in this game, that wasn't the case. How would they handle a team as quick as they were? The same question was asked of the Rangers. The answer was a lot of potential odd-man rushes that were quickly extinguished by the speedy defensemen getting back and the forwards back-checking to prevent any quality scoring chances. But with that much speed from both teams, odd-man rushes will happen and they did; however, both goaltenders stood the test.

So you can match the VGK's speed. No worries. Marc-André Fleury will shut you down.

So your goaltender has an amazing game and gives up only two goals to the VGK, who were averaging 3.52 goals a game. No worries. Fleury will give up only one goal, even though you averaged 3.12 goals a game.

During the last four minutes of the game, the Rangers appeared to take their speed to another level. Fleury, however was so on top of his game that the puck must have looked as big, slow, and predictable as a beach ball to him. He blocked everything the Rangers threw at him. With 1:59 left, the Rangers pulled their goaltender, creating a six on five, and did just about everything humanly possible to get the tying goal. With just seven seconds left, Fleury made a highlight save, his 28th of the 29 shots he faced.

He'd given up two goals or less in his previous five starts and in seven of his last eight, and only 11 goals in his last eight starts. He was 6-1-1 since returning from his injury. His 2-1 win over the Rangers brought his season record to 9-2-1.

The win was also the seventh straight at T-Mobile and increased the VGK's home record to 18-2-1, the best home record in the entire NHL. In the previous 16 games, including this win, Vegas logged a record of 14-1-1, scoring 22 more goals than the opposition. And the Knights now had 60 points, sharing the point lead with Tampa Bay. Some Las

Vegas sports books had posted a line of 72 total points in the Knights' *entire* inaugural season and they were only 12 short — with half the season to go.

Record: 28-10-2

Game 42, Edmonton Oilers at T-Mobile Arena, 1/13/18

On January 13, the Vegas Golden Knights took on the Edmonton Oilers at T-Mobile after a five-day half-season break. Was the five-day break to blame for the VGK appearing to be one step behind throughout the game? Or was it the unbelievable speed of Edmonton's Connor McDavid? His display of speed also came on the second night of back-to-back games for the Oilers. Just how good is he?

Completely good. He plays all 200 feet of the ice surface. He back-checks and forechecks. He draws opposing players to him, then dishes off the puck to one of his wide-open teammates. With what seems like two quick strides, he's at full speed, creating total havoc on the ice. And then he accelerates!

But here's what's really scary about Connor McDavid: The night before this game, he turned 21! Did he go out drinking in Vegas to celebrate? Even if he did, it didn't matter. This hockey phenom hasn't even begun to reach his peak talent-wise. Mark my words, he'll be breaking all or most of #99 Wayne Gretzky's records, which have always seemed unreachable.

In this game, for example, McDavid accumulated his 200th point in his first 173 games. He would have gotten there sooner, except he missed half his rookie year with a broken collar bone.

Even though the VGK earned a point from the 3-2 loss in overtime, that was a gift. The VGK had six power plays without scoring a goal; even worse, Edmonton's penalty kill was the worst in the league.

The VGK's dominance on home ice was interrupted, their home record now 18-3-1. This was their first loss at T-Mobile in more than a month (since December 12), their perfect 6-0 record in OT now had a blemish, and their next four games were on the road.

The good news was that both James Neal and Marc-André Fleury were named to the All Star Team, the third time for both players, and Coach Gallant was selected as the coach for the Pacific Division side.

Record: 29-10-3

Game 43, Predators in Nashville, 1/16/18

In the game against the Edmonton Oilers, the Knights stole a point in their OT loss. They just weren't in sync, perhaps after a week off, and they needed a game to get their legs back under them.

In the next game against the Nashville Predators, they clearly deserved to win, but they didn't even get a point. That's how the hockey gods work sometimes. They reward you when you should be punished and deny you when you play well enough to win a road game in a tough building. Nashville and Vegas may have the most passionate fans in the NHL and the noise in both arenas has an effect on the road team. The VGK played an excellent game and kept the crowd from becoming the sixth skater on the ice for the Predators. But the lack of scoring limited their chance of taking down two points on the road.

The Knights outshot Nashville 43-27. Granted, Nashville was coming off of their own mid-season break and maybe weren't quite in sync themselves. But backup goaltender Juuse Saros made the difference in sending Vegas to their second loss in a row in the 1-0 shutout. He was making the most of his limited playing chances, as veteran Pekka Rinne played most of the games for Nashville.

This was only the second time the VGK were shut out in the season. The other was against the Dallas Stars with Ben Bishop in net.

Defensive games like this are par for the course as the schedule moves into the second half of the season. Goals are hidden treasures. Power-play goals feel like you've struck a goal mine (pun intended).

Record: 29-11-3

Game 44, Lightning in Tampa Bay, 1/18/18

In the Tampa Bay Lightning game on January 18, back in net looking to snap this little two-game losing streak was none other Marc-André Fleury, the world-class goaltender who came gift-wrapped from Pittsburgh. He neither disappointed nor put into question Gallant's decision to come right back with Fleury instead of number-two Malcolm Subban. Fleury was perfect against five on five and the only puck that managed to get by him was a tick-tock goal that featured precision cross-ice passes before finding its way behind him on a power play.

The Knights' penalty-killing unit had been perfect since these two teams met last on December 19 — yes, one day shy of a month and 10 games without giving up a power-play goal. But Ondrej Palat's power-play goal was the only one Tampa Bay scored in their 4-1 loss to Vegas. It was the only thing the Lightning could raise their arms about.

This win was the team's 15th in its last 19 games and Vegas swept the season series against Tampa Bay 2-0, the first series sweep for the VGK.

Record: 30-11-3

Game 45, Panthers in Florida, 1/19/18

Next up: a back-to-back game against the Florida Panthers.

James Neal's goal late in the third period tied it up at 3-3, but Vegas lost in overtime, the second-in-a-row loss in OT after going 6-0. Also, a dark cloud continued to follow the team's power play. The strong goal production when five on five masked the power-play problem, but the

Knights had scored only one power-play goal since December 23 out of their last 32 PP chances. They not only didn't score on multiple chances against Florida, they gave up a shorthanded goal that breathed new life into Florida and knocked the wind out of the Knights.

Malcolm Subban had an off game and looked unsure of himself at times. He faced only 26 shots and surrendered four goals, very unlike the goalie who had been extremely strong in all of his previous starts.

James Neal's goal late in the third was huge for both the team and him personally. It was his 20th of the season and it marked 20 goals in 10 straight seasons with four different teams, making Neal only the sixth active player to boast such a streak. (The other five are icons in the NHL: Alex Ovechkin, Jonathan Toews, Jaromir Jagr, Patrick Kane, and Tomas Vanek.)

Record: 30-11-4

Game 46, Hurricanes in Carolina, 1/21/18

The last time Gerard Gallant walked out of PNC Arena in Raleigh, North Carolina, was on Nov. 27, 2016, the night he was fired as the head coach of the Florida Panthers after a regular-season loss to the Carolina Hurricanes. When he walked out of PNC Arena on January 19, 2018, his job was not only as secure as it could possibly be, but his head was held high with his team currently number-one overall in the National Hockey League and seemingly a lead-pipe cinch to become NHL Coach of the Year.

Firing coaches is common among all the major sports. For the most part, it isn't entirely the coach's fault that the team is doing badly. But management can't exactly fire all the players, so what other choice does it have?

The accomplishments of this team in 46 games were unheard of, almost unimaginable, and their coach was the main reason for them all. He was their foundation. He was Mount Gallant.

After following hockey for six decades, I didn't have to look through the record books to say, with 100% certainty, that there was never a first-year team that, 46 games into a season, led the entire NHL. And they weren't just first in points. They'd scored the most goals in the Western Conference and the second most in the league, while giving up the third fewest goals in the conference. They had the best home record of all 31 teams and were tied for second with the most road wins at 13.

Oh, and they beat the Carolina Hurricanes by a score of 5-1. On the road.

Record: 31-11-4

Game 47, Columbus Blue Jackets at T-Mobile Arena, 1/23/18

We've all been there, men and women alike, jilted by lovers who no longer need or want you around. It's painful when this happens, of course. But then comes a time when you run into your ex, who can't hide the disbelief that you've moved on and are feeling fine and looking good. You can see it in his or her eyes: "Damn, what was I thinking when I let you go?" And, "I never thought you'd be able to live without me."

Well, when William Karlsson met up with his ex, the Columbus Blue Jackets, he made them see red — the red light behind the net that comes on to signal a goal scored. Indeed, Columbus could have gotten a Golden tan with all the red lights going off, six different times in the game. But the two that hurt the most were off Karlsson's stick. Scoring multiple goals in a game is every hockey player's dream, but scoring two against your former team is a night you'll never forget.

In the first period, Columbus looked as fast as the Knights. What I didn't realize was that Vegas wasn't as fast as they normally were, especially in the beginning of games at T-Mobile. The first game home from a road trip, in particular one from the east coast three time zones away, can be troublesome for most teams. The VGK were lucky to survive the first 20 minutes tied at 1-1.

However, when they had the chance to regroup and get their legs under them, it was no longer a contest. In fact, the second period in this game might have been the best the Knights had played up to that point. Wave after wave of offensive attacks was cast upon Columbus. The Blue Jackets looked shocked at the speed of the Knights and who could blame them? They'd just assumed what they observed in the first period would be what they needed to contend with. So sorry. With the 6-3 victory, Vegas recorded its 19th win out of 23 games on home ice, which led the entire NHL at the time.

Brad Hunt had an outstanding game, scoring his first goal of the season, picking up two assists, and allowing the VGK to boast that every VGK skater on the roster had now scored at least one goal—this was a team!

After the game, Columbus Blue Jackets coach John Tortorella was asked about his former player, William Karlsson. He responded, "I don't like him scoring two goals against us tonight. But as his ex-coach, and caring about Bill, I'm thrilled for him." Well-done, John!

Record: 32-11-4

Game 48, New York Islanders at T-Mobile Arena, 1/25/18

The VGK's 48th game against the New York Islanders featured two of the highest-scoring teams in the league. Combined with the fact that the Islanders had also given up a lot of goals, the last score you'd expect would be 2-1 in favor of the visiting team. But that was the result, as New York, which seems to always be involved in 6-5 and 7-5 games, plays some wicked defense. The Islanders threw their bodies in front of everything they could, blocking 20 of the VGK's 59 shots on net. Islander goalie Jaroslav Halak was outstanding.

The VGK hadn't lost at home in regulation in almost two months. Their last home loss before this game on January 25 was way back on November 28 against Dallas. That had to end and in this game, it did.

The good news: The VGK power play, which had seen its share of struggles this season, was finally coming alive. The Knights scored four power-play goals in their last seven attempts and the only goal to beat Halak was on a power play.

Thirty of the 31 teams were in action on this night; the entire NHL went on the All-Star Break the next day.

The VGK's next game, on the road against Calgary, launched a six-game road trip.

Record: 32-12-4

Game 49, Flames in Calgary, 1/30/18

This game called hockey is played in a glass-enclosed rink on an ice surface 200 feet long and 85 feet wide, with at least 10 players whose average height is six-one and average weight is 204 pounds—skating around at speeds in excess of 20 miles per hour. And that's to say nothing of the knife edge on the hockey-skate blade, which has a uniform thickness of approximately 2.9 mm (0.115 inches), and a puck flying around at 100 miles an hour.

In short, when you're out there, you should never blink.

In the VGK's 49th game of the season and the first after the five-day All Star break, the Calgary Flames blinked. With just a minute and 46 seconds left in a game that Calgary should have won and deserved to win, they lost in a blink of an eye.

The Flames' Michael Frolik had the puck on his stick near his own blue line and passed it back toward his net to a defenesman instead of getting it safely out of his defensive zone. Not only did the pass never get to Frolik's teammate, but it became an unexpected shot by a Calgary player on his own net.

Calgary goaltender Mike Smith wasn't, to be sure, prepared for that. Before he could blink, the puck hit him and came right out to the Golden Knights' Erik Haula. Haula's eyes were wide open and he quickly deposited the misplaced pass-shot into the net for his 18th goal of the season to tie the game at 2-2 in the third period.

A mere 10 seconds later, Jonathan Marchessault scored and a 2-1 deficit was now a 3-2 VGK lead. David Perron's empty-net goal closed out the VGK's incredible last-minute heroics.

Marc-André Fleury was the only reason the VGK were still in this game late into the third period. He stopped 31 of 33 shots, including all 12 Calgary shots in the first period.

Also in the blink of an eye, the VGK's puny power play was rendered no longer a problem. The power play had scored six times in the previous four games and in this game against the Flames, the PP unit went 1 for 2, while the penalty-kill unit, the star of the VGK specialty teams, continued to shine, stopping all three of the Flames' power-play chances.

Record: 33-12-4

Game 50, Jets in Winnipeg, 2/1/18

When the VGK took on the Jets in Winnipeg on the first day of February, the Jets had lost only once in their last 16 home games and were 7-2-1 in their last 10 games—one of the hottest teams in the league. Both the VGK and the Jets were, at this point, the season's NHL surprises. Little did anyone know what would develop in the playoffs.

In this game, the VGK penalty-killing unit once again came through when Reilly Smith scored a shorthanded goal to tie the game at 1-1 in the second period and take the wind out of the Winnipeg Jets, who up to that point were dominating. Then the power play, which had been a force of late, scored again to take a 2-1 lead into the third period.

The Jets, fighting hard, tied it up in the third, taking the game into overtime.

David Perron's goal came with only 1:03 left in OT; this was the ninth OT game that the Knights won either during the five-minute period or the shootout.

It was a goal that should have never happened, as it appeared that the Jets had scored in OT. How the puck stayed out of the net I'm not sure, and neither were the Jets players who raised their sticks in celebration. Even the VGK announcer declared it a goal. But Fleury stopped the initial shot, then the puck just kind of lay there in the crease, then Erik Haula threw himself at it, and then it popped out. Intervention from above? Who knows? But those who follow this team know that the impossible is *always* possible.

The Crease

In the NHL, the "crease"—also known as the "blue paint"—is the area of ice directly in front of the net. It has a red border and solid blue interior. An offensive player isn't allowed to precede the puck into the crease. This rule protects the goalie, who's particularly vulnerable during offensive rushes.

The crease rule evolved in such a way as to give referees wider discretion in enforcement, but that led to controversies in which refs were making calls based on their own interpretations. Ultimately, the lack of consistency became glaring.

The most famous blue-paint case involved the deciding goal of the deciding Game 6 in the 1999 Stanley Cup Finals between the Dallas Stars and Buffalo Sabres. The game was tied 1-1 when Brett Hull scored a late goal with his skate barely in the crease. Still, the goal was allowed to stand, giving the Stars the win—and the Cup.

Late in the 2017-2018 season, the NHL assumed authority for the final decision on goalie interference, which it now makes from Toronto in the so-called "War Room." ♣

The defeat of the Jets by the VGK 3-2 in overtime made it two road wins in a row for Vegas. And it was Perron's fourth winning goal of the season.

No one could have projected that the VGK would have so many wins and so few losses after 50 games. Well, maybe Someone could, but He rarely speaks. He just listens most of the time to those who need Him.

Record: 34-12-4

Game 51, Wild in Minnesota, 2/2/18

Vegas could've used Him in the back-to-back game the next night against the Minnesota Wild, in which the VGK sleep-walked to a 5-2 loss. It was over early; the first period was the hardest to watch. The Knights were out-*everythinged*. Add to it that Minnesota had lost only one game at home in two months. But it was just a passing breeze; by game 51, it was foolish to try to find fault with this team. They'd spoiled their fans in so many ways that no matter what they did on the ice, it was a win for Las Vegas.

Record: 34-13-4

Game 52, Capitals in Washington, 2/4/18

The difficult road schedule continued with only one day off before the Knights hit the ice against the Washington Capitals for an afternoon game. The 12:30 p.m. start felt like 9:30 a.m. for the Knights. But it was Super Bowl Sunday, so the NHL was doing what it had to do not to compete with the NFL.

The VGK visited Eastern Conference teams just once during the season, so the meeting in Washington, D.C., with the Capitals was the only one that appeared on the VGK schedule—as of February 4. At that time, I commented in my blog at LasVegasAdvisor.com that of the 16 teams that qualified for the playoffs, one of them would win the Stanley Cup and be invited back to Washington to spend a few hours at the White House with the cherished trophy. Funny how things work out sometimes.

Even 52 games into the season, with the VGK sitting in first place in the Pacific Division, the naysayers insisted that I was getting way ahead of myself for even imagining such a thing. I told them, "Maybe I am, but as a lifelong hockey fan, what you're seeing here with the Golden Knights is so outside the norm that you should please excuse my excitement."

Also, I knew that this team had a big edge on winning playoff games and that was *being* a team. Coach Gallant shuttled all four lines in and out of games, a continuously fresh wave of trios, all of which challenged the workhorse stars of their opponents. As such, just about everyone was scoring. Even Ryan Carpenter, who'd been with the team less than two months, put the puck in the net in Washington to tie the game at 1-1 in the first period, becoming the 23rd VGK to register a goal so far in the season. And Alex Tuch, who hadn't scored in 11 games, landed a huge goal to break the third-period tie and propel the Knights to their 35th win of the season, 4-3.

Marc-André Fleury faced only 23 shots and saved 20 on the way to his 390th career win, passing the legendary Dominic Hasek. The power play was 1 for 1, the 10th PP goal in the last 17 chances over seven games. And the VGK pretty much shut down the potent Washington offense — known to get 20 shots on net in a single period.

The Golden Knights had won five of their last seven

games, three of four on the road trip, and were 20-4-3 since December 3, exactly two months ago. The return of Fleury from a concussion certainly had a lot to do with the torrid pace. The Flower hadn't played in Washington since he shut out the Capitals 2-0 in Game 7 of the 2017 Eastern Conference Championship, making 29 saves. He also beat Washington in Game 7 of the 2009 Eastern Conference Finals with a 6-2 win. Fleury the Capitals-killer. Again, little did we know.

Record: 35-13-4

Game 53, Penguins in Pittsburgh, 2/6/18

Speaking of Fleury, the VGK's next game was one of the most emotional games in which he'd ever played or would ever play. He was returning to Pittsburgh.

Enormous love was shown to Fleury, not only by the Penguin organization with an emotional video tribute, but with an outpouring of affection from the fans, many with tears in their eyes as the video played. They stood, cheered, and chanted his name over and over. Halfway through the video, Fleury sprayed his face with water to mask the tears that swelled up in his own eyes.

The Penguin fans loved him from day one. He was the face of the organization until some guy named Sidney showed up. They loved him for his impressive results over the many years he wore the black and gold and for his character.

Fleury ranked first in the Penguin organization for every goaltender statistic: 691 games, 375 wins, .912 save percentage, 2.58 goals against average, 44 shutouts, three Stanley Cups.

That kind of experience is something money can't buy and the VGK would surely draw from it come April and May, and maybe even into June.

The VGK were and are blessed to have Marc as their starting goaltender. He was one of the reasons that the Golden Knights got to where they were through 53 games. He's a class act on and off the ice and all of his teammates, past and present, have nothing but praise for him.

Unfortunately, the hockey "Oreo-cookie dilemma" ruined the homecoming.

The Oreo cookie refers to two goals by the VGK (cookie), then five unanswered Pittsburgh goals (filling), then two more VGK goals (cookie). Vegas came up one cookie short of an Oreo in the 5-4 loss to the Penguins. So much for the storybook ending. And yes, even some Pittsburgh fans would have been okay if he'd won one against his old team. Actually, the five goals surrendered by Fleury were the most he'd given up since the game in which he was injured, way back on October 13 versus Detroit.

His teammates were visibly disappointed in their performance; they knew how much Fleury would have loved to win this game in Pittsburgh. They knew they'd let him down in the second period, in which their effort left a lot to be desired. Did they get comfortable with a 2-0 lead on the road, even against the defending Stanley Cup champions?

I mentioned earlier that the next team to score in a 2-0

game has a good chance of winning it right there. If the score becomes 3-0, the trailing team knows the night is probably over; teams at this level rarely blow 3-0 leads. The flip side is that if the third goal of the game is scored by the trailing team, now a 2-0 game is 2-1 and all of the emotions and wind are at the back of the pursuer. This was what happened as the Penguins seemed to find an extra jump in their legs when they brought the score back to 2-1 and before the horn blew to end the second, Pittsburgh had deposited three more goals behind Fleury.

Still, William Karlsson scored a VGK power-play goal, his 28th goal of the season, ending a five-game scoring drought. James Neal scored number 23; Jonathan Marchessault scored his 19th and added one assist; Ryan Carpenter scored his second goal in back-to-back games. The Knights were still leading the Pacific Division *and* the Western Conference. Perhaps more important, they remained in the plus column at 3-2 on the six-game road trip.

Record: 35-14-4

Game 54, Sharks in San Jose, 2/8/18

So they came off an emotional game, then sat on the team plane on the tarmac for nearly three hours due to a snowstorm. The plane burned up so much fuel during the delay that it had to stop to refuel in Ohio before finishing the trip by flying another 2,000 miles.

Could anyone blame them for being a step behind the

San Jose Sharks the next day? They didn't even register their first shot on goal until 14 minutes in, after San Jose had already fired 12 shots at Fleury. When the first period ended, San Jose had 16 shots on net and 26 attempts on Fleury. Fleury was the only reason the Shark's didn't blow the game wide open. He was amazing, especially in the first period, in keeping 15 of the 16 shots he faced out of the net.

When Erik Haula scored with six minutes left in the first period to tie the game, it was only the second shot that Sharks goaltender Martin Jones had faced. No one would've blamed the Knights' goalie for anything after the tribute in Pittsburgh, and he did give up three goals there. But Erik Haula scored his 21st, William Karlsson his 29th, James Neal his 24th, Jonathan Marchessault his 20th, a power-play goal, and Brayden McNabb his third, to win the game 5-3.

The win put the VGK ahead of San Jose by 12 points, the largest division lead in the entire NHL. In addition, their one-time Achilles-heel power play was ranked number one in the league (since December 8) and fifth overall, having scored a PPG in nine straight games.

Unlike the last six-game road trip, during which the Knights went 1-4-1, this one was a huge success with four wins, especially considering the teams they faced, the back-to-backs, and the thousands of miles they traveled. With their 76 points, Vegas was the number-two team in the NHL and the VGK steamroller looked almost unstoppable.

Record: 36-14-4

Game 55, Philadelphia Flyers at T-Mobile Arena, 2/11/18

Woulda coulda shoulda.

Vegas woulda won their next game against the Philadelphia Flyers if they'd kept up the pressure on a clearly tired team that was playing back-to-back road games, with their match in Arizona the day before going into overtime. They coulda won if they'd blown open the first period when they had two glorious scoring chances on Michal Neuvirth in the first two minutes, one by James Neal, the other by William Karlsson. Jonathan Marchessault also missed a completely wide-open net on a slick cross-ice pass from Karlsson at the 10-minute mark. All those shots shoulda gone in; if they hadda, the final score of the game woulda most likely been 4-1 Knights, as opposed to 4-1 Flyers.

Instead, they lost their second game in a row at home for the first time all season. The VGK were utterly unaccustomed to trailing by two goals at home. The only other time that had happened at T-Mobile was the 3-0 loss to the Dallas Stars way back on November 28.

The Knights did score first, which seemed like a good path to another win, as their record when scoring first coming into the game was 22-2. Brayden McNabb scored that goal for the Knights, his second goal in back-to-back games, the first time in his career he'd accomplished that. But it was also the only goal to get past Michal Neuvirth, who was exceptional, stopping 38 of the 39 shots he faced. Neuvirth had given up five goals in each of his last two starts. On this night, *that* Neuvirth was nowhere to be found at T-Mobile.

In-the-know hockey fans expect that at least a couple

Hockey players—the toughest SOBs in sports.

Gavin (top left), Joe (top right), and George Maloof (left) are minority owners of the Vegas Golden Knights and were key players in bringing the team to Vegas.

Knights' majority owner Bill Foley (left) and General Manager George McPhee (right) flank Gerard "Turk" Gallant at the press conference announcing Gallant's hiring as the VGK head coach.

Gerard Gallant and assistant coach Mike Kelly had to handle their own luggage and hail a cab to get home after Gallant was fired by the Florida Panthers on a road trip in 2016. Two years later, Gallant was the NHL's Coach of the Year.

T-Mobile Arena lights up on November 22, 2016, as Bill Foley announces the name of the new Las Vegas NHL franchise to 5,000 fans.

A parade at the City National Arena practice facility (above) features Chance the mascot, the Drumline, and the Knights Girls. The Arsenal (below) is the Golden Knights merch outlet at City National.

VGK goalie Marc-André Fleury gets in front of a different kind of shot with BJ Uyal, son of one of the contributors to this book.

Defenseman Brayden McNabb acknowledges a young fan during a game at T-Mobile.

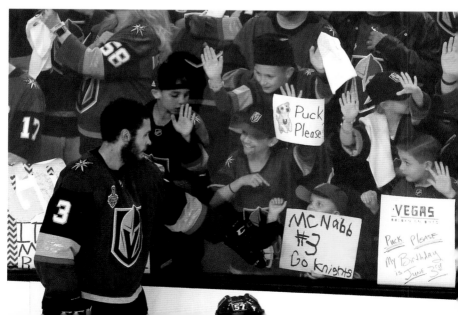

Las Vegan and VGK elder statesman Deryk Engelland addresses the crowd at the memorial ceremony for the 58 people killed on October 1 during the Golden Knights home opener just nine days after the shooting.

Tomas Nosek scores the VGK's first-ever goal at T-Mobile barely three minutes into the game against the Arizona Coyotes, opening the floodgates to an electrifying four-goal first period following the pre-game tribute.

James Neal scores from his knees (top); Cody Eakin goes top shelf against the L.A. Kings (center); David Perron celebrates a game-winning goal (below).

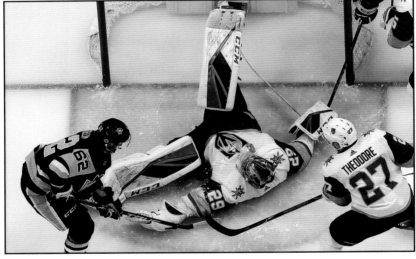

The Goal: William Karlsson goes between his legs to score the consensus "goal of the year" against the San Jose Sharks' Martin Jones in the last home game of the season. The play was nominated for an ESPY.

The Save: Braden Holtby makes what will be forever known as "The Save" to stop a seemingly certain goal by Alex Tuch in Game 2 of the Stanley Cup Finals.

Facing Page: Marc-André Fleury leads the Knights onto the ice at T-Mobile (top), then displays the flexibility and reflexes that made him one of the top goalies in the league.

Fan mania: Julius Caesar clutches a 24-foot-long VGK goalie stick and waves a team flag in front of Caesars Palace during the playoffs.

The replica Statue of Liberty in front of New York-New York wears a 600-pound vinyl VGK jersey, epitomizing Knights mania after the team made the Stanley Cup Finals.

Professional crowd "igniter" Cameron Hughes whips fans into a frenzy in a playoff game against the San Jose Sharks.

Carnell Johnson, also known as "Golden Pipes," was the most popular national anthem singer at T-Mobile.

When Shawn Hickey took it upon himself to become The Knight, he wound up in almost as many photos as Fleury.

The big screen overlooking Toshiba Plaza in front of T-Mobile announces that the VGK would play for the Stanley Cup in their inaugural season.

The glittering arena is packed to the rafters for Game 1 of the Stanley Cup Finals in Vegas; "Welcome to Impossible" became a rallying cry second only to the ubiquitous "Go-Knights-Go."

Vegas' front-row Elvises vie for a stick tossed over the glass by Marc-André Fleury after he shut out the L.A. Kings in Game 1 of the playoffs.

Station Casinos garnered millions in publicity with its free-futures-bet promotion, then saved a million in potential payouts when the VGK didn't win the Cup.

The Washington Capitals' Alex Ovechkin hoists the Cup—*his* Cup—after beating the Vegas Golden Knights four games to one in the 2018 Stanley Cup Finals. It was Washington's first NHL championship in its 44-year history.

Two forlorn fans wait until the last minute to leave T-Mobile for the last time in the VGK's debut season after Game 5 of the Finals.

Author Joe Pane (left) goes all the way back to 1986 with VGK General Manager George McPhee, who was a 28-year-old New York Rangers player at that time.

Clockwise from top left: Gerard Gallant with the Jack Adams Trophy for NHL Coach of the Year; William Karlsson hoists the Lady Byng Trophy for best sportsmanship and gentlemanly conduct, combined with a high standard of playing ability; George McPhee holds his trophy for General Manager of the Year; and Deryk Engelland won the Mark Messier Award for great leadership qualities on and off the ice and for playing a leading role in his community in growing the game of hockey.

The Vegas Golden Knights salute their fans before leaving the ice to allow the Washington Capitals to celebrate their Stanley Cup Finals victory.

of penalties will be called against the Philadelphia Flyers wherever they play. This game's single penalty was rare. When the VGK didn't score, their streak of nine straight games with a PPG ended.

The Knights were playing their first home game after a long road trip, which historically leads to a losing outcome for the home team. Their last game versus San Jose, in which they came from behind to win, was also San Jose's first game home after their long road trip.

Record: 36-15-4

Game 56, Chicago Blackhawks at T-Mobile Arena, 2/13/18

Things weren't looking promising entering the third period of the next game, the Golden Knights' 56th, on February 13. Vegas trailed the Chicago Blackhawks 2-1 after squandering one power-play chance after another. Coming into the third period, the VGK was on the power play that carried over from the second, and though the PP attack was 0-4 thus far in the game, Brad Hunt scored the first of three back-to-back-to-back goals in 4:50 to start the period. In the blink of an eye, the score went from a 2-1 deficit to a 4-2 lead. Tomas Nosek closed out the scoring with an empty-net goal to put the final score at 5-2. Reilly Smith and David Perron sandwiched their goals between Hunt's PPG and Nosek's empty-netter.

Record: 37-15-4

Game 57, Edmonton Oilers at T-Mobile Arena, 2/14/18

The following game was against the Edmonton Oilers, a team that the Golden Knights had yet to beat. As a matter of fact, the only two losses that Vegas had suffered in its own division were to the Oilers, once in regulation in Edmonton and once in OT the last time the two teams played at T-Mobile.

But the game on February 15 was different; the VGK limited Connor McDavid to just two shots on goal and a minus one point for the game—the correct recipe for beating the Edmonton Oilers.

Like the Blackhawks in the previous game, who were on a six-game losing streak, Edmonton came into the game after four losses in a row. T-Mobile wasn't the place to try to snap a losing streak; at the time, the VGK's home record was 20-4-2.

The final score of the game, 4-1, looked like a blowout for the VGK, but it wasn't. If it hadn't been for Marc-André Fleury, Edmonton might have logged its third win against Vegas.

Ryan Carpenter's goal, his fourth in six games, opened the scoring. William Karlsson scored his 30th goal in just 57 games with the VGK. I started hearing murmurs that there was already consideration for post-season awards for William Karlsson as the most improved player in the NHL. His goal in this game was a beauty, shown repeatedly on the week's NHL highlights.

Was "Wild Bill" overachieving or was he a hidden gem discovered by George McPhee and his staff? I'm going—by George!—with a discovery by George.

In the last two games, Fleury stopped 57 of 60 shots. Against the Oilers, he stopped 28 of 29, improving his record to 18-6-2.

Edmonton was pretty much toast after the VGK scored to make it 3-0 (once again supporting my theory about the next team to score in a 2-0 game having a huge edge in winning). It didn't hurt that Vegas was 22-1 when leading after two periods.

Best of all, the Vegas Golden Knights regained sole ownership of the best record of 31. Yes, a first-year expansion team was once again at the top of the NHL.

Record: 38-15-4

Game 58, Montreal Canadiens at T-Mobile Arena, 2/17/18

The next opponent was none other than the team with the most Stanley Cups in the history of the NHL, 23 to be exact.

Even though the Montreal Canadiens hadn't won the Cup in 24 years, this franchise has always been the face of the NHL. It's one of the original six teams and its fan base stretches all over North America. At one time, opposing teams dreaded playing at the Montreal Forum, where the Canadiens hoisted most of their 23 Cups. The hockey gods were even said to live there and opponents could feel the fire and smell the brimstone. The Canadians played 2,366 games in the Forum and won 1,491 of them, while losing only 528, for a .704 win percentage (games ended in ties before overtime became the way to determine a winner).

Ironically, thus far in the season, a case could be made for T-Mobile Arena having taken on the mantle of the Montreal Forum. With their 6-3 win in this game, the Knights had the best home record in the NHL at 22-4-2. They also tied the NHL expansion record for home wins, with 13 more games to play in Sin City.

The current Montreal Canadians are nowhere close to the team that they once were and their new home doesn't have the same effect on visiting teams that the Forum once had. Coming into this game, Montreal had won only eight games on the road all year, tied for last in that statistic. They'd lost 11 of their last 12 road games and were riding a five-game losing streak.

The VGK opened the game by scoring two goals on their first four shots; when they scored their third at the 9:51 mark on only their sixth shot of the first period, Antti Niemi, Montreal's starting goaltender, was headed to the showers. Cary Price replaced Niemi and surrendered three more goals.

Montreal was trying to become only the fourth team to beat the Knights two times this season. The Canadiens won their first meeting in the team's disastrous first east coast road trip when they were playing their third- and fourth-string goaltenders. The only teams that had beaten Vegas twice thus far were the Minnesota Wild, the Edmonton Oilers, and the New York Islanders.

Vegas continued to get scoring up and down the lineup. In their previous game against Edmonton, 11 different players made the score sheet. In this game, 10 different VGK earned at least one point.

Montreal did make it a game by scoring two goals in the first period, which ended 3-2. But when the VGK scored two goals just 39 seconds apart in the second period, it was 5-2 and the game was as good as over. Just the final score of 6-3 remained to be determined.

All the pieces were meshing together, and though 22 games remained in the regular season, the VGK were playing like the best team in the NHL.

Which they were!

Record: 39-15-4

Game 59, Anaheim Ducks at T-Mobile Arena, 2/19/18

The Anaheim Ducks, in the next game on February 19, made a conscious effort to slow the pace and keep the Knights and their shots on the outside of the faceoff circles. This neutralized the speed that made Vegas very difficult to beat, especially on home ice. Before they adjusted to Anaheim's game plan, the VGK kept trying to make that extra pass instead of going to the net on a number of quality scoring chances. Ducks' goalie John Gibson faced just 13 shots in two periods.

For their part, content to keep the game on the outside and in the neutral zone, Anaheim had only 12 shots on Fleury over the same two periods. They were more concerned with shutting down the Knights' potent offense and completely took away any forecheck.

Four VGK starters were out with injuries: high-scoring James Neal, forecheck-minded Pierre-Édouard Bellemare, defenseman Shea Theodore, and William Carrier. The only line that remained intact was Karlsson-Marchessault-Smith and they had a mere five shots total on Gibson. Anaheim's two goals were deflections.

This was a conference game (worth four points in the standings) that had all the elements of a tight playoff contest. Vegas' run-and-gun style is entertaining, but in the run-up to the post-season, I expected to see less of this and more of what the Ducks brought. The 2-0 loss was only the second time all season that Vegas didn't score a goal at T-Mobile.

Record: 39-16-4

Game 60, Calgary Flames at T-Mobile Arena, 2/21/18

The last time the VGK played the Calgary Flames was back on January 30 in Calgary. The Flames were leading 2-1 with just 1:46 left in the game when the VGK pulled off one of the most incredible finishes in the season, scoring three goals in 53 seconds. It may be awhile before that kind of finish is surpassed.

It appeared that Calgary was trying to duplicate what the Anaheim Ducks accomplished so successfully in beating Vegas in the previous game: clogging up the neutral zone, taking away the VGK's effective stretch passes out of their zone, keeping them to the perimeter in the offensive zone, and not allowing any traffic into the blue paint.

This time, the Knights reacted well to the game plan that had snuffed them. They got bodies to the front of the net and took shots from all angles without looking for the next perfect pass. The first goal was scored at the 2:28 mark in the first period, Ryan Carpenter's sixth in his last nine games. Ryan's goal came with his back to the net and he shot the puck between his legs, completely fooling Flames goaltender David Rittich, who never expected *that*. No one did.

Calgary was so intent on slowing down the Knights that they didn't register their first shot on goal until almost 11 minutes into the game. They did score a goal on their fourth shot on Fleury, who once again wasn't too busy, as the Flames wound up with just six shots in the first 20 minutes. The Flames took a different approach in the second and third periods and eventually hit Fleury with 31 total shots; the VGK's amazing goaltender stopped all but three in the 7-3 win.

Yes, from zero goals in their last game to a whopping seven in this one. What a difference getting traffic in the blue paint and players to the front of the net makes. William Karlsson scored his 31st of the season late in the first on a power play, deflecting a Reilly Smith shot. The first period ended 2-1 in favor of Vegas.

Vegas never trailed, but give credit to the Flames, who abandoned their plan when they realized that it'd worked for the Ducks, but Coach Gallant adjusted with a counter plan of his own.

The teams traded goals, tying the score at 3-3 and 4-4. But on advice from his video replay coach Tommy Cruz, Gallant challenged the Flames' fourth goal on the grounds that Calgary entered the zone offside. This was a risky move; if the challenge is denied, the score remains 4-4, but Vegas receives a penalty for a delay of game and puts Calgary on the power play. But when the goal was removed from the scoreboard, the Flames appeared to lose their focus.

Offside

The surface of a hockey rink is divided in half by the red line at center ice. On either side of the red line are two 50-foot-wide neutral zones. Each is defined by the red line in the middle and two blue lines 50 feet from the red line and 64 feet from the goal lines at either end.

A player is judged to be offside if both of his skates completely cross the blue line that divides his team's offensive zone from the neutral zone before the puck completely crosses the same line.

A player deemed to have complete stick control of the puck may enter his offensive zone with both skates before the puck enters the zone; usually, this means the player is skating backwards or laterally. ♣

After giving up on trying to slow the play, Calgary switched gears and attempted to slow down the VGK with crunching body-checks all over the ice. The Flames had averaged 19 hits per game through their first 61 games; against the VGK, they were credited with 41 hits, more than double their average.

Frustrations were evident—and then Travis Hamonic challenged Alex Tuch to a fight with a little more than nine minutes left in the game.

A hat trick in hockey comes when one player scores three goals in a game. Then there's the Gordie Howe Hat Trick: a goal, an assist, and a fight in the same game. Tuch had already scored a goal and had an assist, so when he accepted Hamonic's challenge, the 21-year-old hockey phenom completed the VGK's first-ever Gordie Howe Hat Trick. (Gordie was known for his scoring prowess and his skill at fighting. Still, he accomplished his namesake hat trick just twice in his career.)

The crowd loved it and Tuch was (unofficially) awarded the win as he landed the better shots in a longer-than-normal fight with lots of punches thrown, resulting in a bloody lip for Hamonic, who watched from the penalty box as the Knights scored two goals in three and a half minutes after the fight.

This was Tuch's first NHL fight and he said he was glad to get it out of the way and that he'd held his own. I think he was just being modest—he did real well in throwing some big bombs.

It was a tough night for our Canadian friends in Las Vegas for the game. Their Flames lost and the USA Women's hockey team beat Canada in the 2018 Winter Olympics Gold Medal game in a thrilling shootout. The Canadian women's team had won the gold medal in hockey the last four Olympics: 2002, 2006, 2010, and 2014.

Record: 40-16-4

Game 61, Vancouver Canucks at T-Mobile Arena, 2/23/18

Flurries in the morning, a flurry of goals in the evening, and another win for Fleury.

Yes, Las Vegas had snow flurries on February 23, somewhat rare for the Mojave Desert. But the flurry of goals that night was anything but rare; the VGK put six on the scoreboard on their way to a 6-3 win over Vancouver at T-Mobile.

The 13 goals in this game and last were a response to being shut out at home against Anaheim. The goal production came from the entire team; nine different players made the score sheet, almost a carbon copy of the Calgary game when 10 players registered goals and assists.

In this game, the VGK's 61st, the Canucks tried to skate with Vegas. For a while in the first period, it seemed Vancouver's game plan was working. Both teams were playing a wide-open game and even though Tomas Hyka scored his first NHL goal just 2:29 into the first period, giving Vegas the lead, Vancouver scored the next two to go ahead 2-1.

But then Vegas' top line of Karlsson, Marchessault, and Smith once again became the force that rendered Vancouver's attempt to skate with Vegas a mistake. The line combined for eight points: three goals and five assists. William Karlsson had goals 32 and 33, plus an assist, while Reilly Smith had a career-high three assists and Jonathan Marchessault had a goal and an assist. In the second period, Vegas took complete control of the game, scoring three unanswered goals to take a commanding 5-2 lead into the third period.

For almost all their games, the VGK rolled four lines all night long, every one of which had speed and played all 200 feet of the ice. For a fan, it was mighty entertaining to watch, especially at T-Mobile, where the speed of the game is much more evident than it is on TV. It wasn't so entertaining for the other teams, who never did figure out how to combat the Knights' style.

General Manager George McPhee had already started looking ahead to the playoffs and the big heavy teams in the Western Conference. That was obvious in his trade with Pittsburgh: Tobias Lindberg for Ryan Reaves and a fourth-round pick in the 2018 draft. McPhee didn't acquire Reaves for his scoring ability; thus far in the season, Reaves had eight points on four goals and four assists in the 58 games he'd played with Pittsburgh. No, he was brought to Vegas for the sole purpose of making sure opponents were allowed no liberties with any of the VGK's top forwards. It wasn't exactly explained as such, but in a career that spanned 477 games with St. Louis and Pittsburgh, Reaves collected 59 points (31 goals and 28 assists) and he had a whopping 779 minutes in penalty time. With the acquisition of Reaves, the VGK added a potent dose of toughness and grit.

The opposing teams' freedom was all of a sudden less

free, with Reaves out there to separate them from the puck and not, to be sure, with a fancy stick-check.

In the VGK's seven-game home stand, they won five. The win against the Canucks also moved Vegas back to the top of the entire NHL with 86 points.

Record: 41-16-4

Game 62, Kings in L.A., 2/26/18

What happened in the next game against the division-rival L.A. Kings was another example of what I've said several times, so far: The next team to score in a 2-0 game will mostly likely win.

Back on December 28, only two points separated the VGK and the Kings. The Kings actually led the Pacific Division for a while. Between then and this game, though, they'd gone 11-13-0. During the same stretch, the Knights had a record of 16-7-2, vaulting them to the top not only of the Pacific Division, but the entire Western Conference, while intermittently occupying the number-one spot in the league. During these 25 games, Vegas had a +26 goal differential, while L.A.'s was -1. In this game, however, the Kings overcame a two-goal deficit with eight minutes left in the game to win it in overtime 3-2.

The Kings' netminder, Jonathan Quick, turned in an amazing performance; without him, Vegas could have easily had five or six goals instead of the two that got by him. In the overtime period, Vegas had a few quality scoring chances, but Quick remained solid in the net. Anze Kopitar, the Kings' leading scorer, put the puck behind Fleury for his team-leading 26th goal to tie the score in the third. Then Dustin Brown scored the winning goal in OT.

Oscar Lindberg was blindsided by Kyle Clifford of the L.A. Kings while skating to the bench. Clifford was then challenged several times by Vegas newcomer Ryan Reaves to stand up for his late hit away from the play. Clifford refused. These two teams were obviously starting to dislike each other.

Record: 41-16-5

Game 63, L.A. Kings at T-Mobile Arena, 2/27/18

The VGK played the L.A. Kings again the next night, this time in Vegas. Both teams started backup goaltenders. The Kings' Jack "Soupy" Campbell was starting his first game in 4½ years and only his third NHL start ever. It looked like this might be a good spot for the VGK to rebound from the disappointing loss the night before in L.A.

It started off like it would be, with William Karlsson scoring his team-leading 34th and the first goal of the game just 5:27 in. But that was the only goal Soupy Campbell gave up all night. He stopped all of the other 41 shots Vegas managed to get on net.

Instead of Marc-André Fleury, who had started the last 11 games for Vegas, the VGK started Max Lagacé, who last played on December 9. Unfortunately, Vegas hung Max out to dry with two costly turnovers that resulted in the first two L.A. goals. The Kings also capitalized on an interception of a weak pass when Anze Kopitar scored. L.A. added a fourth goal on a late power play to win it 4-1.

Vegas had lost two games in a row to the Kings. And the Pacific Division rivalry was heating up.

Record: 41-17-5

Game 64, Ottawa Senators at T-Mobile Arena, 3/2/18

In this game, the Ottawa Senators so thoroughly outskated and outhustled the home team that only three Vegas players could call their efforts acceptable.

The Knights managed three shots on Ottawa's goaltender Craig Anderson in the first period, who somehow managed to let two of them get by him. Amazingly, the VGK led 2-1 going into the second. The Knights regrouped and had 18 shots on net in the second, but Anderson turned them all away.

Meanwhile, the Senators scored three goals on their 17 shots on Fleury to take a commanding 4-2 lead going into the third. The third period was almost a carbon copy of the first: Vegas took all of eight shots on goal and somehow managed to tie the game at 4-4. That lasted for less than a minute, when Alexander Burrows scored Ottawa's fifth and final goal to seal the win. Vegas pulled Fleury with 1:49 left in the game and had some quality scoring chances, but were again denied by Craig Anderson, who had a strange game himself, surrendering four goals on only 11 shots in periods one and three. The final score of 5-4 could not be any further from what it should have been.

The three acceptable skaters were Reilly Smith, William Karlsson, and Jonathan Marchessault; the first line combined for two goals and four assists. Coach Gallant rarely speaks negatively about his players, but except for those three, he was obviously upset with the entire team.

This loss stretched the VGK losing streak to three games and it was the first time they'd lost two in a row on home ice in 33 games.

Were they underestimating Ottawa, which had won only three of their previous 25 road games and had only seven road wins all season? Perhaps. But for the VGK, it was their third consecutive stinker and they now had a three-game losing streak staring them in the face as they headed out on a five-game east coast road trip.

Record: 41-18-5

Game 65, Devils in New Jersey, 3/4/18

Against the New Jersey Devils, the Knights needed passion and a renewed commitment to the team's system on the first east coast game. They got it, but it took awhile.

Marc-André Fleury once again saved the day for the VGK, especially in the first period, when he was the only reason Vegas wasn't blown out of the Prudential Center.

It appeared the VGK, other than Fleury, had missed

their wake-up call. Granted, the start time was 2 p.m. for VGK body clocks. NHL players have routines on game days and the time change, along with the long flight across the country, seemed to really affect them. They even bypassed the normal morning skate.

Fleury, starting his 13th game of the last 14, had to be especially sharp until his teammates' alarms clock started ringing. During the last 15:28 of the first period, the Knights mustered only two shots on goal. All the scoring in the game took place in the second period. Fleury covered the first and third periods for a final score of 3-2, Vegas. If you didn't already believe that Coach Gallant was passionate about the entire process of building a winner, looking at his reaction at the end of the game, you'd have thought they'd just *lost* the game.

Vegas scored first. The team scoring first in a hockey game has a strong win ratio. Still, the VGK had also scored the first goal in their previous three losses. In their short history, Vegas had never lost four in a row and Fleury wasn't about to let that happen on his watch. The good news was that Vegas now had a 24-2-2 record entering the third period with a lead and Fleury recorded his 10th win against three losses and a tie on the road.

In a season that, to me, felt like it had just started (winning does make time fly), only 17 games remained on this schedule of myriad highs and trifling lows—nine on the road and eight at home. Eight of the games would be against Pacific Division teams, another eight against teams with winning records. So the race to the finish line would be anything but a cake walk. Even so, in Vegas, we were preparing for the first-ever Stanley Cup playoff games at T-Mobile. Just the thought of it gave me a warm feeling, like a cup of hot chocolate on a cold winter day.

Record: 42-18-5

Game 66, Blue Jackets in Columbus, 3/6/18

The Knights hit another small speed bump in their second road game against the Columbus Blue Jackets.

Though Pierre-Édouard Bellemare had returned to the lineup, a number of players were still on the mend and Reilly Smith left this game late in the second period after taking a hard hit. He went straight to the locker room and didn't return. Losing Smith immediately created a huge void right through the remaining three lines, as Tomas Tatar was moved up to the first line. Injuries are part of the game, but of late, Vegas seemed to be on the wrong side of that curve. Reilly Smith joined a growing list of injured Knights: James Neal, Oscar Lindberg, Luca Sbisa, Nate Schmidt, and Malcolm Subban.

The game was almost over before the end of the first period, as the Blue Jackets came flying out of the gate and scored just 16 seconds in. Columbus also scored the second goal to go up 2-0 and Fleury appeared less than sharp.

The momentum of the game was clearly on the side of Columbus, until VGK video replay coach Tommy Cruz once again notified Coach Gallant that he believed the play was offside. The challenge was upheld and the second goal was removed from the scoreboard. Cruz had been nearly perfect in his assessments of calls subject to a coach's challenge. In my opinion, he changed the entire complexion of this game, as the Knights seemed to get their legs after the second goal was disallowed. The period ended with VGK trailing 1-0, but they were now engaged.

Indeed, the second period was just 90 seconds old when Erik Haula scored his 24th goal of the season. Unfortunately, that was Vegas' only goal against backup goaltender Joonos Korpisalo, who was inserted into the lineup when Columbus' starting goaltender, Seregi Bobrovsky, took ill. Joonos, who'd lost his three previous starts, was outstanding, stopping 37 of the 38 shots he faced. He was the main reason Vegas dropped this game. The other reason was that Fleury had an off night, surrendering three goals on the initial 12 shots; the last goal in the 4-1 loss was into an empty net.

Record: 42-19-5

Game 67, Red Wings in Detroit, 3/8/18

The Detroit Red Wings were the first team to beat Vegas way back on October 12 when the VGK surrendered four third-period goals to lose 6-3. In this game against Detroit, Vegas obviously remembered their first meeting very well. At this point, the Red Wings were already far from a playoff team and sure to miss the Stanley Cup post-season for the second year in a row — after they'd made the playoffs an amazing 25 consecutive years.

What a difference from one game to another. Even though Tomas Tatar still didn't look comfortable with the top line that was missing an injured Reilly Smith, the entire team seemed like it had decided that enough was enough. They'd lost four of their last five games and scored only 11 goals, a big contrast to the 13-goal juggernaut in the two games prior.

Alex Tuch scored the first goal early, just 2:24 in, his 12th of the season. Cody Eakin added a shorthanded goal, his eighth, at the 10:40 mark of the second period. But this game was far from over.

With the score 2-0 and 4:40 left in the second, Fleury made three amazing saves in a matter of 10 seconds that could have shifted the momentum back to the Red Wings.

Shortly after Fleury's saves, Cody Eakin scored his second goal of the game. Entering the third period with a 4-0 lead looked promising for the Knights, who were 25-2-2 when entering the last period with any lead, while Detroit's record of coming back in the third while trailing was nearly the opposite, 1-24-5. The only question was, could Fleury maintain the shutout? He did; it was his career 47th, stopping all 28 shots he faced.

Both Eakin and Tuch, who also added another goal for his second of the game, had gone through long stretches without scoring. Alex's first goal was his first in his last 14 games and Eakin hadn't scored in 25 games. With the Knights still missing James Neal, along with Smith and defensemen Nate Schmidt and Luca Sbisa, getting contributions from the rest of the lineup was essential.

Record: 43-19-5

Game 68, Sabres in Buffalo, 3/10/18

I've never understood NHL games being played in the afternoon, or in this game for the VGK, at 10 a.m. Pacific time. Hockey players are highly conditioned athletes who have game-day routines, so odd start times are disruptive.

On a normal game day, players have a morning skate in the arena. This allows them to scrutinize the equipment they'll use for the game. It also gives them the opportunity to check the texture of the boards that are different in every arena; passes off the boards are key components of starting breakouts and getting the puck to teammates in the offensive zone. The skates are typically followed by an afternoon nap, then a team meal.

The start for game 68 in Buffalo against the Sabres was six hours earlier than normal. That meant there was none of the above for either team and Vegas' body clocks were off by nine hours.

Not only does this create problems for the players, it's unreasonable for the fans. Attending a hockey game is hardly an inexpensive day or night out. So charging big bucks when the players probably aren't performing at their peak levels is misguided.

The Golden Knights-Sabres game was one of several matinees in the NHL that day, most likely scheduled so as not to compete with March Madness. In the first 20-minute period, there were 35 stoppages of play, one every 57 seconds. That's boring hockey for fans and unsettling for players.

Another indication of topsy-turviness: This game went 40 minutes without a goal—in a league that has adjusted its rules to create more offense. Why not just keep the games starting at a time the players are comfortable with?

The only player on either team who seemed to have any energy in the first period was Alex Tuch. That made sense; it was a homecoming for him. He played a lot of his amateur hockey in the Syracuse-Buffalo area and had no less than 450 family and friends in attendance. He later said he'd been looking forward to this game since October. Tuch didn't need any incentive to be ready and he took four of Vegas' 11 shots in the first period.

The other 39 players? They were working off of a cold cup of coffee for the first two periods and most of the third.

Marc-André Fleury once again saved the day for his team, stopping 31 of Buffalo's 32 shots in regulation play, though Buffalo scored first in the third to take a 1-0 lead. Then, with less than five minutes left in the game, Deryk Engelland stepped up and scored a lucky goal off a deflection to send the game into overtime, which was scoreless. No surprise.

The shootout took five long rounds to determine the winner; when Erik Haula buried one, it was a heartbreaker for Sabres' goalie Robin Lehner, who'd saved 33 of the VGK's 34 shots.

Record: 44-19-5

Game 69, Flyers in Philadelphia, 3/12/18

The drudgery of the Buffalo game seemed gone when the VGK took the ice to play the Philadelphia Flyers a couple nights later.

Over the five previous games, the VGK power play had been sluggish, scoring only two PPGs in the last 12 attempts. Granted, some of the forwards on the power-play unit were out with injuries and the 2-for-12 was as good an indication as any of how much James Neal and Reilly Smith meant to the power play. But in the Flyers game, the power-play unit paved the way to a victory to close out the five-game road trip with four wins and one loss. In the process, it also helped Marc-André Fleury goaltend his 400th career win. He became only the 13th player in NHL history to achieve this lofty record and he did it in 728 games, second fastest to the mark.

Entering the game, Fleury had an impressive 24-9-3 record for Vegas with a 2.16 GAA and .930 save percentage. Against the Flyers, he stopped 38 of 40 shots — in total, three goals allowed on 100 shots. Also, he'd surrendered only one goal on the 60 shots he faced in the last two games. Not bad for a netminder who was out for almost two months with a concussion. It didn't hurt that Vegas scored two goals in the third period to win it 3-2.

Pierre-Édouard Bellemare was playing against his old team, which was evident in his energy from the opening faceoff. And in a class move that many probably didn't notice, on his way off the ice after the game, Bellemare handed a young fan his gloves. The look on that boy's face was priceless and I'm certain that he'll never forget this gesture by a class guy who was playing for a class organization.

Record: 45-19-5

Game 70, New Jersey Devils at T-Mobile Arena, 3/14/18

I've mentioned that the first home game after a long road trip usually isn't a team's best. This proved true again in the March 14 game at T-Mobile against New Jersey. The Devils scored the first four goals of the game in the first and second periods, forcing out Fleury; it was a truly rare sight, seeing the fabulous Fleury sitting down in the middle of play. He was replaced by third-string goalie Max Lagacé (Malcolm Subban was still out with an injury).

The VGK came back at the end of the second period with a couple quick scores by Erik Haula and Colin Miller, making the score 4-2 and turning the momentum, but the Devils roared back in the third with four goals. Vegas scored a final meaningless goal to end the game at 8-3. It was New Jersey's highest-scoring game of the year.

And that, my fellow hockey fans, is all that needs to be said about the VGK's worst loss of the season.

Record: 45-20-5

Game 71, Minnesota Wild at T-Mobile Arena, 3/16/18

That loss carried over to the Knights' 71st game against the Minnesota Wild on March 16, when Vegas didn't start playing until the last few minutes of the third period. They were extremely lucky to survive the first period trailing by only one goal. Their failure to test the Wild's second-string goalie early in the game made their job going forward even more difficult, as Alex Stalock became so comfortable that he was initiating stretch passes to forwards in the neutral zone, creating odd-man rushes — borrowing liberally from the Knights' playbook.

Vegas managed only eight shots on goal in the first period. Things got worse in the second and they registered a two-period total of 15 shots, compared to Minnesota's 24. But Minnesota's two goals on its first three shots of the second period put Vegas in an almost insurmountable hole. Only the penalty-kill unit prevented this from being a blowout. Strong all year, it almost provided a miracle as it kept the game close, with the VGK closing the gap to 3-2 with 55 seconds left to play. But with Zach Parise's empty-net goal 22 seconds later, the 4-2 loss was sealed and the VGK's double-digit lead in the Pacific Division was down to just eight points over the San Jose Sharks.

Minnesota forward Jason Zucker is the only Las Vegas-born player in the NHL and he came to town with a little extra zip in his legs. That was evident right from the drop of the puck. Zucker scored his 29th goal of the season and got an assist on a night he was certainly looking forward to and one he'll remember for a long time, having his whole family there, along with a lot of friends he grew up with.

Record: 45-21-5

Game 72, Flames in Calgary, 3/18/18

I went into the VGK's next game against the Calgary Flames with a bit of trepidation, taking a wait-and-see attitude with regard to Vegas' chances to end a four-home-game losing streak. After watching all 72 games this team played in its inaugural season, I had no doubt that they could. But as the first 20 minutes rolled by, I began to wonder if maybe I was wrong. The VGK were so bad that they allowed the Flames a season-high 20 shots on goal in the first period, while mustering only a pair of shots on Calgary goaltender Mike Smith in the first eight minutes and four more the rest of the period.

They weren't getting the puck deep into the zone and when they dumped it in, Smith quickly moved it to one of his players, who headed back to make Fleury face several high-quality scoring chances. Calgary was swarming all over the VGK, and only luck and Fleury prevented Vegas from being behind by two or three goals at the end of the first period.

Early in the second period, Calgary had two quality scoring chances on Fleury, who remained perfect on shots

21 and 22. And then a Knight stepped up.

The arrival of this particular player was accompanied by a lot of opinions, pro and con. Some fans and media, myself included, loved what he brought to the team. Others weren't thrilled; since he'd joined the team at the trade deadline, and with the VGK losing the next three games, it was easy to blame him for the imbalance in the team's chemistry. But no one could have faulted him in this game.

At the 3:06 mark of the second period, Ryan Reaves knew something had to be done to light a fire under his teammates and get the T-Mobile crowd rocking. He delivered a thunderous open-ice hit on TJ Brody, who had the puck and was attempting to break out from behind his net. Reaves' hit separated TJ from the puck, the fans rose to their feet, the entire VGK bench jumped up, and the game changed. Calgary was never the same and neither was TJ, who left and didn't return.

This is what Ryan Reaves brought to the VGK that was lacking. Vegas had two big defensemen in Deryk Engelland and Brayden McNabb, who delivered big hits, but they were pretty much limited to operating in the defensive zone. A check like Reaves' in the offensive zone makes players attempting to break out a little more apprehensive, forcing them to keep their heads up and on a swivel instead of down and skating hard toward the net.

Players like Reaves get paid a lot of money to change the direction of the game when it's needed. In this game, at this time in the season, the VGK needed it badly and Reaves delivered.

That hit won the game right then and there. The VGK

went on to score four goals on 10 shots, two within 53 seconds of each other. Three of the four were scored by William Karlsson—his second hat trick of the season. With goals 37, 38, and 39, Karlsson suddenly led the league with a +39 rating.

Fleury's shutout was the 48th of his career and his fourth of the season. It was also his 401st win, which moved him into a tie for 12th on the all-time win list with Chris Osgood, who played for 14 years with the Detroit Red Wings during a career that spanned 18 years. Osgood played a total of 744 games, while Fleury played 732 to achieve his 401st win.

The 4-0 win snapped the four-home-game losing streak against a Pacific Division foe as a bonus. Their record was now an amazing 17-3-2 in the Pacific Division and they continued to lead the division by eight points.

Record: 46-21-5

Game 73, Vancouver Canucks at T-Mobile Arena, 3/20/18

Speaking of Fleury, the game on March 20 appeared, initially, to be an easy night at the office for the VGK goaltender. The Canucks were already eliminated from the playoffs; they'd lost six games in a row and nine of the last 10, shut out in their last three road games. They also had the unfortunate distinction of scoring two goals or less 37 times in the season and were ranked 29th in goal production.

Yes, Vancouver's offense, in which Fleury faced seven

shots, was no real danger—except one of those shots hit him flush on the face-mask portion of his helmet.

The face mask offers ample protection from cuts by pucks traveling at 100 mph, but it's less effective against the impact suffered by a goalie's brain. At first, Fleury didn't seem bothered by the shot and I observed him adjusting the straps on his face mask after the play went to the other end of the ice. On the next whistle, he further adjusted his mask and all seemed to be okay.

But as we now know after many years of ignorance about safety issues when players receive blows to the head, those who've had previous incidents tend to be more at risk going forward. Concussions are a serious threat to one's ability to play and subsequent concussions usually take more recovery time than those previous. Plenty of players' careers have been curtailed by repetitive concussions.

Five goaltenders appearing in a single season due to injuries is almost unheard of. Teams certainly go on a merry-go-round of goaltenders when they're floundering, but one thing that didn't plague Vegas this season was floundering.

Even so, considering their use of third-, fourth, and fifth-string goalies, it was a miracle that the VGK were where they were—with nine games remaining and with a sure path to the playoffs.

Second-stringer Malcolm Subban replaced Fleury at the start of the second period. He was playing for the first time since February 2 and it was his first time at T-Mobile since he beat Toronto on New Year's Eve. Subban was perfect in the second, turning away all 11 shots he faced; then he stopped 11 of 12 in the third.

Tomas Tatar finally got his first goal at T-Mobile and his second as a VGK. He looked much more comfortable on the top line, which allowed Coach Gallant to reunite the highly successful line of Neal, Haula, and Perron.

At that point, Vegas had scored 133 goals at T-Mobile, the second most home goals scored among the 31 teams in the league; Tampa Bay led with 137. Overall, Tampa Bay had scored 264 goals. Vegas was second with 248.

Record: 47-21-5

Game 74, Sharks in San Jose, 3/22/18

Roughly 99.9% of the time, defining moments for a player, those which will always be remembered as a highlight of his entire career, occur on the winning side of games.

In the game against the San Jose Sharks, with the status of the VGK's number-one goalie in question, the team looked to their number-two, Malcolm Subban, to step up. And step up he did. His performance in this game will be remembered by Subban, his teammates, and every VGK fan who watched it or will watch it in the future. It was an amazing effort that solidified his spot on this team. By now, everyone knew that Fleury was the top goalie for Vegas, but having a player who could raise his level the way Subban did had to give every teammate, plus Coach Gallant and General Manager McPhee, an enviable level of confidence.

Coach Gallant's plan was to slowly ease Subban back

into the lineup, giving him a chance to work out the rust caused by his inactivity after his second injury. Subban hadn't played since February 2 when he was rushed into action to finish the previous game against Vancouver. He faced 25 shots and gave up only one meaningless goal late in the third period. But due to Fleury's continued absence, Gallant had no other choice in a crucial game against the San Jose Sharks, who were breathing down Vegas' neck, trailing by eight points with nine games to go. Plus, San Jose was on a five-game winning streak and had scored 27 goals in that time. The last time SJ scored 27 goals in five games was in 1998.

It didn't start off well for the VGK, as Subban looked shaky on the first shot he faced and San Jose had the Knights on their heels for the first two minutes of the game. But the VGK opened the scoring when Tomas Tatar put a backhander past Sharks goaltender Martin Jones at the 3:47 mark of the first period. That was Vegas' only goal.

For his part, Subban blocked shot after shot, saving 42 of the 43 he faced in regulation. The only goal he surrendered in the first 60 minutes was one in which his teammates had at least three valid attempts to clear the puck out of their zone, which would have allowed a line change and some fresh legs. San Jose's relentless forecheck prevented that. Brent Burns' slap shot from the point eluded Subban, who appeared to be screened.

The Knights allowed San Jose six power plays. One lasted four minutes and another created a 5-on-3 advantage for 25 seconds. Vegas was the second least penalized team in the league, but you wouldn't know that looking at the game's box score. Subban faced 13 shots on the power plays. In the first 12 minutes of the second period, San Jose outshot Vegas 13-1. Still, it was all tied up at 1-1 at the end of regulation.

The game went into overtime, which didn't last long. On San Jose's only rush into Vegas' zone, Logan Couture lifted a backhand past Subban.

It just wasn't right for the game to end like it did. Subban was the best player on the ice, but San Jose was the better team.

The only bright spot to the 2-1 loss was that the game went to overtime, allowing the potential four-point conference game to become a one-point game. San Jose still trailed Vegas in the Pacific Division by seven points.

Record: 47-21-6

Game 75, Avalanche in Colorado, 3/24/18

It was a vast relief to see Marc-André Fleury back in the lineup after missing one and a half games due to an undisclosed injury. He was so sharp that, like Subban in the previous game against San Jose, he alone kept the VGK in the game.

The Avalanche that Vegas thrashed 7-0 way back on October 27 was a totally different team than the one Vegas faced in this game. They'd come together after getting past the major distraction that star player Matt Duchene caused by demanding to be traded. After Matt was dealt to Ottawa

14 games into the season, Colorado went 33-20-8, putting them right in the mix for a playoff spot.

This game could have been the opening round for Vegas. Indeed, the first two periods were playoff-like, with tight checking and the Avs controlling the puck and tempo. The third period, however, was wide open; the Knights were aggressive with the puck and were getting their defensemen into the play. Of their 40 total shots, 22 came from the defense.

Vegas' lone goal that tied it up at 1-1 was scored by Jonathan Marchessault 1:15 into the third period; it was his 24th.

There was no scoring in the five-minute OT period and the only goal scored in the shootout came on Colorado's final attempt of the three that each team is allotted. It was scored by Gabe Landeskog, whom Fleury had robbed early in the third period.

Final score: Colorado 2, Vegas 1.

Record: 47-21-7

Game 76, Colorado Avalanche at T-Mobile Arena, 3/26/18

Two nights later, the Avalanche and Golden Knights were back at it, only this time at T-Mobile.

It didn't start off well. The VGK appeared to be a step behind Colorado, which kept putting out its top line — though that line combined for zero points and only six shots on Fleury. Meanwhile, Coach Gallant stayed with his program of rolling four lines throughout the game. He also inserted Alex Tuch into the top line and Alex responded like he wanted to show Gallant that he was the guy who could fill the void left by Reilly Smith. Tuch scored a power-play goal, had five shots on net and four hits, and provided a screen for a goal by Jonathan Marchessault.

Fleury surrendered only one goal on the 29 shots he faced to notch his 403rd victory, tying him for 11th place on the all-time wins list with Grant Fuhr.

The Knights racked up their 103rd point, with six games still to be played in the season. And if you want to know how impressive 103 points in one season is, the Toronto Maple Leafs entered the NHL in 1917. In those 100 years, they reached 103 points only one time — 86 years later in the 2003-2004 season.

In addition, the VGK remained at the top of the Pacific Division, which they'd led since December 28. They trailed Nashville for the lead in the entire NHL by only four points.

Best of all, with the 4-1 victory over Colorado, in the NHL standings, Vegas had a big beautiful "X" next to it. Playoffs, baby!

Record: 48-21-7

Game 77, Arizona Coyotes at T-Mobile Arena, 3/28/18

It came as no surprise that, in the VGK's 77th game against the Arizona Coyotes, they had, perhaps, a slight playoff-bound hangover. Did they take Arizona lightly, knowing they'd beaten them four times? Whatever it was, in the 3-2 loss, Vegas once again failed to play the entire 60 minutes. This had happened in at least their last three games and it was anything but a good way to prepare for the post-season.

Arizona outshot Vegas 15-5 in the first period. Granted, Arizona had been playing much better of late — they started the season with a 1-11-1 record, but were 9-5-1 over their last 15 games. Arizona goaltender Antti Raanta had a solid performance, stopping 27 of the 29 shots and winning the seventh of his last eight starts.

Fleury was starting his 28th of the last 31 games. Coach Gallant certainly wanted to win the Pacific Division, which guaranteed home-ice advantage for at least the first two rounds of the playoffs. But getting Fleury some much-needed rest before he rode into the post-season was just as important. The lead in the Pacific Division was down to five points over San Jose.

Vegas continued to deal with holes in its lineup. Even though Oscar Lindberg returned for the first time since February 26, David Perron was a scratch. Reilly Smith was still missing from the number-one line. Also gone were defenseman Luca Sbisa and forward William Carrier.

On some positive notes, Jonathan Marchessault extended his point streak to six games with an assist, giving him eight points over that stretch. Alex Tuch, who had two goals in his last two games, had accumulated 33 points in his rookie season.

Early in the life of the Golden Knights, there was some

speculation that hockey in Las Vegas was a gamble. This game's full house at T-Mobile finally laid that notion to rest: More than 700,000 fans had attended games there, with two home games yet to be played.

Record: 48-22-7

Game 78, St. Louis Blues at T-Mobile Arena, 3/30/18

The Knights rebounded against the St. Louis Blues, winning 4-3 in overtime.

Malcolm Subban was in net, finally giving Marc-André Fleury a night off in preparation for the big game against the San Jose Sharks. James Neal was back and found his legs and timing after returning from his injury. Neal's goal was his first in 13 games, his first since February 8, and his 25th of the year; he'd now scored 25 or more goals in five of his 10 NHL seasons.

Just 22 seconds into overtime, Jonathan Marchessault scored his second goal of the game, propelling the VGK to victory. The VGK top line continued to shine, with William Karlsson registering three points on his third shorthanded goal of the season, along with two assists. It was Karlsson's 41st goal of the season; he was only four goals behind the Washington Capitals' Alex Ovechkin, who led the NHL. In addition, his play away from the puck made him an even more valuable piece in this group of castoffs.

With this win, Vegas improved its record to 49-22-7

for 105 points; it was also the 28th win at T-Mobile. Only the Winnipeg Jets had more wins at home: 30. The VGK needed one more point to lock up the Pacific Division; second-place San Jose had 98 points with four games remaining. Even if San Jose won all of its remaining games, they'd wind up with 106 points. Vegas needed one point in any of its own final games to achieve 106, since it owned the tiebreaker.

Still, the San Jose Sharks were on their way to T-Mobile for Vegas' last home game of the season. It was, by far, the hottest ticket in town, with history possibly about to be made.

Record: 49-22-7

Game 79, San Jose Sharks at T-Mobile Arena, 3/31/18

March 31 was once again a special moment at T-Mobile for multiple reasons.

First, as the last home game of the season, it was something of a reprise of the season's home opener, when the Vegas Golden Knights honored the Metro police officers, EMT workers, doctors, and nurses who responded to the Mandalay Bay shooter's reign of terror and death. The bond that developed that night between this team and this city continued to become stronger and stronger throughout the season. So, as it would have been written if this were a novel, the memory of the 58 souls who were taken from us that Sunday night were honored before the last home game as they were before the first—a banner with #58 was raised to the rafters of T-Mobile.

Team owner Bill Foley will no doubt raise many banners in the name of his hockey team. He'll never raise one with more symbolism, and connection to the city of Las Vegas, than the one that went into the rafters of T-Mobile on March 31, 2018.

No player will ever wear the number 58 for the VGK.

Excuse me if the details of this game are overshadowed by the emotions of the pre-game ceremony. But the second reason this was a special moment was that, in a storybook ending at the last home game of the inaugural season, the VGK were crowned the number-one team in the Pacific Division.

This game was easily the VGK's most important during the regular season. Vegas had led the Pacific Division since December 28 and held it until the end. Meanwhile, San Jose was coming in with a record of 8-1-1 in its previous 10 games, accumulating 17 out of a possible 20 points and chopping down the double-digit lead that the VGK once enjoyed. If San Jose were to win this game, the 12-point Pacific Division lead that Vegas once had would dwindle to a mere five points with three games left.

Vegas knew the importance of getting off to a good start in order to get the crowd into the game and juiced up.

And what a start! The Knights scored on the very first shot of the game, 2:21 in, when Shea Theodore nailed a slap shot from the point. Theodore's roommate Alex Tuch set up a screen that prevented San Jose goalie Martin Jones from seeing the shot.

San Jose tied the game in the first period. In the second, Shea Theodore took a long shot from the left-wing boards. The puck went between the legs of a Shark and past Ryan Reaves and another San Jose player. Oscar Lindberg appeared to ever so slightly touch it and change its direction, allowing it to sneak past Jones. It was Lindberg's first goal since December 23.

San Jose scored again about seven minutes later. This goal was challenged by Coach Gallant for goalie interference, but it held up. The game was tied at 2-2 entering the third.

And then the most incredible thing happened.

Team-leading scorer William Karlsson was helping to kill off a San Jose power play when he stole the puck in his defensive zone and skated down the left wing at full speed. He swooped in on Martin Jones and made a move that qualified for goal of the year for the entire NHL. While Jones was attempting to poke-check the puck away, in Harlem Globetrotter fashion, Karlsson put the puck between his legs, then shot it from behind his trailing leg. All that—at full speed!

I've watched this goal many many times and it still amazes me that William Karlsson was left unprotected in the expansion draft, considered not good enough to protect. Forty-two Karlsson goals later, it was quite clear that someone made a huge mistake on that decision. It was not only the game-winning goal, but also the one that clinched the Pacific Division for Vegas.

Only five players scored more goals than Karlsson on teams in their inaugural season: Blaine Stoughton (56 for the 1979-80 Hartford Whalers), Wayne Gretzky (51 for the 1979-80 Edmonton Oilers), Blair MacDonald (46 for the 1979-80 Oilers), Mike Rogers (44 for the 1979-80 Whalers), and Joe Malone (44 for the 1917-18 Montreal Canadiens).

With this win, the Knights assured themselves of home-ice advantage in at least the first two rounds. And with a record of 50-22-7, the VGK became the third team in the NHL to get to 50 wins this season.

Vegas played to its largest crowd ever, with an attendance of 18,458.

Record: 50-22-7

Game 80, Canucks in Vancouver, 4/3/18

The VGK took to the road for their last three games of the season.

The first, against the Vancouver Canucks, had no real significance for the VGK: They'd already clinched the Pacific Division and their chance of catching Nashville for the Western Conference lead seemed all but unreachable. Nashville led Vegas by six points, 113 to 107. Vegas would have to win all three of their remaining games, while Nashville lost all three. Vegas owned the tiebreaker if the teams wound up tied in points, but that was unlikely to come into play.

By the looks of the lineup, Coach Gallant had determined that resting players such as Jonathan Marchessault,

Erik Haula, David Perron, and Marc-André Fleury was more important than trying to catch Nashville.

This decision allowed Brandon Pirri to be called up from the Chicago Wolves, the AHL affiliate of the VGK. Pirri had prior NHL experience. He was drafted by the Chicago Blackhawks in the second round, the 59th pick overall in the 2009 draft. He played in only seven NHL games during the span of three seasons with Chicago (2010-2013) and played for four NHL teams (Chicago, Florida, Anaheim, and the New York Rangers) before joining the VGK. So it was a "golden" opportunity for Pirri to make a statement.

It always amazes me how some athletes just seize the moment. It also didn't hurt Pirri that Coach Gallant, who could have easily put Tomas Tatar back onto the first line, left Tatar where he'd been playing and put Pirri on the line with Tuch and Karlsson. Pirri rewarded Gallant's decision by scoring two goals in a 5-4 win in overtime and it further proved that Alex Tuch can play his top game with *anyone*.

Vegas held a 4-1 lead with just under 18 minutes left in the game, prompting them to lose concentration and surrender three goals to Vancouver in just under seven minutes of the third period.

Luckily, the keen eye of VGK video coach Tommy Cruz picked up another goal, fourth of the season, on which Vancouver was offsides. The goal was challenged, the call on the ice was overruled, and the goal was disallowed.

The game went into overtime. It appeared that the VGK had won the game when Tomas Tatar snapped a wrist shot into the net, only to have it waived off immediately by the referee for goaltender interference. Then, with just nine seconds left in overtime, Colin Miller appeared to beat Jacob Markstrom with a blistering shot, but the Vancouver goalie made an amazing glove save, sending the game to a shootout.

The first three shooters for both teams failed to score. Shea Theodore, who'd had a hot stick of late, was the fourth shooter. He made Gallant's choice look just as good as the decision to play Pirri on the first line when he found the back of the net to beat the Canucks by one.

Record: 51-22-7

Game 81, Oilers in Edmonton, 4/5/18

In the VGK's next-to-last game in Edmonton, the Oilers won 4-3, dashing any hopes of the Knights capturing the President's Trophy, awarded to the team with the most points for the season. Of course, Vegas' probability of winning it this year was never even a consideration for 99.99% of the hockey—and gambling—world.

Actually, there wasn't much thought outside of the VGK organization that this team would even make the playoffs. But we know how that worked out for the so-called hockey pundits. Also, with its win, Edmonton became the only team on the Knights' schedule to beat them three out of four games during the season. Connor "NASCAR" McDavid, who seems to skate as fast as a human possibly can, once again caused multiple problems for Vegas.

In this game, like the last, Coach Gallant was resting

several of his top players. Only Colin Miller and William Karlsson saw ice time; both had played in every game thus far. Karlsson was chasing the Rocket Richard Trophy for leading the league in goals, but his point streak ended and winning the award was no longer a possibility.

Brandon Pirri was again in the lineup and he scored a goal on his first shot; he'd scored two goals in the previous game on his first three shots. He even had a glorious chance to tie the game with just 14 seconds remaining, but Edmonton goaltender Cam Talbot made a pad save to deny Pirri back-to-back two-goal performances.

This game also saw the debut of Zach Whitecloud, the VGK's six-one 200-pound college free agent signee. Coach Gallant said about the decision to insert Whitecloud into the lineup, "We want to see if the kid can play." And play he did, with nearly 17 minutes of ice time and a +3 differential. Whitecloud was a highly sought-after free agent, who now had the full attention of the VGK coaching staff.

Record: 51-23-7

Game 82, Flames in Calgary, 4/7/18

When the VGK closed out its amazing season on April 7 at Calgary, the game brought to mind a well-known saying in showbiz, "Bad rehearsals lead to strong performances." I certainly hoped it would prove true for the VGK, because their final game was pretty bad. It might go down as the only game in the 82-game season for which the Knights were totally unprepared and in which they looked completely disinterested.

The Flames scorched Vegas early and often—three goals in 3:28 of the first period, with the first two coming just 10 seconds apart. Calgary came into the game having won only 11 of their last 36 and was long out of the playoffs; they were playing for pride and consideration of next year's starting roster.

Calgary forward Mark Jankowski pretty much locked in his spot by closing out the season with a four-goal performance; he nearly scored his fifth late in the third period, only to be denied by Malcolm Subban, who replaced Fleury after two periods. Fleury surrendered six goals on just 18 shots, a showing that was unlike anything we'd seen from him during the season. No worries—this "off knight" would no doubt stimulate his competitive juices.

This game had no bearing on the standings or who Vegas would face in Round 1 of the playoffs. Still, it was a bit disconcerting that the team didn't show up. But in the end, they lost 7-1; Vegas' only goal was scored by Cody Eakin.

Final regular-season record: 51-24-7

Game over, season over, it was time to buckle up!

The L.A. Kings were up first and were sure to be a challenge for the Golden Knights, with a ton of playoff experience and two Stanley Cups in recent years. The Golden

Knights had only 480 games worth of playoff experience on their roster. Anaheim had 1,168 games, Pittsburgh 1,153, Tampa Bay 1,152, Nashville 1,016, and San Jose 978.

During the season, Vegas had a record of 2-1-1 against L.A. The Kings outscored Vegas 11-10 in their four games.

The bottom line for Round 1 of the 2018 Stanley Cup playoffs? Two-world class goaltenders facing each other and some big bodies colliding at full speed. What more could anyone ask for?

Chapter 5
The Fans

It's safe to say that most eventual fans of the Golden Knights had rarely, if ever, watched an NHL hockey game. LasVegasAdvisor.com blogger Kevin Lewis summed up the prevailing phenomenon at the start of the season in the following parody piece, "Everyone Gives a Puck."

"I've never been a hockey fan. Here's what I know about it. Hockey ball is played with big sticks and a 'puck,' which looks like a frozen Ding Dong. The players skate back and forth and hit the puck with their sticks. There are various things like the 'blue line,' which delivers a painful electric shock to anyone crossing it at the wrong time; 'icing,' which is interacting improperly with the ice; and 'offside,' which no one knows what it means. Every game contains at least one mandatory mass brawl, after which the referees determine which team started it, then force members of the other team to sit in the 'penalty box.' In particularly egregious cases, the refs put the entire team there, which leads to the occasional lopsided 26-0 score."

But even though hockey was new to most Las Vegans, the Golden Knights had a fascinating effect on the City of Sin. People like Kevin Lewis, who barely knew the difference between a faceoff and a forecheck at the beginning of the debut season, felt a deeper and deeper sense of pride as the VGK won game after game, set record after record, and kept playing as a seamless unit with less collective ego than at an enlightenment-focused ashram—especially in a city that could easily be nickmaned the Me-First Capital of the World.

What's more, the Golden Knights phenomenon went way beyond rooting for the home team. Tens of millions of people from all over the globe have a strong affinity for Las Vegas and it's not a stretch that, especially if they didn't have a team of their own, they'd root for the VGK.

With a new team, everything is new, not the least of which is fan engagement and excitement. It was a vibrant kind of celebration after every Knights' goal. For some of the players, like Alex Tuch and Vadim Shipachyov, it was their first in the NHL, which created a bond among new players and new fans that, at the risk of sounding melodramatic, will be everlasting.

One of the ways in which fan support and team loyalty manifest is with logo merchandise. And if the figures are any indication, the Vegas Golden Knights won the NHL popularity contest by a long shot—and not just with its own fans.

According to the National Hockey League based on data from Fanatics.com, one of the world's largest sports-apparel companies that operates Internet merchandising for all 31 NHL teams, the VGK ranked first in the league in team merchandise sales throughout the 2017-2018 season. And Golden Knights' paraphernalia outsold the merch of all the other Stanley Cup contenders *combined* throughout the playoffs.

The Golden Knights also topped the NHL in retail spending at their home games, making $4 more per attendee than the next closest team. And it started right at the beginning, at the first home game on October 10, as fans at the arena spent close to $20 per person on merchandise alone.

Las Vegas, naturally, was the top market for VGK merchandise; in the enormous Fashion Show Mall on the Las Vegas Strip, with eight department stores and 250 shops, Golden Knights' gear in the dedicated USA Hockey Store made up more than 90% of sales throughout the season. In addition, there are team stores at the City National and T-Mobile arenas; in keeping with the quasi-military motif of the brand, they're called the Arsenal and Armory, respectively. Knights' apparel and paraphernalia are also hawked at a dozen authorized retailers, from Fanzz to Sam's Club, from Dick's Sporting Goods to, of all places, Cracker Barrel. All the MGM Resorts casinos have outlets, as the VGK play at MGM-owned T-Mobile; McCarran International Airport also has one. Everywhere you look, Knights products are for sale—and Las Vegans are wearing the stuff, which is suitable for everyone from newborns to Great-Grandma.

Los Angeles, New York, Pittsburgh, and Chicago rounded out the VGK's top five merch markets—all with highly established and successful NHL teams of their own. Farther afield, Golden Knights' wares were purchased by fans in nearly 100 countries.

Merchandising was part of the plan from the very beginning, as a way to set a serious revenue-generating machine in motion and, at the same time, proliferate the brand by turning as many fans as possible into walking advertisements. And there's no shortage of selections of logo products: hats, hoodies, sweatshirts, short- and long-sleeved T-shirts, jerseys, polos, gym shorts, argyle socks, rally towels, neckties, infant bodysuits, trucker and blockhead hats, snapback and slouch caps, patches, pins, earrings, handbags, commemorative coins, flags, pendants, banners, lanyards, decals, playing cards, photographs, posters, collages, license-plate frames, travel tumblers, shot, pint, and mixing glasses, coffee mugs, bottle openers, keychains, Stanley Cup programs, autographed pucks, and the ever-popular rosewood cornhole game sets—all adorned with various expressions of the Knights' brand. And I could go on; these were from just the first four pages on the Fanatics website.

Also contributing to the VGK's showcase success in marketing and branding was a lack of competition from another Las Vegas major-league team (the L.A. Kings, for example, compete with the Angels, Dodgers, Lakers, Clippers, Chargers, Rams, and Ducks, plus the FC and Galaxy soccer teams and the WNBA Sparks) for fans' merchandise dollars. In addition, VGKwear took on a life of its own that not only encompassed but blew past hockey fandom. This is a culture, especially but not limited to Millennials and younger, that embraces the latest thing, the cool new gear.

All this engendered some brickbats from arbiters of the national mood, as rampant consumerism is wont to do. But no one—not the critics, cynics, or skeptics—could argue with the *basis* of the demand for the swag: A first-year expansion team was conquering the world. Everyone loves—and plenty of people identify with—a triumphant underdog.

Just as the Vegas Golden Knights' fan base extended far beyond Las Vegas, the VGK meme far surpassed paraphernalia. According to the NHL, the Golden Knights led the league in interactions on social media, even though the team had the smallest user base. Television ratings for the Knights' first-round series against the L.A. Kings were 200% higher than the regular season. And the numbers for the Stanley Cup Finals series were higher than hockey had ever seen.

But what told the real story of fan fixation were the ticket prices.

When season tickets went on sale on February 10, 2015, Las Vegans were asked to put down a 10% deposit on a non-existent no-name team that, if it received approval from the league, might play in an arena that wouldn't be completed for at least another year.

And that arena? It was right on the Las Vegas Strip.

Local Las Vegans avoid the Strip at all costs. They don't like going to the Strip, they don't like being on the Strip, they don't even like *crossing* the Strip *in their cars*. Most only wind up there when they have to meet visitors who are staying in a Strip casino, but they don't like the traffic or the crowds or especially the prices. And this was a couple years *before* the casinos started charging to park on the Strip, putting an end to a comp, an entitlement, that Las Vegans and visitors had enjoyed for nearly 90 years and expected to enjoy forever. Pay to park at a gambling hall whose entire reason for being is to pick your pocket? I've never seen a bigger uproar in all my years in Vegas.

T-Mobile Arena has an official capacity for hockey games of 17,500 seats. Subtract 16,000 season tickets and, even accounting for the roughly 2,000 half- and quarter-season-ticket deposits and others that would be purchased with the full intention of reselling them on the secondary market, plus blocks held back for the visiting team, league guests, network and media affiliates, additional media, and corporate sponsors, that left … not too many seats for the general public. Perhaps 1,000, though even before the season began, when single tickets first went on sale, so few were available that the VGK website was pushing buyers toward season and partial-season seats or standing-room-only.

There were two SRO choices: a $50 option for way up on the upper level or a $150 all-inclusive deal on the mezzanine "party" level that included all-you-can-eat hot dogs, popcorn, and cookies, and all-you-can-drink beer.

Including the single, season, and standing-room-only tickets, the VGK ranked fourth in the league for average arena capacity at 103.7%; Chicago was first (109.7%), then Minnesota (105.9%), then Washington (104.6%). In other words, the home games consistently sold out T-Mobile's entire seating capacity, plus hundreds of SRO tickets.

In addition, with the league-average single-ticket price in the $70s, the VGK's average was $88. Even before the season started, the team ranked 11th in the league with an average resale price of $162 per ticket.

Want more? All 44 luxury suites were reserved early on for prices ranging from $7,000 to $20,000 per game, depending on size and location in the arena. Each has a seating area for 16, a full kitchen complete with an attendant who cooks and serves, food and beverage are included, and suite guests park in reserved spots in the New York-New York garage and enter through a VIP entrance that bypasses the lines and crowds.

And that was during the regular season. For the playoffs, these were the hottest tickets in Las Vegas, in the NHL, and possibly in sports. Which is why the Golden Knights organization offered the Knights Vow program to the 16,000-plus season-ticket holders.

The Vow came to life toward the end of the regular season, after 30-odd home games. T-Mobile always had large contingents of visiting-team fans, which neutralized, to a certain extent, the home-ice advantage. In addition, from the start, the VGK were trying to build a fan base; it wasn't in their long-term interests for people to buy and resell game tickets. And no team, or headliner or act for that matter, likes to see their ticket prices grossly inflated on the secondary market. Most pride themselves on offering a reasonable cost so that fans and aficionados can afford to experience the show. When ticket prices double or triple, it defeats that purpose.

On the other hand, Las Vegas is a destination city. Almost everyone, from Bill Foley to the Edmonton Oilers' fans looking to escape 30-below in January to see their team play in balmy southern Nevada, recognized the extraordinary potential of an expansion team in Las Vegas. And though they might be cheering for the VGK's opponents, they're still buying plenty of beer and hot dogs and merchandise; one night I saw a young guy wearing a Connor McDavid jersey buying a James Neal pullover hoodie.

So the VGK had to tread a fine line between welcoming visitors to a travel destination built on entertainment and inclusiveness and sacrificing the team's advantage gained by playing on home ice. The Florida Panthers are also a case in point, but plenty of other teams face the same conundrum; eventually, the resale market can erode local fan support to the extent that, when it passes a point of no return, a team might have to move.

As a season-ticket holder, it's virtually impossible to make all 41 regular-season games. The Golden Knights didn't allow resale of the roughly 1,000 tickets sold on game days, but there wasn't much they could do to prevent their season tickets from being sold on StubHub, the team's authorized partner and the only place fans can resell electronic VGK tickets. StubHub shares its ticket data with the organization: how many tickets were resold and who bought them. By all accounts, the VGK closely monitored the resale situation—and why wouldn't they, with every game at nearly 104% of capacity? If the team spotted too much profiteering, no doubt they warned ticket sellers and, in egregious cases, blacklisted them.

During the regular season, Bill Foley and the VGK tolerated the situation, but as it became clear that the team would play in the post-season, they wanted to recoup their home-ice advantage and had to come up with a plan to persuade the season-ticket holders not to go to the resale market. So on March 29, just after the Knights clinched a spot in the playoffs, the team introduced the Knights Vow program.

If season-ticket holders took the Vow—in other words, made a promise not to resell tickets—they could buy playoff tickets for 25% more than their regular-season prices, a substantial saving, between 40% and 70% less than single-game ticket prices. Fans who didn't take the Vow paid full retail. Also, the price of any tickets resold under the Vow program, if discovered, would revert to the higher price paid by the general public, which immediately skyrocketed due to the howling demand for the limited supply.

The Vow cut into the VGK's profit margin a bit, but one intended consequence was that it didn't take long for the rest of the available season tickets for the 2018-19 season to sell out. Also, it accomplished the team's core objective—rewarding their most loyal fans with the best prices for the playoffs. The local Vegas fan who wasn't a season-ticket holder, though, was pretty much priced out of seeing the VGK live at T-Mobile during the playoffs, especially during the Stanley Cup Finals. The success of the VGK created a situation for which there was no viable solution.

In a second part of the Vow program, season-ticket holders received their tickets electronically via FlashSeats shortly after the dates and times of the playoff games were set. In conjunction with this was the "Cheer Now, Pay Later" deal, in which season-ticket holders attended home playoff games, but didn't have to actually pay for their tickets until after the rounds were completed.

It all created such an unstoppable demand for seasons tickets for 2018-19 that the team had to cancel its planned three-day campaign after selling out in the first day.

And here's another number to consider. Alan Snel of LVSportsBiz.com did a very rough calculation. He multiplied the VGK's announced average ticket price of $88 times total announced attendance during the regular season and came up with approximately $65 million in total ticket revenue. Remember, that doesn't include the 10 playoff games, with the astronomical ticket prices.

A question on a lot of people's minds was how much of total ticket revenues, regular-season and post-season games, went to the team?

Well, according to Pat Christenson of Las Vegas Events, "Professional sports teams cut deals with venues no other events can even hope to receive. The teams take all of the suite, signage, merchandise, and parking revenue. They get the majority of food and beverage revenue. They pay a flat nominal fee in rent that covers all staffing, security, and venue setup."

The VGK organization did well for itself with both merchandise and ticket proceeds. I'm sure it went at least part way toward paying back that $500 million entry fee.

The main show was the hockey, of course, but the side shows were no less worthy of the Entertainment Capital of the World.

Kevin Allen of *USA Today* wrote, "The Vegas game plan is similar to the Nashville Predators (country music), in that the Golden Knights have married their city's identity with their hockey identity. Everything about the Golden Knights is about entertainment."

The whole game-day protocol started at Toshiba Plaza, a two-acre "entertainment activation" space outside T-Mobile Arena's main entrance. In a multi-million-dollar 10-year sponsorship deal, Toshiba became the arena's exclusive supplier for digital signs and displays (and printers and copiers). Its namesake plaza connects the arena to the New York-New York parking garage and The Park, the six-acre $100 million tree-lined outdoor dining and entertainment district between the Las Vegas Strip (and Tropicana Avenue) and the arena.

Those without tickets to the game settled into Toshiba Plaza, sitting in portable folding camp chairs, drinking and eating takeout from Bruxie, Beerhaus, California Pizza

Vow Ticket Prices

The Golden Knights were a hot commodity and their ticket prices were the most expensive in the league for the playoffs.

Case in point: During Round 2 against the San Jose Sharks, tickets on resale sites were twice as expensive for the games at T-Mobile than they were for games at SAP Center in San Jose; they ranged from $434 to $631 for Vegas home games and only $207-$249 for Sharks home games. For Game 5 at T-Mobile, VividSeats prices averaged $328, while for Game 6 at SAP Center, $153.

By comparison, season-ticket holders who took the Vow were charged only $75 during Round 1 for tickets that cost $55 during the regular season and $150 for tickets that cost $120 for regular-season home games.

Prices went up for Round 2. The $75 tickets in Round 1 became $110 and the $150 tickets were now $225. That's still less than half and in some cases only a third of what they cost on StubHub and Vivid.

Inflation also hit Round 3 tickets: Round 2 $110 tickets went up to $170, while $225 tickets became $320.

The Vow price for the Round 3 $170 tickets rose to $235; the $320 tickets went up to $415.

And if you were looking to attend a Stanley Cup Finals game and didn't have a season ticket, prices on vegasgolden knights.com, the team website, started at $275 and skyrocketed to $1,000.

But again, those were bargains compared to the resale prices. A week prior to Game 1 of the Finals, the first-day tickets were available, 2,300 were listed on StubHub. Prices started at $836 and averaged nearly $1,200; the highest I saw was more than $10,000—and that was before the series between the Washington Capitals and Tampa Bay Lightning was over. Ticket buyers didn't even know who the Knights would be playing. On other resales sites, such as TickPick and Vivid, ticket prices averaged between $1,000 and $2,000.

For Game 5 of the Finals at T-Mobile, the $235 tickets charged to season-ticket holders were reselling for $875-$975 and the $415 tickets were listed on StubHub in the range of $1,675 to $2,500.

The Vow program accomplished, mostly, what it set out to. During the first three rounds, the number of visiting-team fans was minuscule compared to the regular season. During Games 1, 2, and 5 of the Stanley Cup Finals, more Washington fans crowded T-Mobile, an estimated 6,000, than in the first three rounds, but nowhere near what was seen during the season. Besides, by then, ticket prices were so through the roof that even I couldn't blame season-ticket holders for taking a little advantage. If Capitals fans wanted to pay the price, well, this was Vegas, after all. ♣

Kitchen, and Sake Rok in The Park, while watching the game on the giant video screen set up outside the arena. It was, to my knowledge, the NHL's first and only tailgating party without a car in sight. During the playoffs, fans got their faces painted with the Golden Knights logo or colors, along with bona fide tattoos, compliments of the team. There were free concerts before the games — by Las Vegas band Imagine Dragon and rappers such as Lil Jon and Logic — and spontaneous dance parties after. Even long-time residents who couldn't remember the last time they'd ventured onto the Strip now flocked there, whether they had a ticket to the game or not. At the end, thousands of fans jammed Toshiba Plaza before, during, and after the home games.

Those with tickets lined up in The Park, then marched into the arena behind the Knight Line, the in-house VGK percussion crew, along with the team cheerleaders, the "Golden Knight" character in medieval armor who opened every home game (real name, Lee Orchard), and Chance, the VGK's gila-monster mascot (real name Clint McComb, a professional sports mascot who traded himself from the L.A. Rams to the Golden Knights when he was offered the job). The drummers, unique to the NHL and more appropriate, perhaps, to half-time at a college football game, had been playing around Las Vegas as the Drumbots when they received a call from the VGK, asking if they'd like to perform at the home opener on October 10. The drummers went over so well that it turned into a season-long gig in which they acted as the pulse or heartbeat of the game—even if they did look like alien robots with light-up glasses and neon costumes. The Knight Line performed from the upper arena level in front of the Fortress, the Golden Knights' castle, pounding out its rhythms, starting some of the chants, and no doubt contributing to the hangovers of the all-you-can-drink beer fans in the nearby standing-room-only party section.

To start the pregame ceremony at T-Mobile, inner-arena hosts Mark Shunock and his sidekick, known as Big D, led the 10-second countdown to "Knight Time." Shunock was one of the stars of the production show "Rock of Ages," the gig that brought him to Vegas, in which he sang epic '80s' anthems. Originally from Canada, he's another family hockey guy; his father was involved in Canadian hockey and Shunock himself was a third-string goaltender in the Canadian Hockey League.

The lights went out, the Golden Knight lifted the sword, the Knight Tron broadcast previous game highlights, the Knight Line gave a drum roll, and the VGK finally entered the arena to their intro song, "John Wick Mode" by Le Castle Vania. The VGK also used what's reportedly the loudest goal horn in hockey: the Kahlenberg KPH-130C Triton Electric Piston, which has an output of over 150 decibels, about as loud as a jet airplane taking off 100 feet away.

During the national anthem, it became a tradition for the arena to erupt during the line, "… gave proof through the …" and yell "KNIGHTS!" at the proper time. At first, some people thought it might be disrespectful, so the fans responded by singing along throughout the song and just … emphasizing … that word a little extra. And this being Vegas, the favorite anthem crooner was a singing gondolier, "Pippo," who steers gondolas along the faux waterway that runs down the middle of the Grand Canal Shoppes at the Venetian Hotel-Casino up the Strip a ways. *Las Vegas Review-Journal* sports writer Ron Kantowski tallied it up: When Pippo (also known as the "Golden Pipes," whose real name is Carnell Johnson) sang the anthem, the Knights were 3-1 in the regular season and 3-1 in the playoffs, for a winning percentage of .750.

The VGK organization added to the natural excitement

of NHL hockey with so many interactive experiences that fans couldn't wait to see what might happen next. "The pregame show," wrote Jason Gay of the *Wall Street Journal*, "resembles a renaissance fair co-managed by Cher and Elton John." And Reed Koutelas of DigitalSport.com commented, "The pregame festivities in Vegas belong in a Cirque du Soleil show, not in the old-fashioned world of hockey."

In the 18-minute intermissions between periods, random fans participated in contests for prizes, merchandise, or vacations sponsored by local casinos. They had to identify locations around the world from travel photos or movies from short clips; 18,000 fans played along and helped supply the correct answers.

During play, the popular Dance Cam broadcast images of fans on the Knight Tron scoreboard showing off their moves. For the Flex cam, attendees displayed their muscles. Themed games, such as "Name That Tune," drew costumed fans who competed for prizes during timeouts. Lyrics were rewritten for sing-alongs; the favorite was "Sweet Golden Knights," where "Golden Knights" replaced "Caroline" in Neil Diamond's 1969 number-one hit.

Requests posted on the Knight Tron got the women screaming, the men booming, and the lower level pitted against the upper. Next, married people were asked to cheer, then singles: "This is a better than any dating app you've ever used," the Knight Tron quipped. "If you're a visitor, scream" prompted a smattering of shouts and hoots, but "If you're a local, scream" caused the entire building to shake off its moorings. That response always gave me goosebumps.

Fans whose mugs made it onto the Knight Tron during the game, in a random shot or cheering, dancing, or losing their minds in one way or another, could download the image onto their phones using an app called "15 Seconds of Fame." Officially part of the show, they were a fine souvenir photo VGK-style.

One season-ticket holder looked like Hulk Hogan as he ripped up his T-shirt as soon as he believed the score was sufficient to assure a victory. With the VGK's winning record at home, he certainly went through a lot of T-shirts during the season.

Then there was Cameron Hughes, whom everyone saw jump out of seats around the arena, dance down the aisles, pull layered VGK T-shirts over his head, and throw them into the crowd, whipping the arena into a frenzy. Most fans at T-Mobile probably thought the guy was just outrageously excitable, but Hughes is actually a full-time professional crowd "igniter" who has performed at 1,700 NHL and NBA games in a 20-year career. Hoo-wee!

Of course, there were the usual marriage proposals, but one stood out, because both the proposal *and* the wedding occurred during the game. In the first period on a break from play, the couple was participating in a "Name That Tune" game when Bruno Mars' "Marry You" came over the PA system. The guy took a knee and proposed. The gal said yes. During the second intermission, now dressed in a tux and wedding gown, the couple tied the knot in front of the Fortress on the upper level. The Elvis impersonator from the Elvis Wedding Chapel officiated. The team presented the newlyweds with their first wedding gift: Mr. and Mrs.

Golden Knights jerseys. The whole thing was broadcast on the Knight Tron. All the girls cried.

Of course, the season-ticket holders, who sat among one another throughout the season, developed friendships. They jumped up and cheered together, sat down and sweat the outcomes together, especially during playoff games that went into overtime, and cried together during the heart-breakers — in short, bled the VGK team colors together.

The kids lined up against the glass, hoping to catch a puck some players tossed to their young fans before the game or receive a stick from other players afterward.

All that was just at the games in and around the arena. VGK mania gripped Las Vegas from day one and got more and more intense as the winning season progressed.

All the big casino marquees on the Strip continuously wished the Knights good luck in the playoffs.

A giant 600-pound Knights jersey showed up on the 150-foot-tall replica of the Statue of Liberty at New York-New York. A statue of Julius Caesar at the entrance to Caesars Palace held a 24-foot-long Golden Knights' goalie stick in one hand and a team flag in the other. A statue of Benny Binion, founder of Binion's Horseshoe Hotel-Casino, astride a steed at South Point Hotel-Casino wore a Knights sweatshirt. The saffron robe of the Buddha, sitting in the full lotus at the entrance of TAO restaurant and nightclub at the Venetian Hotel-Casino, matched the gold armbands on his VGK V-neck tee. The giant MGM lion, Leo, was decked out in the Knights' logo behind a 15-foot-tall puck. Even Céline Dion performed in a loose logo sweater that doubled as a mini-skirt.

Every other person on the street was wearing an iteration of Golden Knights apparel, including T-shirts reading "Welcome to Impossible." Random fans adopted medieval-knight costumes: T-face barbuta, helmets, breast plates, surcoats over armor, leather baldrics, and of course swordsman gauntlets; they looked like they'd just wandered in

The Knight

When it was announced that the NHL had approved Las Vegas for the league's next expansion team, local Shawn Hickey ordered a suit of armor from a British company that creates props and costumes for film and TV.

Hickey wore the costume to the 2017 NHL Awards show in Vegas, which coincided with the announcement of the expansion-draft player selections, and realized that he was ahead of the ball—or in this case, the puck. The team didn't even have a mascot yet.

Appearing in armor during the preseason, he got a lot of media exposure—photos, interviews, profiles, even an entry in the NHL's Top 100 Weirdest Things of the first six months of the 2017-2018 season.

Hickey said, "It was a blast. The president of the team [Kerry Bubolz] gave me his seats for a game. I traveled to away games in armor. Everyone wanted pictures, so I created Instagram and Twitter social-media sites to share them ("VGKUltimatefan"). It was a great experience."

Hickey made a commitment to himself to play out the Knight character through the first season. It remains to be seen if he'll continue into the second. ♣

from the *Tournament of Kings* jousting show at Excalibur Hotel-Casino.

Pet owners outfitted their doggies, kitties, bunnies, hamsters, and turtles in VGK colors and logos. A 10-year-old Jack Russell terrier dubbed Bark-André Furry, whose owner started bringing him to VGK practices at City National Arena, went viral when his photo, in a custom jersey, was posted on Instagram by a Golden Knights reporter. When a new German shepherd was added to the Metropolitan Police Department's canine unit, he was named "Knight" and was put into a VGK jersey with his paws sticking out of the end of the sleeves.

Casinos held nearly non-stop Golden Knights promotions. One of the coolest was hatched by Station Casinos, the big locals-casino operator: Anyone earning 100 players club points (by playing slot or video poker machines) received a futures bet on the Golden Knights to win the Stanley Cup that would pay on free bets of 4-1 from $5 to $250. Savvy locals knew that meant $5, though some of the bigger bets were in the mix and Station stood to pay out more than $1 million should the Knights pull it off. Silverton Hotel-Casino had a "Hat Trick Giveaway": Rack up 1,000 points on three designated days in a row and earn an entry into a drawing for two T-Mobile luxury-suite tickets. Fan fests and viewing parties were held at casinos with beer-bucket and shot specials. At the D casino's Downtown Events Center, viewing parties for the playoffs attracted thousands, including Vince Neil, lead vocalist of heavy-metal band of Mötley Crüe and a sports fiend involved in arena football. The ultimate watch party took place at T-Mobile Arena for

Bugsy Would Be Tickled

According to popular legend, Ben "Bugsy" Siegel invented Las Vegas when he opened the Fabulous Flamingo on the incipient Strip in 1946. Though it's been long debunked, it's still a good story—and the flamingo is an enduring representation of the city.

Plastic pink flamingo lawn ornaments are ubiquitous in Las Vegas, so I suppose it was only a matter of time before they started showing up at T-Mobile for VGK home games.

The tradition started in mid-March. Following a two-game losing streak at home, a fan named Drew Johnson snuck the flamingo past security and threw it onto the ice after the game, which the Knights won. "Showgirls are a little heavy to toss over the glass," Johnson explained.

Flamingos on the ice caught on enough as a way to celebrate wins that the Armory, the Knights' store at T-Mobile, started selling plastic flamingos wearing a team sweater. ♣

Game 4 of the Stanley Cup Finals on Monday June 4; 10,000 fans sat in air-conditioned comfort (in 102-degree weather) to watch the game on the huge video screen.

Bars all over town had a wear-your-VGK-apparel-and-get-a-draft-beer-free special, or complimentary Jello shots for every Knights' goal, or 24-ounce Stanley Cup replica mugs filled with Bud or Bud Light ($20, $3 for refills). The Beerhaus had an Ovechkin Special: a white Russian, no cup. And they all had the games going on every TV in the joint. Strip clubs offered dollar lap dances on game nights.

The newly legalized recreational-marijuana dispensaries got into the act, with special discounts on bud and edibles after VGK playoff victories.

Nail salons advertised custom polish in VGK colors.

Food and drink specials popped up with Golden Knights' themes: power-play cocktails, McFleury alcohol milkshakes, Cloudy with a Chance of Fleury craft beer, puck-shaped mini-cakes with the VGK logo. The Patisserie at Bellagio Hotel-Casino displayed a five-foot-tall 90-pound chocolate sculpture of Marc-André Fleury, on which two pastry chefs worked for five weeks, including 20 pounds of Rice Krispie Treats, Styrofoam, wires, and some intricate carving on the helmet. Individual Chocolate Fleurys were on sale for $40.

Party stores rolled out VGK-themed napkins, tablecloths, cups, plates, banners, and car flags.

Finally, to give fans watching the game in bars a way to keep the celebration going, the Maloofs gave away bottles of their hangover drink, DrinkAde, "The Official Drink Before You Drink," throughout Game 4 against the Capitals at four popular Las Vegas tavern chains.

The Elvises

What would a Vegas party be without Elvis? One of the staples of the wild and raucous T-Mobile home-game scene was the line-up of Elvises positioned in the front row adjacent to the visiting-team's bench. If you watched a Knights playoff game, you probably saw them. During each post-season game at home, the Elvises were the surest bet on the board to get television exposure.

The Elvises were the brainchild of a former professional blackjack player of fine repute who's known in gambling circles as "KC." He hatched the idea heading into the playoffs for the Elvis line-up, pitched it to his seat neighbors (who bought in) and VGK brass (who sold them a second row of seats at a sweetheart price to accommodate more Elvises), and had costumes made. Throughout the playoffs, home and sometimes away, as many of 12 from the original group were in attendance, while at least three other copycat Elvis groups showed up (plus another in Washington with Elvis-Capitals garb).

"We did it to support the team," KC said. And it wasn't his only attempt to do so.

"During the season, I started tapping my wedding ring on the glass," he said. "It wasn't that loud, but it was a steady and monotonous tap that obviously was getting under the skin of the visiting players, who one by one got up and moved to the other side of the bench. How do I know it got to them? Because they complained—and twice I was escorted out of the T for doing it."

In a bizarre postscript after the Capitals won Game 5 to take the Cup, KC ran into Alex Ovechkin in the high-roller room at Aria.

"I sat next to you during the games," KC confided to the Capitals' captain.

"Yes, you were dressed like Elvis," Ovi responded. "You were very annoying." ♣

Chapter 6
The Playoffs

Could a first-year team on an impossible mission con-
summate one of the greatest sports Cinderella stories of all
time?

As the 2018 Stanley Cup playoffs got underway, no one
knew.

But millions of fans from around the world were already
enjoying the ride. And Las Vegans would remember it no
matter how deep their team made it in the rounds. The
Vegas Golden Knights had already surpassed everyone's
wildest dreams.

Round 1, Game 1, L.A. Kings at T-Mobile Arena

When you think of medieval times, you can't help but
imagine kings and knights.

Usually, the kings and knights are on the same team. In Game 1, Round 1, of the 2018 Stanley Cup playoffs, the only thing that the L.A. Kings and Vegas Golden Knights shared was the ice at T-Mobile Arena.

It was a classic playoff game that had the T-Mobile crowd at a fever pitch, even though the two world-class goaltenders with five Stanley Cups between them kept the score to a bare minimum. On the only goal, scored just 3:23 into the game, Shea Theodore's slap shot from the point hit one of his own players and slightly changed direction to give the Knights an early lead that they never relinquished. One would think a 1-0 game wouldn't create a lot of action and excitement, but the game had both in spades.

The physicality of the game was called into question when Ryan Reaves, who was acquired at the trade deadline exactly for possible playoff matchups against teams like the Kings and Sharks, was a healthy scratch. Coach Gallant made a game-time decision not to match Vegas brawn with Kings brawn. His plan was clearly to outskate L.A. and not engage them in a game that would feature scrums and glove-washings to the face at every whistle.

However, William Carrier, inserted into the lineup in place of Reaves, had his own game plan. Carrier was a one-man wrecking ball, throwing his body into any L.A. King he could find. His name appeared nowhere on the score sheet, but he contributed to Shea Theodore's goal with a huge hit on L.A. defenseman Christian Folin along the side boards, creating the turnover that led to the winning goal.

Carrier had a game-high 10 hits, even though he left halfway through the third period after taking a shoulder to his head from Drew Doughty. Doughty was clearly frustrated as he'd been a target of Carrier's. The hit that knocked Carrier from the game was ruled dirty and Doughty was handed a one-game suspension.

And speaking of Drew Doughty, few fans at T-Mobile had forgotten that, way back on December 28 after the VGK beat L.A. in overtime, he said, "There's no way they'll be a better team than us at the end of the season." Well, here it was, just after the end of a season in which the VGK topped the Pacific Division, while the Kings slipped in as a wild-card. And now L.A. had lost the first game and had to win four out of the next six for Doughty not to have to eat his words.

Even without Reaves in the lineup, the hits kept coming at a high frequency. The Kings led the NHL in hits over the past few years with an average of 32.1 per game, though it did drop a bit to 25.7 in the 2017-2018 regular season. Vegas had an average of 21 hits per game. L.A. had 68 hits on Vegas and Vegas responded with 59 of their own—127 hits dished out by both teams.

As far as I was concerned, the only reason Fleury was named the number-one star of the game was the shutout. All shutouts are difficult to achieve, especially in the play-offs, but in this one, Fleury didn't have to make a lot of difficult saves; his team continuously frustrated the Kings on the offensive side of the puck. That was why I felt that Carrier deserved the number-one nod. He got off his 10 hits in less than nine minutes of ice time.

Still, Fleury earned his 63rd playoff win with 30 saves and the 11th postseason shutout of his career.

So one win was in the books. Only 15 more would take down the most cherished trophy in team sports.

Record: Vegas 1, L.A. 0

Round 1, Game 2, L.A. Kings at T-Mobile Arena

Game two was a saga, an epic, a mammoth marathon that required 95 minutes and 23 seconds to determine the winner.

Jonathan Quick almost single-handedly stole this game from the VGK. He faced 56 shots and stopped 54 of them. He rejected shot after shot after shot after shot.

The one goal that beat him in the first period was on a power play off an offensive-zone penalty by the Kings for goaltender interference. A shot from the point by Jonathan Marchessault went wide of the net, rebounded off the wall, and slid right to Alex Tuch, positioned behind a Kings defenseman. Tuch tapped it in for the first goal of the game and the first power-play goal that Vegas had scored against L.A. all year. They were 0-13 during the regular season and 0-3 in Game 1 and for good reason: L.A.'s penalty-killing unit was ranked number one of all 31 teams in the league. The Kings' lone goal was also on a power play, scoring on a lucky bounce on a shot from the point that glanced off of Deryk Engelland's leg to get past Fleury.

It was also Alex Tuch's first NHL playoff goal. He and his rookie housemate Shea Theodore scored the Knights' first two goals in their first two playoff games.

The score remained tied at 1-1 through the third period and the first 20-minute overtime period. In NHL playoffs, overtime is the same as regulation periods—20 minutes with full 18-minute intermissions between them. There is no shootout. As many OT periods as necessary are played until a winner is determined in sudden death; first team to score wins.

The winning goal in the second OT started when a blocked shot bounced out to James Neal, who skated into the neutral zone with Erik Haula and Alex Tuch trailing the play. Neal crossed, drawing both defensemen toward him. He dished the puck over to Haula, bearing down on Quick with speed off the right wing. Quick attempted to poke-check the puck away from Haula, losing his position, and Haula slipped the puck between Quick's legs for the dramatic double-overtime win.

The roof practically exploded off T-Mobile as the crowd went wild. It was Haula's first-ever playoff OT goal and the 13th playoff goal in his career. The game was the longest in the L.A. Kings' franchise history. In their previous longest OT game, they beat the New York Rangers in 2014 to win the Stanley Cup.

The Kings were missing three of their starting defensemen, two due to injuries (Jake Muzzin and Derek Forbort). Drew Doughty, one of the best defensemen in the league, was sitting out on a one-game suspension for his overzealous check on Vegas forward William Carrier in Game 1. Added up, it forced the Kings to play four defensemen who'd appeared in a total of just five NHL playoff games among them. It showed again and again, as Vegas kept the puck in the Kings' defensive zone and had a number of quality scoring chances that Quick rejected—one after another after another. Quick surrendered just three goals in two games and was 0-2. Fleury and Quick were putting on a veritable goaltending clinic.

If, somehow, L.A. had won this game, it would have been a crushing defeat for the Knights, who clearly dominated and, just like in Game 1, carried the play the entire game. Wave after wave of VGK players swarmed the Kings' defensive zone, firing a total of 111 shots toward Quick, and the physicality of the series continued, with 136 hits between the two teams—L.A. 80, Vegas 56.

Vegas now had a stranglehold on the series; L.A. had to win four of the five remaining games to advance to Round 2. In the NHL, teams that win the first two games are an 88.7% favorite to win the series. But hockey fans know better than to take anything for granted. Only four years ago in 2014, L.A. lost the first *three* games to the San Jose Sharks before winning the last four of that series, then going on to win the Stanley Cup.

This game was played on April 13. One year and a day earlier, on April 12, 2017, Gerard Gallant was hired as the head coach of the Vegas Golden Knights. Coach was no doubt pleased with the anniversary gift from his team.

Record: Vegas 2, L.A. 0

Round 1, Game 3, Kings in L.A.

In Game 3, the L.A. Kings played their best game in the series in front of the home crowd. The only reason the first two games were even close was Jonathan Quick's goaltending. The Kings played a total of 168 minutes and 37 seconds without having a lead in the series. They hadn't scored a 5-on-5 goal until they finally got one past Fleury at the 13:14 mark of the first period.

L.A. found their forecheck, missing in the first two games, and gave Vegas a challenge in the first 20 minutes. Quickly clearing the puck, they neutralized the Vegas forecheck, which had bogged down the Kings' ability to break out of their defensive zone in Games 1 and 2. It didn't hurt that Drew Doughty was back after serving his one-game suspension and Jake Muzzin returned after missing the first two games. Their presence in the lineup made a big difference in getting the puck up and out of their zone.

The score remained 1-0 going into the third, until Cody Eakin opened it up for Vegas. With the score now tied at 1-1, James "Big Game" Neal, who set up the winning goal in Game 2, made a great move coming down the right wing, turning his back on the L.A. defenseman, then quickly pivoting by him on his way to Quick. Earlier in the period, Neal came down on Quick from the same side of the ice, but passed the puck. This time he took matters into his own hands and, just like Haula in Game 2, fired the puck between Quick's legs for the lead that Vegas would not lose. When Karlsson scored just 19 seconds after Neal's goal to go ahead 3-1, you could see the air get sucked out of the L.A. Kings' sails. It was the first goal for Karlsson in the series.

L.A. added a second goal with Quick pulled for an extra skater when, with 2:04 left in the game, Oscar Fantenberg's shot was deflected in off Anze Kopitar in front of the net, giving Kopitar his second point of the night. But Vegas killed off the last two minutes and, with the exciting 3-2 win at Staples Center, vaulted to a commanding 3-0 lead.

L.A.'s physical play was once again evident, with 28 hits in the first period; 14 of their 18 skaters registered at least one. Vegas dished out a few in return. Jonathan Marchessault, the smallest player on the team, is listed at five-nine and 174 pounds. I've stood right next to him in the locker room and five-nine is a stretch. Still, he delivered some huge hits against players to whom he gave up a few inches and a lot of pounds.

Vegas was held scoreless for the first 40 minutes, but Fleury, being Fleury, stopped just about everything the Kings sent his way. He clearly kept Vegas in the game through the second period, giving his team its chance for a third-period surge. Fleury faced 39 shots; Quick faced 26.

This team was such a pleasure to watch. They could and did play whatever kind of game was presented to them. And they could and did win.

Record: Vegas 3, L.A. 0

Round 1, Game 4, Kings in L.A.

"There's no way they're going to be a better team than us by the end of the season."

On December 28, 2017, L.A. King Drew Doughty scored a goal late in the third period to tie the game against Vegas and send it into overtime. The Knights won, but Drew thought it was a fluke. He might have even still believed it — until Game 3 of this playoff series.

It was an important win, but Doughty's declaration in December turned out to be even more important. You never want to give your opponent any *extra* incentive to want to beat you. There are enough reasons to begin with without adding to the list. And never in Doughty's wildest dreams four months earlier could he have foreseen that his ill-considered statement would echo all over Las Vegas and come back to haunt him so strongly. The VGK players would never admit that they used these words as a motivation tool, but trust me, they did.

Doughty's was just one expression of all the non-believers. "It's an impossible mission." "It's all just a fluke." "The collapse is just around the corner."

And in a fitting end that makes it all even sweeter, the winning goal — in fact, the only goal — in Game 4 was scored by former L.A. King Brayden McNabb. McNabb had appeared in a sum total of five playoff games in his entire NHL career, all with the Kings during the 2015-2016 season. During those games, he registered zero goals and zero assists. It's poetic justice that his first-ever playoff goal came against the team that cast him off.

Years from now, people who didn't have the privilege of witnessing the dismantling of the Kings in this series might look back and think, even though Vegas won all four games, it must have been close: 1-0 in Game 1; 2-1 in

Game 2; 3-2 in Game 3; and 1-0 in the series clincher. Nothing could be further from the truth.

During the 14 periods in this four-game series, L.A. was the better team in one of them. In the other 13, the Golden Misfits put on a complete-team show. Leading up to the playoffs, it was clear that all four lines would have to contribute for the Knights to advance through the round. And that happened: Each of Vegas' seven goals in the series was scored by a different player. Oh, and Fleury standing on his head in all of them didn't hurt.

The Kings were completely dominated. The only thing that was close was the goaltending. Jonathan Quick and Fleury put on a clinic for the ages.

The first period of the fourth game in the series was *that* period, the one out of 14 where L.A. was the better team. The Kings gave it all they had. In the first 12 minutes, they took 22 shots at Fleury, while Vegas had only four on Quick. But it was like running too fast in the first part of a marathon; they had nothing left in the later stages of the race.

L.A.'s forecheck caused multiple turnovers that resulted in quality scoring chances on Fleury. Though he was left with no support, he was a rock wall. During the break after the first period, Coach Gallant settled the team down and when they returned to the ice, they looked like the same bunch that had outplayed L.A. in the previous 11 periods.

The player who created all scoring in this game, four minutes into the second period, isn't recognized on the scoresheet. Jonathan Marchessault made a breakout pass to William Karlsson, and with Reilly Smith tagging along, they came down the left wing. Quick had to focus on both

Smith and Karlsson who were bearing down on him. Both L.A. defensemen slid over to their right. Brayden McNabb joined the rush entering the zone from the right wing. Karlsson passed the puck to Smith and in one swift motion, Smith slid the puck over to McNabb. Like a gunslinger, the ex-King had his stick up, poised to blast the pass from Smith. Before Quick could even move, McNabb's one timer was in the net. Thirty-five minutes and 56 seconds later, the VGK swept the Kings in four straight.

The Kings had a number of quality scoring chances. In the first, Fleury snapped a wicked uncontested shot by Anze Kopitar out of the air like a wiffle ball in a baseball glove. The last save with just 15 seconds left before advancing to Round 2 was off the stick of Dustin Brown. This time, Fleury didn't glove it, but he got just enough of it to send it a few inches wide of the left post. As the final seconds ticked down in an ironic ending, Drew Doughty wound up with the puck on his stick, but all he could muster was a weak backhand that never made it to Fleury.

By sweeping the series, Vegas earned itself a week off, since Round 2 in the Stanley Cup playoffs doesn't begin until all Round 1 games are completed. They would also enjoy home-ice advantage again in Round 2.

Best of all, the Vegas Golden Knights were just eight wins away from playing in the Stanley Cup Finals.

Round 1 final record: Vegas 4, L.A. 0

Round 2, Game 1, San Jose Sharks at T-Mobile Arena

The VGK feasted on the San Jose Sharks in the first game of the second round of the Stanley Cup playoffs. Even before all the invited guests were seated, the buffet began and the defensive battle that the pundits predicted never materialized. Instead, there was blood in the water. Under normal conditions, sharks are most dangerous when the sea is red. In this game, however, the blood was streaming from the Sharks themselves, who were netted, harpooned, and hung by their tails in front of the 18,000-plus fans at T-Mobile.

The building started rocking from the last note of the national anthem and it never stopped, as the SS Gallant and its crew of 20 made its way over the frozen waters of T-Mobile. Even though the crew had been off for eight days, the captain and his sailors made the Sharks look like guppies. Their speed on the game's first two shifts spelled trouble for the Sharks, who seemed like fish out of water. Vegas beat San Jose by a whopping 7-0.

In the first round of the playoffs, both the Sharks and Knights quickly disposed of their opponents. San Jose surrendered only four goals in their four-game sweep of Anaheim; Vegas allowed only three, as Marc-André Fleury had two shutouts in their own four-game sweep.

One had to assume that the San Jose scouts were well aware of the L.A. Kings' game plan: trying to force Vegas away from their speed and into playing a defensive game, and that it failed miserably. When they combined the Kings' loss with their own domination in the first round, they probably believed they could play speed against speed and trust that their goaltender, Martin Jones, would keep up his torrid puck-stopping pace.

Fair enough. The plan had only one problem. Vegas' speed had given its opponents problems for the past 86 games. After the Game 1 in Round 2, it was 87.

Actually, there were two problems. The second? As had been the case many times before, this was a complete team effort. In Round 1, Vegas scored seven goals in four games, all seven by different players. Now they'd scored seven in the first game alone and guess what? All seven goals, *again*, were scored by different players.

Unbelievable.

That said, make no mistake about it: The superstar of this team is Marc-André Fleury. With the thrashing of the Sharks, Fleury recorded his third shutout in the first five games of the playoffs. The last time that happened was 14 years ago, by Nikolai Khabibulin (Tampa Bay) and Ed

---

Ferrall on Fleury

Marc-André Fleury was the toast of Vegas town, but it didn't stop there. Sports-talk-radio host Scott Ferrall of CBS, an avowed hockey nut, couldn't have been more effusive. After the VGK swept the L.A. Kings in Round 1 of the playoffs, including two shutouts, Ferrall told his audience, "They're going to ride Fleury all the way. He's just too good, isn't he? I mean, you can't score on that guy."

In later broadcasts, he called Fleury "one of the game's greatest goalies" and "one of the top five goalies of all time." ♣

Belfour (Toronto). Keep in mind, established teams were playing in front of these goaltenders back in 2004. The expansion team in front of Fleury was put together less than a year earlier. The shutout was Fleury's 13th in postseason play. It was also his 67th playoff win.

In the first five games of the playoffs, Fleury had a goals against average of 0.54 and a save percentage of .982.

Astonishing.

San Jose's Martin Jones gave up four goals on the first seven shots he faced and five goals on just 13 shots. His night ended early. Aaron Dell replaced Jones and made 19 saves on 21 shots.

Vegas' speed led to three goals within 1:31: Cody Eakin scored at 4:31, Erik Haula at 4:57, and Jonathan Marchessault at 6:02. Alex Tuch closed the scoring in the first period when, on the power play, he exploded through four San Jose players who tried to stand him up at the blue line. Instead of standing him up, they looked like they were standing still as Alex blew right through them and nailed his shot before Martin Jones even knew what was coming.

San Jose had a respectable 17 shots on Fleury in the first period, but could only muster eight in the second and eight in the third. They were demoralized and it showed as the game dragged on and on for them. Out of their frustration, they handed Vegas 10 power-play chances.

The real letdown came in the third period when Evander Kane took a five-minute major for cross-checking Pierre-Édouard Bellemare across the face long after the whistle had blown and a scrum ensued. Kane was more than 30 feet away from the scrum and skated directly to Bellemare, who had his back turned. It was clearly a dirty hit that earned him a seat in the press box for the next game.

Sometimes shots registered can be a telling statistic as to which team controlled the flow of the game. The shot totals ended up 34-33 in favor of Vegas, so one might assume that San Jose was competitive in this game. Far from it. The Sharks were done at the "Star-Spangled Banner." The crowd played a major factor in making sure there was no letdown when the score got to 4-0. They were engaged the entire 60 minutes and had a well-organized wave going through the arena. I couldn't believe my eyes when Marc-André Fleury actually joined in on the wave while play was in action at the other end. If you didn't notice that this team was loose, you weren't paying attention.

This continued to be the best sports story in the U.S. in years, and for sure the best sports story in the 113-year history of Las Vegas. No one knew when it would end, but from this game, it appeared that it wouldn't be any time soon.

Record: Vegas 1, San Jose 0

Round 2, Game 2, San Jose Sharks at T-Mobile Arena

Just when it seemed that nothing could interfere with this team's improbable mission, along came a game that seriously challenged its unimaginable path.

Having two goaltender interference calls in one game is extraordinary, but for both to go against the same team is almost unheard of. It happened to the Knights in Game 2.

Vegas also sent a parade of players to the penalty box—seven different times. You're playing with fire when you undergo an unforgivable breakdown of discipline, hand the opposition one power play after another, and surrender two power-play goals.

During the regular season, Vegas was one of the least penalized teams in the NHL, a total of 560 minutes for the entire 82-game season, which averaged out to 6.8 minutes per game. The only team with fewer penalty minutes was Carolina with 512. In Game 2 of Round 2, the Knights tripled their average: 18 minutes of penalty time.

It clearly showed as they seemed completely out of sync, almost discombobulated at times. Their passes, usually tape to tape and a key factor in the breakouts, were missing. The uneven flow of the game played right into San Jose's hands; Vegas' speed, which had given the Sharks all they could handle in Game 1, was MIA.

The game turned around a bit with 2:01 left in the first period, when Colin Miller intentionally shot the puck wide of the net, hoping the rebound off the end boards would create a favorable bounce. It seemed like a long shot, but it was the safest play, since he had no clear path to Sharks goaltender Martin Jones. It also turned into one of the game's rare lucky moments for Vegas. The puck came out to William Karlsson, positioned to the right of Jones, and with an almost impossible shooting angle, Karlsson found the tiny opening.

It was the only goal of the first period on the five shots that Vegas managed to muster. San Jose had nine shots in the first and most of them were quality scoring chances that Fleury snuffed.

Fleury had been perfect in the VGK's prior seven periods. The last goal he gave up was way back on April 15, 13 days earlier, with 2:04 seconds left in Game 3 against the Kings. He had back-to-back shutouts in Game 4 of the first round and Game 1 of the second, plus a perfect first period in this Game 2.

William Karlsson scored again, just 26 seconds into the second period to jump ahead of the Sharks 2-0.

But wait. Here it comes again, my theory, which more often than not seems to be spot on: The next team to score in a 2-0 game is usually the winner. So when San Jose scored the first of their two power-play goals just 1:34 after Karlsson's goal, I thought Vegas might be in trouble.

Fleury's fantastic, but he's not perfect, and he had a small hiccup on a shot by the Sharks. He clearly had the puck in his possession and both Vegas defensemen relaxed. But the VGK goalie had other plans and pushed the puck to his left at the feet of Deryk Engelland, who was flat-footed and unable to control it. Tomas Hertl swooped in, took the puck, and moved it out to Logan Couture, who put it past Fleury to tie the game at 2-2.

Three minutes later, Brent Burns scored his second goal of the night—the first of the controversial goal-interference decisions. Shark forward Timo Meier was pushed into Fleury, preventing him from covering the now-open net. Coach Gallant's challenge was denied and the Sharks, who had trailed 2-0, were now ahead 3-2 and with Vegas still out of sync, things weren't looking so good.

The third period seemed to be salvaged when Nate Schmidt took a Shea Theodore pass and timed a slap shot from the blue line that beat Martin Jones to tie the game with just 6:32 left in regulation.

Since they'd played maybe 10 minutes of the first 60, the Knights were mighty lucky to move the game into overtime. They didn't deserve to win, but it appeared they did just that when Jonathan Marchessault came out from behind the net with defenseman Brenden Dillon right behind him. Shea Theodore's slap shot hit Marchessault and fell at his feet; he quickly backhanded the loose puck past Martin Jones, who immediately raised his stick to claim he was interfered with. The crowd went wild, the Vegas bench emptied in celebration, but now we were facing our second goaltender-interference call of the night.

The longer the replay officials took to decide, the more likely it appeared that they were going to overturn the goal, and after what seemed like a near eternity of agonizing torture, the 18,000-plus crowd and the 20 Vegas players were informed the goal had been disallowed and play resumed. Two goaltender-interference calls both going against Vegas? You just had a feeling this wasn't going to be their night.

The game went into a second overtime, which lasted only 5:05, during which Vegas committed two penalties and pretty much handed the Sharks a loaded gun in a fight where the Knights had a sword. Logan Couture took a cross-ice pass on the power play and beat Fleury for his second goal of the game to end a "knightmare" of a game for Fleury and his team. This was the first loss in the post-season for Vegas.

A bright spot? The VGK forced the Sharks into five periods of hockey to beat them.

The series, now tied, moved to San Jose for two games.

Record: Vegas 1, San Jose 1

Round 2, Game 3, Sharks in San Jose

Game 3 had multiple storylines. The one that ran straight through the night was this: More than a few VGK fans probably had to schedule EKGs with their cardiologists to check for lasting damage to their hearts from this game. Those whose heart rates didn't flutter a few times in Vegas' 4-3 win over the San Jose Sharks have nerves of steel and ice water in their veins.

I've had countless viewing experiences of NHL playoff hockey in the past 50-plus years, but after this one, I could have auditioned for a Jack in the Box commercial. I was up. I was down. I was pacing like an expectant father. I was yelling at the TV. I admit I really erupted a few times, especially after the ruling that there was *no goalie interference* when Evander Kane scored, closing the 3-1 Vegas lead to 3-2.

The original storyline started early in the game. Once again, Marc André-Fleury was amazing. He saved the day, literally by himself, in the first period as San Jose created scoring chance after scoring chance and had 16 shots. Fleury stopped them all.

Part of the Knights' problem in the first was the continuation of the parade to the penalty box that started in

Game 2. The VGK committed three penalties in the second period alone. They killed off the first on Reilly Smith for hooking. But when Timo Meier scored the Sharks' first goal, William Carrier was off for tripping.

A similar story was that San Jose joined the parade. They committed three minor penalties in the second period, during which Colin Miller and Jonathan Marchessault scored back-to-back power-play goals only 3 minutes and 29 seconds apart to put the VGK ahead 2-1. And one minute and 17 seconds after Marchessault's goal, Reilly Smith scored, making it 3-1. Smith had missed a number of games after being injured and it was his first goal since March 2.

This is where the plot began to look familiar. The two-goal lead in the second period was the same as Vegas held in Game 2. I assumed that they wouldn't blow another two-goal lead in a crucial swing game in this series. If they didn't, it would make Marchessault's the winning goal—fair enough, as Marchessault's score in double OT was taken off the board when the NHL ruled he interfered with Martin Jones.

Evander Kane cut the lead to just one goal with a wicked snap shot that somehow found a small opening just over Fleury's left shoulder. But Logan Couture bumped into Fleury just as Kane's shot entered the net, leading to goaltender-interference-review number three in just three games. On the replay, it appeared that this one would be the first to go in favor of the VGK. When that didn't happen, the two-goal lead was down to just one with 12 minutes and 11 seconds to play.

Tomas Hertl made a power move from behind the net,

beating both Deryk Engelland and Shea Theodore in a mad scramble, tying the game with 1:57 remaining.

William Karlsson almost won it with just a few seconds left in regulation; he came out from behind the San Jose net, only to be denied by Martin Jones.

On to overtime, yet another storyline and a familiar one at that—the second OT in a row, the VGK's third in the play-offs, and more EKG appointments texted to Vegas doctors.

Back to the Fleury subplot, he made the save of the entire 2018 playoffs up to that point when he robbed Game 2 double-overtime winner Logan Couture. Couture was wide open 15 feet in front of Fleury, who made a spectacular glove save. The look on Couture's face was priceless. He, along with everyone else watching, thought San Jose had just won Game 3.

Enter James Neal, who'd been an absolute beast in this series. He rang one off the post that could have ended the game and regained home-ice advantage for Vegas.

Someone tweeted that the overtime had so far taken 10 years off his son's life—and his son is only a year old.

Back to Fleury, whose magic was not to be denied. The hockey gods owed a game to Vegas and in a play that was reminiscent of the winner in Game 2 against the Kings, James Neal was flying through the neutral zone and drew both Shark defensemen toward him as he approached the blue line. Just like his pass to Erik Haula streaking down the right wing against the Kings, he dished the puck to William Karlsson, who ripped a perfect shot over the stick side and right shoulder of Jones to win the game at the 8:17 mark of OT.

I always tried to be neutral and unbiased when I covered this team, but I must admit, it was far from easy. The VGK captured the hearts and souls of Las Vegas and of fans worldwide.

Enne Bond, a dealer at Mandalay Bay who got into hockey because of the Golden Knights, was curious between Rounds 1 and 2 and asked fans on social media where they lived. He heard from Australia, Canada, Denmark, England, Finland, Germany, Ireland, Japan, Kuwait, Lithuania, New Zealand, Norway, the Philippines, Puerto Rico, Scotland, South Africa, Sweden, and Switzerland.

Even the Golden Knights organization tapped into this worldwide appeal. They asked fans via Twitter: "Where's everyone watching the game from tonight?" They were stunned at the reach—countries all around the world. They contacted fans from faraway places via direct message, sent them shirts, and created the hashtag #VGKWorldwide.

Record: Vegas 2, San Jose 1

Round 2, Game 4, Sharks in San Jose

How often, in hockey, do you hear the phrase "keeping up with the Joneses"? Not very. It usually refers to the struggle to maintain your daily responsibilities, while keeping pace with your neighbors, who for simplicity's sake we call the Joneses.

But in Game 4 with the Sharks, the Golden Knights' first in the month of May, Martin Jones was the better goaltender. Yes, in no games of the Knights' first seven in the playoffs could you say that Marc André-Fleury wasn't the number-one goaltender on the ice. But you could in the second game played in San Jose and no one would give you an argument. The Sharks were the better team all around: They shut out the Knights by a score of 4-0. This was the Knights' worst playoff appearance.

With just six seconds left in the first period, Vegas allowed Joonas Donskoi to skate the entire length of the ice, starting from deep in his own zone to just inside the blue line, where he fired a seemingly innocent shot at Fleury that should have ended the period with San Jose leading 1-0. But Fleury didn't pick up the puck as it went through the legs of Brayden McNabb. For all intents and purposes, the game was over right there, as Vegas never recovered from that goal. Goals late in a period, especially in the playoffs, are huge for the momentum of the scoring team and have the complete opposite effect on the team that's scored on.

All season long and in the playoffs, the Knights produced offense from their power play and even when they didn't score, it often changed the momentum of the games in their favor. In this game, San Jose offered up five power-play opportunities on a "golden" platter, of which Vegas failed to take advantage. There also could have been at least one, or possibly two, additional penalties called on San Jose for using a play that's 100% legal in the NBA, but 100% illegal in the NHL: the pick.

On the first San Jose goal, Alex Tuch was clearly picked off, preventing him from staying with his check on San Jose forward Marcus Sorensen. This illegal pick allowed

Sorensen time and space to carry the puck across the zone and beat Fleury on his stick side. If Tuch had been allowed to continue his check, this play would likely never have developed. Coach Gallant was both visibly and vocally upset at the non-call, which might have paid dividends; just 1:06 after Sorensen's goal, Mikkel Boedker was assessed a penalty for interference. But the VGK couldn't capitalize on this opportunity or on their other four power plays. San Jose continued to use this pick play throughout the game, but was called on it one time in the third period, when Timo Meier was whistled for the infraction.

Throughout the season and especially in the playoffs, the Knights' success both offensively and defensively was due, in large part, to contributions from all four offensive lines and from the first, second, and third defensive tandems. In this shutout, four Vegas forwards—Tatar, Tuch, Perron, and Bellemare—didn't register a single shot on goal. The defensemen had also added to the VGK's offensive output by being aggressive on the offensive side of the puck, but three—McNabb, Merrill, and Schmidt—took no shots in this game. And it wasn't often that an opposing team's fourth line outplayed the VGK's fourth line, but that occurred as the VGK's fourth couldn't establish a forecheck. The results of the forecheck never seem to make the score sheet, except when the other team is scoring, because of the unimpeded path toward their offensive zone. San Jose faced little resistance to that portion of their game.

The Sharks had to win this game. If they'd lost, it would have put them down 3-1, with two of the next three games played at T-Mobile. That would have been an almost insurmountable lead for San Jose to overcome. Likewise, the VGK missed a golden opportunity to lock up the series. San Jose played a desperate game and it came up with a complete 60-minute effort.

This was Vegas' first playoff loss on the road and the first time they'd been shut out since February 19, a little less than three months earlier. The Golden Knights weren't often this unprepared or emotionally flat for games.

Of course, Round 2 was a long way from being over and if history held true, the VGK would be back on course, especially with two of the three remaining games played at home. Being back at T-Mobile with 18,000 fans rocking the building figured to be exactly what they needed to regain focus and return to the kind of hockey that got them where they were after 82 regular-season games and seven playoff games.

Record: Vegas 2, San Jose 2

Round 2, Game 5, San Jose Sharks at T-Mobile Arena

Throughout the season, Coach Gerard Gallant never seemed to get too high when his team won or too low when they lost. In Game 5 against the San Jose Sharks, he retained that posture, which by this time had also been adopted by his charges.

With a complete roster of healthy players, Gallant inserted Luca Sbisa, who hadn't played since February, in place of Jon Merrill. He also put in Oscar Lindberg, who hadn't played since April 7 in the regular-season final game, and took out Tomas Tatar. And Ryan Carpenter replaced Tomas Nosek, who'd played in 67 of the 82 regular-season games and was a key contributor to Vegas' fourth line and penalty-killing unit.

Nosek's removal from the lineup was a clear statement about the lack of forechecking in Game 4 by the Knights. That seemed to get the players' attention as the forecheck was back in this home game.

Give credit not only to Coach Gallant for his uncanny knack of pushing the right buttons at the right time with this team, but also to the replacement players themselves, along with their conditioning staff, for making a seamless transition into the lineup without upsetting the overall chemistry of the team.

Gallant also tinkered with his lines and that seemed to really work for Alex Tuch, who was reunited with Cody Eakin. Granted, Tuch seemed to play well with anyone he was lined up with. This diamond in the rough hadn't even quite grown into his body, but with just a few days before his 22nd birthday, he was playing like he had a few hundred NHL games under his belt, instead of 78 regular-season games, plus all eight playoff games, for a total of 86.

Though the Knights won Game 5 by a score of 5-3, the victory didn't, to be sure, come without drama. The raucous crowd at T-Mobile, in a festive mood during the first two and a half periods, began to experience some sweaty palms as the Knights' 4-0 lead as late as 9:35 into the third became 4-3 within 6 minutes and 9 seconds. Vegas had committed only one penalty in the first two periods, but took three in the third, and when San Jose scored a power-play goal 29 seconds after James Neal's slashing penalty, the calm seas all of a sudden turned choppy. It doesn't take much to breathe some life into a desperate team and with three goals in a six-minute span, all of a sudden an impending storm was on the T-Mobile horizon.

This time, the blood in the water wasn't the Sharks'. Fleury, who'd been strong in the net, stopping all 17 shots in the first two periods, was under siege by San Jose's desperate push to remain a factor, not only in this game but for the balance of the series. Fleury did as Fleury does and rose to the occasion, eventually making 27 saves of the 30 shots he faced, earning him his 69th playoff win and moving him into 10th place overall in goaltender victories in the post-season.

San Jose pulled Martin Jones for the second time in the five-game series when none other than Alex Tuch scored his second goal of the game at the 8:36 mark of the third. That turned out to be the game winner, though at the time it was scored, not one of the 18,000-plus fans in attendance had a clue. Jones had surrendered four goals on 31 shots. Tuch's goal seemed like additional icing on the cake. Jones was replaced by Aaron Dell, who stopped all seven shots he faced.

Teams that win Game 5 and go up 3 games to 2 have a 78.9% success rate in winning the series. If this stat held true, the VGK would be just eight wins away from turning a mission impossible into a team, to mix a metaphor, for all seasons.

Record: Vegas 3, San Jose 2

Round 2, Game 6, San Jose Sharks at T-Mobile Arena

Marc-André Fleury, who was unshakable in net during the first two rounds of the playoffs, had three friends join him in eliminating the San Jose Sharks in Game 6 by a score of 3-0. For Fleury, it was yet another series-clinching game and his fourth shutout in the 10 playoff games.

Marc-André's three friends weren't found anywhere on the official game summary, but they were on the ice for the entire 60 minutes of the game. They were Left Post, Right Post, and Crossbar. They, along with Fleury, were the main reason that Vegas was now one of only four teams left that would compete for the Stanley Cup.

Not many VGK fans could have even had this on their radar in October. The initial hope was for a competitive team; the dream was to at least compete for a playoff position. Accomplishing that alone was so farfetched that in our hearts, we knew we were reaching for the stars.

Who could have possibly imagined that this group of castoffs, who dubbed themselves the "Golden Misfits," would come together as a team that looked like they'd been playing together for years? Who could have foreseen that, in the process, they'd galvanize an entire city? The city fed off the team just as the team fed off the city and the combined energy shook T-Mobile Arena down to its very foundation—in every game.

In Game 5, Coach Gallant had inserted three new skaters into the lineup. In this game, he added only one new player, but once again it seemed to be the perfect addition to the 20-man lineup. With William Carrier suffering an undisclosed injury in the previous game, Gallant once again faced a "next-man-up" situation. He was looking at three choices at least.

The obvious one was to put Tomas Nosek back on the fourth line and hope sitting him down for the lackluster forecheck in Game 4 would prove to be a wakeup call. Gallant's second choice was to play Tomas Tatar, but that would probably have meant juggling the line combinations that seemed to gel in Game 5. Coach's last choice — and one that seemed to be the least favorite for the fans — was Ryan Reaves.

As I've mentioned, Reaves was never fully accepted by the VGK fan base. So sorry, because Reaves filled what might have been the team's only hole: a player who could not only add a solid forecheck, but also be a threatening presence on the ice to give opposing teams pause before manhandling the best skaters. He'd performed that task for the St. Louis Blues and when Pittsburgh needed some protection for their star player Sidney Crosby, the Penguins went out and traded for him. When Pittsburgh, in turn, wanted to obtain Derick Brassard for enhanced offense for their playoff run, they needed some cap relief to add him to the lineup. VGK had plenty of cap space available and the deal was worked out: Vegas assumed a portion of Brassard's salary and obtained Reaves in return. To me, it was a smart move by GM George McPhee, who contributed to some grit the team lacked without screwing with its celebrated chemistry.

In Game 6, Reaves was inserted into the lineup for the exact reason he was obtained. The forechecking line of Carpenter and Bellemare needed a replacement on the right wing for the injured Carrier and in the first five games of this series, the Sharks had been extra physical with some of the VGK players.

In this game, the Carpenter-Bellemare-Reaves line set the tone for the forecheck that shut down San Jose for the final 40 minutes. Fleury and his three friends took care of the first 20 minutes, when San Jose controlled the game. Those four stonewalled San Jose, which had 31 attempted shots on Fleury, while Vegas attempted only 19 shots at Martin Jones. Shots on goal were 11 for San Jose in the first period, while Vegas tallied 12.

In the second period, the Vegas forecheck took over the game, allowing only seven shots on Fleury. With everything to lose for San Jose, you'd have expected that Fleury would be severely tested by pucks to the net. But the Sharks could get off only 10 shots. They were smothered by the entire team playing all 200 feet of the ice, and especially the line of Carpenter-Bellemare-Reaves.

I hadn't seen Reaves play too many of his 498 NHL games or 36 playoff games, but the talking heads on NBC Sports Network and the NHL Network insisted that what they were witnessing was the best Ryan Reaves had ever been.

Between McPhee and Gallant, their decisions from June 2017 to May 2018 had been almost flawless—especially Gallant's, who had to fill out the lineup card for 92 games, thus far. He just seemed to know whom to plug in and where.

Granted, in this game, for maybe the first time in 10 playoff games, the breaks all seemed to go Vegas' way and not only with the uncredited assists from Goal Posts and Crossbar, but also on the second Vegas goal, when Nate Schmidt on the point appeared to ring his shot off the crossbar and back out of the zone. It seemed that the crossbar that had been so helpful to Fleury was returning the favor for the Sharks and the game continued until the horn was blown right in the middle of play. That made me thrust my fist into the air. One of the few reasons play is stopped is when a goal is scored and no one had realized it.

The last 40 minutes of the game were dominated by the Knights; they threw a blanket over San Jose. A wet one.

Vegas' first goal came from their number-one line. William Karlsson stripped the puck from highly reliable San Jose defenseman Marc-Edouard Vlasic, who was attempting to leave his defensive zone. Karlsson chipped the puck to Reilly Smith, who found Jonathan Marchessault in the slot. Marchessault quickly slipped the puck through Martin Jones' pads. It was Marchessault's fourth goal of the 2018 playoffs. At the time, this line had combined for 25 points in 10 games.

The Knights added their third goal when Martin Jones was pulled for the extra skater. Ryan Carpenter, who happened to be playing against the team that released him on December 13, 2017, had a wide-open net to shoot at and could have waited until Brent Burns slid by him to score. Instead, and in an unselfish move, he passed it to Cody Eakin, who closed the scoring and ended the San Jose Sharks' season.

This wasn't only a complete team effort. It might also have been the VGK's best game in the playoffs.

Eliminating San Jose ended an eight-year streak of California-based teams making it to the Conference Finals.

Fleury's four shutouts this postseason were in the first and last games of both rounds.

After winning Round 2 in six games, it was time to hope for the two series in the round that still remained to go to their respective seventh games. The hockey playoffs are a war of attrition and the more the opposing teams play, the more they're worn down. Rest at this time would be *golden*.

Round 2 final record: Vegas 4, San Jose 2

Round 3, Game 1, Jets in Winnipeg

The night that was expected to be the barometer on how the Western Conference Championship would play out went as badly as it could have for the Golden Knights, on the road against the Winnipeg Jets. Whoa!

This was especially true of the first seven minutes of the first period, in which Vegas surrendered the same number of goals they allowed in the entire L.A. Kings series: three. That's right: At the 7:35 mark, the score was already 3-0, Jets.

Yet *again*, a goalie-interference decision needed to be resolved and for the fourth time in the playoffs, the call went against the Golden Knights. The Knights were also on the wrong side of the final result, losing Game 1 of the series by a score of 4-2.

On the very first shift, Jonathan Marchessault entered the Winnipeg zone with the puck and had three options: dish off to James Neal, who was open on his right and heading fast toward the net; shoot; or to try to force a pass past two Jet defenders to Erik Haula on his left. He chose the third, probably the least favorable of the three, which turned into the first of 11 VGK giveaways. To make matters worse, this particular giveaway led to a quick transition from defense to offense for Winnipeg. Rather than back-check on his giveaway, Marchessault went to the bench for a line change, allowing the Jets more open ice. Dustin Byfuglien, who was a force throughout the game, took a drop pass and when his slap shot evaded Fleury just 65 seconds into the game, the Jets were off and running.

Of Vegas' 11 giveaways, nine were from their defensemen, which magnified the forecheck with which Winnipeg was so successful in limiting the VGK speed and offense.

The first goal got the already pumped-up crowd into the game and the home team fed off the emotion. Just 5:44 later, Patrik Laine scored the first of the two power-play goals that put Vegas in the unfamiliar position of chasing the game. The first Vegas penalty, called on Alex Tuch for hooking, was questionable; it appeared his stick was being held as he attempted to enter Winnipeg's zone. Nonetheless, it became a costly penalty when Laine scored. This put Vegas behind 2-0, though that wasn't insurmountable; the game had almost 54 minutes still to be played.

On Winnipeg's third goal, Joel Armia skated through the blue paint and bumped into Fleury just as he was prepared to accept a blind behind-the-back pass from Ben Chiarot, a defenseman deep in the offensive zone. Chiarot's blind pass hit Armia's skate and slithered into the net. It was instantaneously waved off as no goal by the referee, who was only 10 feet away. Without a doubt, Fleury's position was impeded by Armia. So it appeared the score would still be a manageable 2-0—and not the dreaded three-goal lead. But Winnipeg coach Paul Maurice challenged the interference ruling.

Like every other goalie-interference call so far in these playoffs, the call went against Vegas and the 3-0 lead was now a problem.

Vegas regrouped during the challenge delay. Coach Gallant settled down his team, which had been caught flat-footed by the Jets and the emotion of the crowd.

Still, the VGK seemed unprepared for Winnipeg's explosive speed and scoring capabilities. The Knights were the slower team, especially for most of the first period. That was rarely the case throughout the season and the first 10 playoff games, during which they won more than their fair share of battles for loose pucks and neutralized the opposing team's forecheck with quick breakouts and stretch passes. In this game, Vegas seemed to have trouble getting through the neutral zone. The Jets had a chokehold on the offensive side, limiting the Knights to just 21 shots for the entire game, the lowest shot total of all the playoff games thus far. In the L.A. Kings series, consisting of four hard-fought defensive games, the Knights had 28 shots on Jonathan Quick in their win in Game 1, 26 shots in Game 3, and 21 shots in their 1-0 Game 4 series-clinching win.

You can survive with a low shot total against a team

like the Kings, which play 1-0 and 2-1 games. With the Jets, that style didn't work. Other than Reilly Smith's five shots on goal, William Karlsson had two and only five other forwards had just one shot each on goal. Connor Hellebuyck is a fine goalie, but you make him seem unbeatable when you can't register more than eight shots in a third period that you entered trailing by two goals. Vegas had only six shots on goal in the first and seven in the second.

It also seemed like Winnipeg's forwards revealed the lack of speed among the VGK defensemen, with only eight hits registered by the six combined for the entire game. Winnipeg's forwards could not be given that much time and space in the offensive zone. Fleury is great, but he needed a little help.

Vegas did seem to adjust its game in the second and third periods, but spotting a team three goals is usually too big of a hole out of which to climb, especially in a Conference championship game on the road.

In their first two rounds, no single opposing player dominated any of the games, allowing Vegas to win eight of 10. In the first round, L.A. Kings star Drew Doughty was held without a point in the three games he played. In Round 2, San Jose's star Brent Burns wasn't a factor in any of the games. That, however, changed in this game, in which Dustin Byfuglien had three shots on goal and scored one, assisted on another, blocked two shots, and played 27 shifts with just shy of 25 minutes of ice time. Byfuglien had 17 points up to that point in the playoffs. By comparison, the entire defensive core of the VGK had 15 points *combined*. This absolutely had to change if they were to defeat the Jets.

Winnipeg led the league in first-period goals during the season with 92 and led all playoff teams with 14 first-period playoff goals.

Brayden McNabb, with his second goal of the playoffs, and William Karlsson his fifth of power-play goal in the post-season scored for the Knights in the failed effort.

Record: Winnipeg 1, Vegas 0

Round 3, Game 2, Jets in Winnipeg

Holy Schmidt!

Nate Schmidt played no part in the scoring that beat the Winnipeg Jets by a score of 3-1 to even the Conference Championship series at 1-1. And what he accomplished might have gone unnoticed by the casual hockey fan who didn't watch the game and simply checked the Internet or local paper for the box score and final results.

Those showed that Schmidt had two shots on goal, two blocked shots, and a takeaway, while logging 23:17 of ice time. It all looked like a normal night for a defenseman, but ...

Look again.

Schmidt's hockey stick appeared to be eight feet long in this game, always in the passing lanes, always preventing uncontested shots on Fleury. He even had a 200-foot rush that resulted in a quality scoring chance on Connor Hellebuyck. This kind of Bobby Orr end-to-end rush is rarely seen by a defenseman these days — unless his name is

Erik Karlsson of the Ottawa Senators.

Nate wasn't in the lineup for his offensive skills, although he did have a huge goal in Game 6 versus San Jose. Instead, he played to mute those skills in others and in this game, he was instrumental in keeping the explosive offense of the Winnipeg Jets from taking control, not only of this game, but the series itself; a Winnipeg win would have forced the Golden Knights to win four of the remaining five games. Now, with the series tied at 1-1, three of the next four games would be played in Las Vegas at T-Mobile Arena. Winnipeg has its "Whiteout," which, by the way, was noticeably quiet for most of the game. But Vegas has "Knight Time," which, if you haven't noticed or heard, shakes the entire arena. The team fed directly off the energy that Knights fans brought to every home game.

Once again, Coach Gallant proved that he can work magic with his team, no matter how he juggles the lineup. After Game 1, though he used a clear and calm voice to announce that he needed all 20 guys working, which he didn't have in the loss, the players heard him loud and clear. Also, he inserted Tomas Tatar and Tomas Nosek into the lineup; they replaced Oscar Lindberg, a healthy scratch, and David Perron, who according to Gallant wasn't feeling well.

The Tomases stepped up to have a major impact, especially Tatar, whose seeming preference for playing offense rather than forechecking had earned him a seat in the press box instead of one on the bench. Tatar not only scored Vegas' first goal, he put on a clinic in forechecking. On the goal, he knocked down Patrik Laine's attempted breakout pass to keep the puck deep in the Winnipeg zone, then out-muscled Paul Stastny for possession of the puck deep in the corner. Ryan Carpenter passed the puck to Shea Theodore, who got it back to Tatar. Tomas' original shot hit the side of the net and went behind it. Tatar chased after it, took it off the back wall, and brought it around to the front of the net. Hellebuyck made the initial save on Tatar, but when he failed to cover the puck, Tatar reached around and pushed it in for the 1-0 lead. What a play!

That was Tatar's first playoff goal since 2015. It was also just his fifth playoff game for Vegas out of the 12 up to that point. When he skated for Detroit, he didn't have to earn his ice time. With this team, *everyone* had to earn his ice time, even those acquired for three high draft picks. Not only didn't Gallant play favorites, he never felt obligated to play someone just because GM George McPhee paid a king's ransom to get him.

It was Coach Gallant's way — a 20-man effort. You work hard, he always said, you earn your ice time.

Tomas Nosek, the other addition to the Game 2 lineup, had three shots on goal and two blocked shots and was an integral part of the resurrected forecheck. Along with having a very valuable 11:10 minutes of ice time, he also played 2:24 minutes on the penalty kill, which nullified two of Winnipeg's three power plays.

All four lines were engaged, allowing Gallant the luxury of wave after wave of his 18 skaters to harass the Jets' offense. The one goal they did score was a complete fluke that I'm 100% sure Fleury would stop the next 100 times that shot came at him. It first hit the top of his right pad, then bounced up to the VGK logo on his chest, and somehow slid between his arm and the post.

Jonathan Marchessault also had an amazing night, especially considering that his giveaway in Game 1 led to Winnipeg's first goal, from which Vegas never recovered. He seemed to take full personal responsibility for that loss and he looked nothing if not determined to make a statement in the following game. And did he ever, aided by Reilly Smith who had three takeaways, two of which contributed directly to Marchessault's goals. Jonathan became the 10th player in NHL history to collect at least 15 points in his club's first trip to the playoffs. The entire line of Marchessault, Smith, and Karlsson had logged 41 points thus far in the playoffs.

Even though the next two games were at T-Mobile and it was tempting to look ahead, home ice hadn't been a huge advantage to the home teams. With the VGK's road victory in Game 2 of the Conference Championship, the visiting teams owned a 38-33 playoff record. Indeed, Winnipeg had now lost three of their last four home games, after having won the previous 13 and having the best home record in the NHL.

The VGK hadn't lost two games in a row during these playoffs and were now 3-0 following a loss.

It was Fleury's 71st career playoff win.

With the series tied up 1-1, the rest of the NHL and the hockey pundits continued to wait for the VGK bubble to burst, but we fans continued to see a good team that refused to get rattled. With just three more wins, everyone would be wondering how in the world this could have happened.

Record: Vegas 1, Winnipeg 1

Round 3, Game 3, Winnipeg Jets at T-Mobile Arena

On the back of Marc-André Fleury's amazing performance at T-Mobile on May 16, the Vegas Golden Knights took a 2-1 series lead with a 4-2 win over the Winnipeg Jets. Prior to this third game in the Western Conference Championship, the Jets were 4-0 following a loss.

Yes, Mark Scheifele, the leading playoff goal scorer with 14 goals in 15 games, scored two goals. But Fleury's incredible back-to-back saves off Scheifele's stick halfway through the third period with the score 3-2 denied him his 15th goal and a hat trick that would have erased the 3-1 lead the Knights enjoyed entering the third.

"Are Fleury's saves the most incredible you've seen as the Vegas Golden Knights' coach?" Coach Gallant was asked in the post-game presser.

"He's made unbelievable saves and they were obviously important at a key time for us," he said. "That's Fleury. He's been great throughout the playoffs and all year for us. He's also a guy who has fun out there. I'm sweating on the bench, yelling my head off, and I look down there and he's just having fun."

A mere 30 seconds into the game, Brayden NcNabb intercepted a weak pass from Scheifele just inside the blue line and stretched a pass out to Jonathan Marchessault. Marchessault beat the Jet defenseman, broke in on Connor Hellebuyck, and as with his two goals in Game 2, went to his backhand. When Hellebuyck tried and failed to poke-check the puck away, Jonathan had an open net. He just slid the puck and was in like Flynn.

Vegas completely dominated the first period, allowing the Jets only three shots on Fleury in the first 20 minutes.

Mark Scheifele scored his first goal to tie the game 1-1 at the 5:28 mark of the second period when he made an amazing tip that went between his legs and somehow got behind Fleury. Scheifele's score could have changed the momentum of the game that Vegas had on its side.

But the VGK response was swift. Just 12 seconds after Winnipeg tied it up, James Neal buried one.

Neal had to leave the game in the first period when he took Dustin Byfuglien's elbow to his face. Post-game, Neal had a noticeable bruise under his left eye. As per concussion protocol, he had to be examined and his return approved by the medical staff. But he came back strong. Erik Haula intercepted a pass by goaltender Connor Hellebuyck, who went behind the net in an attempt to help move the puck to his defenseman. With his back to Neal, Haula passed it out front and Neal had a completely open net.

James "Big Game" Neal has that name for a reason: He thrives in high-pressure situations. In the VGK's 13 playoff games, he had four goals and five assists. Career-wise, he had 29 goals and 24 assists in 93 playoff games.

Just two minutes 33 seconds after Neal's goal that broke the tie, Nate Schmidt stripped the puck from a Jet player inside the blue line. Schmidt chipped it up to Neal in the neutral zone. Even though "Big Game" wasn't one of Vegas' fastest skaters, he blew by Jets defenseman Toby Enstrom down the right wing and came in alone on Hellebuyck, who made the save on Neal's shot. But he picked up his own rebound, went behind the net with the puck, and found Alex Tuch trailing the play and alone. Both Enstrom and Byfuglien were facing Neal, which allowed Tuch an uncontested shot.

With the score now 3-1 entering the third period, Mark Scheifele scored his second goal just 18 seconds in and all of a sudden, it was white-knuckle time once again at T-Mobile.

The Jets dominated the first 14 minutes and saw a complete flip-flop of the first period, as Vegas went more than 10 minutes without a shot on net. Wave after wave of Winnipeg players roared into the Vegas defensive zone, only to be denied by Fleury time after time. Then, with 9:30 left in the game, Fleury made those back-to-back saves.

Winnipeg wasn't going down without a fight and the physicality, which was intense throughout the game, heated up in the third period, then exploded when the game ended with a 10-player scrum at center ice after Jonathan Marchessault scored his second of the game and his fourth in the last two games into an empty net. And with that goal, Marchessault became the first player in the NHL's entire history to score in the first minute and the last minute of the same playoff game.

Both coaches had the big boys out for the last 2.7 seconds and they didn't disappoint. Ryan Reaves went after Adam Lowry, joining Deryk Engelland who got a few in on Lowry as soon as the puck was dropped. Lowry had been a little too rough with a few of the Vegas players throughout the game and with just 2.7 seconds left, it seemed like the appropriate time to respond.

In Game 2, Winnipeg had 19 hits and Vegas had seven. In this game, the Jets got in 48 and the Knights responded with 41 of their own. Winnipeg was exhibiting a lot of frustration over not being able to handle Vegas' speed and forecheck.

For the eighth time in 13 playoff games, Fleury gave up two or fewer goals. A few of his 15 saves in the third period could easily be categorized as spectacular.

The VGK were now 5-1 at home in the playoffs, having lost only to the San Jose Sharks in Game 2 of Round 2. In the six playoff home games, Vegas scored nine first-period goals, while surrendering none. Zero. Zilch. Zippo. Scoring first in the playoffs has a huge effect on the final outcome. This year, the team scoring first had thus far won 57 games and lost 19, for a 75% win ratio.

The VGK led for 59 minutes and 13 seconds of this 60-minute game.

In their first 12 playoff games, Vegas had a goals against average of 1.83, which led all teams; Vegas' four shutouts led all teams; and Vegas' average of 41 hits per game led all teams.

Record: Vegas 2, Winnipeg 1

Round 3, Game 4, Winnipeg Jets at T-Mobile Arena

At first, many called the early success of the Vegas Golden Knights a fluke. Others said it was a bubble that would eventually burst. Some suggested that the VGK all had a chip on their shoulders, which would be knocked off sooner than later. More than a few purists thought that everything about the VGK was a conspiracy, hatched by the NHL to generate renewed excitement for the sport.

Well, following the fourth game of the Conference Championship series, I had a question for all the doubters. It went like this: After 96 games total, 82 in the regular season and 14 in the post-season, including the 3-2 win over the Winnipeg Jets and now just one win away from playing for the Stanley Cup ... are you still waiting?

These were the know-it-alls who started out by insisting that the Golden Knights would be the worst team in the league, "potentially historically so," in the words of Deadspin. After the expansion-draft selections were announced, the random bunch of no-names, other than Fleury and Neal, didn't inspire much more confidence. But now that the team had come so far, these same experts were suggesting that the whole thing was rigged from the start. Some fans of other teams even had the audacity to say that Vegas' success this year was an embarrassment to the NHL, as if the Knights' astonishing success cast a dubious shadow over the rest of the league. I'm usually patient with bullshit, but I have to admit, that one got me a little exercised. What Vegas accomplished in its first season put the entire NHL in a shining spotlight in front of the nation and the world. It was one of the greatest sports stories ever! Not just in Vegas. And not just in the NHL. In any city in any sport. After all, this is supposed to be the toughest championship of them all to win, so a team that started playing together a mere eight months ago couldn't possibly even come close.

In the first round, the L.A. Kings were supposed to be the bigger and better team. We know how that worked out: a 4-0 sweep, with Fleury pitching two shutouts in just four games.

In the second round, the big bad bloodthirsty San Jose Sharks, who made it all the way to the Stanley Cup final in 2016, were expected to deliver the knockout punch. What happened? The Sharks were outplayed in all but Game 4 in San Jose and the one other game they won was a *gift*. Fleury and his Team Resiliency shut them out twice as well.

All the while, Coach Gallant kept pulling magical lineup changes out of his metaphorical top hat. One game it was Ryan Reaves, the next it was Tomas Nosek, then Tomas Tatar, then Luca Sbisa. Nate Schmidt, who had trouble making the starting lineup for the Washington Capitals, was giving us 200-foot rushes up the ice. Jonathan Marchessault, a minus 21 last year with Florida, was a plus 36 this year—a whopping 57-point differential.

Granted, Winnipeg got off to a blistering start in Game 1 of the Championship series. After that, though, the VGK led 86.2% of the time and the score was tied 13.8% of the time. That adds up to 100%—Winnipeg never led, not even for a second, after Game 1.

In this game against the Jets, Game 5 of the series, the VGK had a big problem that Fleury turned into a small problem. Once again, the Knights had a less than stellar third period. When Tyler Myers tied the score at 2-2, 5:34 into the third, 18,000-plus pair of palms got sweaty again at T-Mobile.

The Knights didn't respond quickly to Myers' goal and

it seemed like the entire period was spent in the VGK zone. But with just under seven minutes left and Winnipeg firing shot after shot on Fleury, the puck was passed out to Dustin Byfuglien. "The Buff" has a big booming shot and Reilly Smith was heading toward Dustin, prepared to get in front of it. Just as Dustin wound up to blast the puck, it bounced over his stick. Smith, moving in that direction, had speed, while Byfuglien was flat-footed. Reilly swept up the puck, skated into the offensive zone, and before the trailing defenseman could catch him, he blasted his own perfect shot over Hellebuyck's right shoulder for the 3-2 lead and the final score.

Winnipeg tried to get Hellebuyck off the ice with two minutes to go, but the Knights kept the puck deep in Winnipeg's zone; the Jets' goaltender didn't manage to exit the game until 1:02 was left on the clock. Even when the Jets did get the extra skater on, they had no chance to score.

Going into Game 5, the VGK's series lead of three games to one had a long tradition of being insurmountable for the opposing team. The only time a team came back from a 3-1 deficit in a Conference final was when the New Jersey Devils beat the Philadelphia Flyers in 2000, 18 playoff series ago.

Record: Vegas 3, Winnipeg 1

Round 3, Game 5, Jets in Winnipeg

Nothing is impossible, but countless things aren't probable. What happened in Game 5 wasn't impossible, but it was about as close as you can get.

In fact, the Vegas Golden Knights removed the "im" from impossible when they eliminated the Winnipeg Jets in Game 5 of the Western Conference Championship series by a score of 2-1. Just 227 days after playing their first-ever regular season game (Oct. 6, 2017) as the Vegas Golden Knights, this team would now be vying for the honor of lifting the Stanley Cup. Teams have gone decades without playing for the Cup. Vegas would be playing for it in its inaugural season.

The Vegas Golden Knights started out as a small group of random players from all over the league looking for a home, assembled by George McPhee on an idea in the dark recesses of the minds of the Maloof family and Bill Foley. At that time, Las Vegas was, and had always been, a city of strangers. Before the Knights' season began, few residents knew their neighbors' names. That all changed: The team that came here with no family created one, a big one. The VGK players, who were in Las Vegas only a short time before the tragic event of October 1, turned themselves into the glue that this city needed to hold itself together.

Throughout the season, they galvanized the entire city and a lot of the state with their winning ways and appreciation of their fan base. In the moments immediately after earning a trip to the Stanley Cup Finals, player after player mentioned how much the Las Vegans had energized and pushed them along. They loved their new family and Las Vegas loved its new family members.

The only people who weren't thrilled about this magical run were the sports book managers who made the VGK

500-1 to win the Stanley Cup before they played their first game. The word on the Strip was that if the VGK won the Cup, the sports books stood to lose millions. This story started with heartbreak and tears, but was now creating lifelong friends — and maybe a few million worth of winning sports-bet bucks for good measure.

Unlike Game 1 in Winnipeg where Vegas appeared a step slower and out of sync, for Game 5 back in Winnipeg, they were ready. They pretty much silenced the crowd by dominating the first 10 minutes of the game. In the first eight minutes, the Jets had only one shot on Fleury. It wasn't until Colin Miller took a minor penalty for interference that Winnipeg became engaged and took back the momentum, logging 13 shots in the final 12 minutes.

But before that, Alex Tuch forced Connor Hellebuyck into hurrying a pass; it bounced off his own player's skate and over to Ryan Carpenter, who found Tuch alone in the slot in front of the net. Though Tuch's back was turned, he did a quick 180, slammed the puck home, and Vegas, just like it had in Games 2, 3, and 4, scored first. In this 5-game series, the team scoring first won every game. Overall in the first three rounds, the VGK were 10-1 when scoring the first goal of the game.

Winnipeg tied the game late in the first period on a goal by Josh Morrissey off a set play when Bryan Little won the faceoff to Fleury's right. He passed the puck to Morrissey, who was just inside the blue line. Marchessault skated toward Morrissey and for some unknown reason, Jonathan lifted his left skate off the ice, which allowed the shot to get to Fleury with no attempt by Marchessault to block it. This was, in the end, the VGK's only mistake in the game.

It also turned out to be the only shot that Fleury missed; he had 31 saves on 32 shots. The win was his 74th in playoffs, moving him into eighth place overall, tied with Chris Osgood.

The second period ended with the VGK leading 2-1. Entering the third period with a lead, Vegas was 9-0; Winnipeg was 0-7 when they trailed entering the third period during the 2018 playoffs. Those zeroes held true; with no scoring in the third, the VGK won the game, the series, and maybe even the doubters. We'd see.

Vegas lost Game 1, even giving up three goals in the first 7:38 of the first period. After that game, however, Winnipeg *never* led. Fleury surrendered four goals in Game 1. In the next four games, Fleury surrendered only six goals and had a 1.50 GAA and a .956 save percentage. In the three clinching games in these playoffs, Fleury surrendered only one goal on 90 shots and racked up two shutouts.

In another piece that fit right into this magical ride, Winnipeg native Ryan Reaves, who had never scored a goal for Vegas, tipped a Luca Sbisa slap shot from the left point. His first goal as a VGK was only his second in the 42 playoff games in his career — and the winning goal of the game that clinched the Western Conference Championship.

The win was Vegas' 12th against three losses in the 2018 post-season.

On October 10 at the first home game at T-Mobile, longtime Las Vegan Deryk Engelland picked up the mic to tell the crowd about the team's commitment to the city in helping it heal from the October 1 shooting. At the end of this game, he picked up the Clarence S. Campbell Bowl that's awarded to the Western Conference Champion. It was perfectly fitting that Deryk was selected by the other players to accept it.

Finally, the VGK became the seventh team in NHL history to win the first three rounds of a season's playoffs on the road. Five of the previous six teams went on to win the Stanley Cup.

Round 3 final record: Vegas 4, Winnipeg 1

Chapter 7
The Bookmakers

Vegas Golden Knights mania — the merchandise feeding frenzy, the ticket tango, the themed gimmicks, the instant traditions — also stormed the sports books. The bookies had never seen the likes of this kind of betting handle on the National Hockey League.

Football betting, professional and collegiate, accounts for the majority of money wagered in the legal sports books of Nevada, even though most of the games are played on just two days a week, Saturday and Sunday. Basketball is a distant second, even though you can wager on games seven days a week between October and June. Horserace betting, available 365 days a year, is ranked third in money wagered. Fourth-place baseball has a bit of an advantage for nearly three months a year; once the NBA and NHL playoffs are completed, it's the only major sport on which to wager. Soccer is fifth, followed by boxing and mixed martial arts. Finally, the red-headed stepchild, hockey, arrives, in seventh place on the sports betting hit parade. In fact, hockey isn't even its own category in the Nevada Gaming Control Board's monthly revenue reports; it's lumped together with golf and tennis under "Other."

All that changed when the Vegas Golden Knights became an NHL franchise. All of a sudden, a lot of money started pouring in on hockey. A lot of that was bet on the home team. And a lot of *that* was paid out by the sports books, which were bombarded by VGK money.

ESPN's Doug Kezirian interviewed Jason Simbal of CG Technology, which operates eight sports books in Las Vegas. Simbal said that he finally became aware of how the VGK had changed the landscape of hockey betting on December 31, 2017. With 300,000 out-of-towners crowding Vegas for New Year's Eve, more sports bettors placed wagers on the Golden Knights than on the NFL's Week 17.

"The Vegas Golden Knights were drawing an average of 15 times more bets than their opponents," Kezirian reported. "Simbal said the Knights alone accounted for 30% of CG Technology's hockey handle, about three times more than any team in any sport. By comparison, the New England Patriots, the most bet-on team in the NFL, garnered just 8% of the total NFL handle."

The "Other" category's handle was $214 million during the six-month period that roughly matched the NHL's regular season (October 2017 through March 2018). That was a 36% increase from the $157 million for the previous hockey season. The $57 million in additional handle wasn't, to be sure, from any big flurry of betting on golf or tennis. The regulators might need to hand hockey its own category.

Jimmy Vaccaro, who helped the Las Vegas sports betting business make the transition from independent standalone sports books to casino-affiliated operations in the 1970s and is now one of the elder statesmen of the industry, told Kezirian, "When I started in the seventies, we didn't book hockey. Hockey wasn't on our minds. Nobody even asked for it." Hockey lines weren't posted until the mid-1980s. "There's absolutely no doubt in my mind," Vaccaro added, "that about forty percent of the people betting hockey now never bet it before the Golden Knights came."

Jay Konegay, director of Westgate Las Vegas' huge Superbook, echoed the sentiment in a mid-May interview, "Whenever the Knights are playing, we have to put them on the main screen with audio. This is the first time we've featured hockey games over the NBA playoffs."

It didn't hurt that fans of visiting teams taking in games at T-Mobile Arena had to pass by at least one of Las Vegas' 60-odd sports books, including the one at New York-New York, which they had to walk right past on the way into the game.

Almost 100% of the large contingents of visiting-team supporters cannot legally bet on their teams in their home cities and states. That might (or might not) change, now that the United States Supreme Court, in a recent ruling, flung open the door to legalized sports betting around the country. But in the VGK's inaugural season, with all the excitement surrounding the expansion team, and hockey fans from all over North America placing bets a few steps from the entrance to T-Mobile, the mania came home to roost on the balance sheets of the Las Vegas sports books.

The Day the Bookies Wept was a 1939 comedy (of sorts) in which Betty Grable's character, Ina, figures out that Hiccup, the "race horse" her New York City cab driver boyfriend was scammed into buying in Kentucky, can actually win horse races — as long as his belly is full of beer. She bets $2,000 at long odds, Hiccup wins, and bookies weep.

The movie title was an apt description of what would have happened if the Vegas Golden Knights won the Stanley Cup. The exposure of the sports books to futures bettors who, for a souvenir, sentimentality, or just a lark, bet the VGK to win it all before the season at astronomical odds was, concurrently, a major liability for the bookies.

The highest odds went off at 500-1, meaning you could bet $100 to *win* $50,000 if the Knights hoisted the Cup. Those odds were posted as soon as the NHL announced that Las Vegas would, indeed, get the new team. They came down quite a bit after the expansion draft, to between 200-1 and 175-1, and they continued dropping all season long. In late February, when the Knights were well ahead of the San Jose Sharks at the top of the Pacific Division, they were the lowest *in the league*: 9-2, making the VGK a slight betting favorite over the league-leading Tampa Bay Lightning at 5-1 to win the Cup. In fact, so much money was coming in on Vegas that it was the largest liability the books had ever held on NHL futures.

Conversely, before the season, the Westgate sports book also posted odds on the opposite outcome — that the Golden

Knights would *not* win the Stanley Cup. Here, you had to bet in excess of $50,000 to win $100, a huge outlay for a minuscule return, even on an event as seemingly preposterous and inconceivable, at the time, as the Las Vegas Misfits beating the best and most established teams in the NHL to win the Cup. Which is why, according to Jeff Sherman, manager of the Westgate Superbook, they didn't book a single No bet on the Knights.

As money poured in on futures backing the VGK to win the Stanley Cup, the bookmakers naturally tried to reduce their exposure with No bets. After the -50,000 at the Westgate was taken down, they started out at -550. Now you could bet $550 to win $100, which was too attractive for the "wiseguys" (also known as "smart money") to pass up. So much action came in on the No that the lay price quickly rose to -750. That was a far cry from -50,000, on which no one took a chance, but I suspect the books kept getting action, otherwise there wouldn't have been so much attention on how the bookmakers were sweating it throughout the season.

Nowhere was this truer than at William Hill, biggest sports book operator in Nevada with more than 100 locations. Will Hill booked more than 300 bets on the Knights to win the Stanley Cup at odds of 100-1, or higher.

On the other hand, the sports books had had a lot of experience with longshots. Mackenzie Kraemer, an ESPN staff writer, pulled together some stats. In the most recent years for all four major league American sports, 12 teams began the seasons bucking 500-1, or longer, odds to win their championships. "Only two," Kraemer found, "even made the playoffs (Vegas and the Indiana Pacers) and only Vegas won a playoff series.

"The New York Jets were 1,000-to-1 odds to win a title at the start of the 2017 season. No other team was longer than 200-to-1. The Jets went 5-11 and finished last in the AFC East.

"The Chicago White Sox and San Diego Padres were both 500-to-1 to win the World Series at the start of the 2017 season. They finished a combined 48 games below .500."

Kraemer also cited teams that did beat similar odds. "The 1999 St. Louis Rams dropped to 300-1 to win the Super Bowl following an injury to quarterback Trent Green. However, backup Kurt Warner led the Rams to a Super Bowl victory. And the Minnesota Twins are responsible for two of the most surprising World Series wins ever. In 1987, the Twins won it all as 500-to-1 longshots. Four years later, they did it again, this time as 300-to-1 underdogs."

So, in 31 years, it had only happened three times, out of how many thousands of games in all the sports.

Still, there were some pretty big bets out there. The Westgate Superbook's largest bet was $400 at 300-1, paying $120,000 on a winner. GC Technology booked a $500 bet at 200-1 for $100,000. South Point's $400 at 150-1 would be good for $60k. And the Golden Nugget's $250 at 200-1 and William Hill's $1,000 at 50-1 would cost them $50,000. All on bets of $100.

On the other hand, the sports-betting world had seen a lot worse. United Kingdom books took an estimated $38 million shellacking when the Leicester City Foxes won the championship of the Premier League, the top level of

English football (soccer), in May 2016. The Foxes started the season as *5,000-to-1 underdogs*, so a $100 futures bet to win the championship paid out a half-million dollars. "That put Leicester City more in line with the odds one might see in the novelty category often offered by British bookies — bets on things that are so outlandish and unlikely as to be unimaginable," wrote Sam Borden of *The New York Times*. "But even there, Leicester City was a long shot. The odds that Simon Cowell, the acid-tongued producer of 'American Idol,' would become the next British prime minister were only 500-to-1, for example, while those that Hugh Hefner, who founded *Playboy* magazine, would reveal that he was a virgin were set at 1,000-to-1." The Foxes, according to the UK bookies, were five times *less* likely to win than Hefner being a virgin.

Actually, the Westgate Superbook opened with the Golden Knights at 300-1 and got so little action that it moved the line to 500-1. Even then, the Westgate booked only 13 bets.

Todd Dewey, who writes about sports betting for the *Las Vegas Review-Journal,* tracked down a few of the 13. A boyfriend placed two bets, $50 to win $25,000 for himself and $20 to win $10,000 for his girlfriend. They broke up during the season, but the boyfriend still handed over the $20 ticket to his now ex-girlfriend. The girlfriend hung onto hers till the bitter end, but the boyfriend sold his for $550 in November on PropSwap, a Las Vegas-based startup that provides a platform for a secondary market for active sports bets in Las Vegas. He cleared $500, with which he paid a month's rent. "The logic in making the bet wasn't that the Golden Knights would win the Stanley Cup. It was just that they would get better and I could sell the ticket," he explained.

Another couple stayed together. They parlayed some football winnings in October and picked up two tickets, one for $300, the other for $100, on the Knights at 100-1 to win $40,000 total. They said they "had a feeling—Marc-André Fleury and James Neal were in the 2017 Cup playoffs and now we had them both." They, too, sold the $300 ticket on PropSwap for $12,600, but let the $100 ticket ride for the $10k.

The sports books' liability of an estimated $5 million to $10 million on futures bets alone was only part of the story. The bookies were also taking a pretty cold bath on the game-by-game betting. According to Covers.com, a one-stop shop for current sports-betting information, the VGK beat the puck line, otherwise known as the hockey pointspread, in 23 out of the 41 home games (56%) during the regular season. They also went 29-10-2 against the moneyline (a whopping 74%). In the wagering proclivities of "the public" (in bookie lingo, this means the great unwashed masses of bettors, also known as "squares," who make their wagers based on team loyalty and feelings, or hunches, as opposed to the wise-guys, or "sharps," who do everything in their power to get an edge when betting), there's a strong natural tendency to bet the favorite and over. Hence, the betting lines tend to be skewed, to varying degrees, to exploit that bias. The bookies got beat not only by the local bias, but also by the Knights'

high-flying offense, which typically paid off the over bets. The locals were cleaning up.

Chris Andrews, sports book director at the South Point Hotel-Casino, one of the major bastions of sports betting in Las Vegas, agreed with the assessment that the bookies undervalued the Golden Knights, at least early on, as a way to entice more money on the Vegas underdogs. "The wiseguys were betting against the Knights quite a bit at the season's opening," he said. "I remember one game in Phoenix where they were +165 or so, a huge dog to the worst team in the league. Of course, the public and wiseguys soon woke up to exactly how good they really were, but the bookmakers still had their ratings on the Knights pretty low. We did adjust quickly, so the undervaluing of the Knights didn't last too long, in my opinion."

Then there were the divided loyalties of the bookmakers themselves.

This was where it started to get interesting. The sports book managers and directors are locals too, so you'd expect them to want to root for the home team. On the other hand, with all the liability of the futures bets and the losses their books were sustaining during the season, one had to wonder: Was it a major energy drain for the bookies to be on both sides, the head saying one thing and the heart saying another? Or were they so inured to this conundrum that they could take it in stride? Was the situation with the Golden Knights unusual enough that they had an atypical internal struggle with it?

Various directors were interviewed by reporters and to a man, they all admitted to rooting for the Knights, while hoping they didn't win the Stanley Cup.

Chris Andrews of the South Point and author of a book-maker memoir titled *Then One Day*, said, "I don't know how anyone's deal works but mine. I don't have an actual stake in the win and loss as a part of my pay. At my previous job, my salary was relatively small and the bulk of my income was based on how much money the sports book made. In that case, you can bet your ass I'd have been rooting against the Knights. But in my case as it is, I get to root for the Knights. It's great for the town."

Tony Miller, director of the race and sports book at the Golden Nugget Hotel-Casino, told the *L.A. Times* that his heart was with the Knights, while his head was with the bottom line.

Bob Scucci, director of race and sports books at Boyd Gaming, said, "I can't speak for the company, but on my own, personally, I can't root against this team for what they mean to this community. Whatever happens, we're going to book the games the way they need to be booked, but it's hard not to root for this team."

The position of Art Manteris, vice president of race and sports book operations for Las Vegas locals-casino giant Station Casinos, was summed up in an article in *The New York Times*. "The liability was the largest for any futures bet accepted by a sports book Manteris managed since moving to Las Vegas in 1978. Still he claimed that no one in his business will root against the Knights, considering how the team has infused the city with an energy level he has not seen since Jerry Tarkanian's UNLV Running Rebels dominated college basketball in the 1990s." He seemed to express the prevailing sentiment among his sports book brethren with, "'I loved that and I'll love the Knights too—just maybe starting next year.'"

It's doubtful that anyone was feeling too sorry for the bookies' exposure on the futures bets.

One sports betting expert told *Forbes*, "A seven-figure loss for a big sportsbook sounds a lot worse than it really is. They'd take a similar hit on a bad NFL Sunday. There's a reason Nevada sports books haven't had a losing month since July 2013. Even with a Knights' Stanley Cup win, I'd be willing to wager that Nevada books finish the month in the black again. Sports books generally love stories like this due to the publicity they can get."

It didn't take a genius to estimate the value of the publicity that the futures "liability" was generating. *The New York Times, L.A. Times, Washington Post*, even the *Wall Street Journal* all wrote about it. How much was *that* worth? Besides, the reason I put liability in quotes was because no one, that I saw anyway, was mentioning how much money the books stood to *win* from the losing futures bets on the other 30 teams in the NHL. Not to mention all the square money that flowed into the books from the intensified attention on the NHL due to the Knights historic run; hockey betting during the 2017-2018 season was up 35% across the board. The casinos also booked increased volume on professional and college regular-season and playoff basketball games while the public was coming in to bet the Knights.

In the overall realm of casino gambling, the sports book is just a blip: In 2017, Nevada raked in $11.6 billion in gambling revenues, of which sports betting accounted for $249 million—slightly more than 2.2%. And on the Las Vegas Strip, even with all those punters passing by the book at New York-New York on their way into the games, it was a mere 1.78% of the gambling win.

And how much money did the casinos vacuum from the gamblers who played a little blackjack, craps, or the bandits on their way in and out of the joint? No doubt Station Casinos, for one, did just fine on its giveaway of $5 futures bets with 4-1 odds—even with its seven-figure exposure—for accruing a certain amount of points on players club cards.

And what about all the food and beverage revenue from the watch parties—dinner on the way into the casino and the celebration or commiseration drinking on the way out? And what about hotel revenues from out-of-town fans coming to Las Vegas for a brand new kind of entertainment? Plus collected fees from the locals who put their paid-parking boycott aside to attend the games?

The sports books are in the casinos, and the casinos are like the IRS: They have every nuance of every transaction in their vast universe wired in every possible direction. Even so, there's no denying that the inaugural season for the Las Vegas hockey expansion team was a wild roller-coaster ride—in more ways than one.

Betting Hockey

For years the major sports leagues publically shunned Vegas as a potential franchise city due to its legalized gambling, despite the reality that thousands gamble on their games daily and gambling is a powerful marketing element that increases viewership. Now, with a U.S. Supreme Court decision paving the way to widespread sports wagering in the U.S., betting on games will become part of the routine for a whole new universe of players.

The following explanation of how hockey lines are presented in a sports book is excerpted from the upcoming Huntington Press book, *Bet on Sports*, by Blair Rodman.

Hockey has always been a lower-tier sport among bettors. However, the historic success of the expansion Las Vegas Golden Knights has ignited an interest in the game around the country.

Prior to the 2005-2006 season, ties were common in the NHL. From that point forward, regular-season games tied at the end of regulation have gone to a five-minute, four-skater (including the goalie), sudden-death overtime (OT). If still tied, there's a shootout with each team taking three shots by separate players. If tied after three shots, the shootout goes to sudden death. In a shootout, regardless of the number of shootout goals scored, the winning team is awarded only one goal that's added to the final score for the game's side and total determinations. Games must complete 55 minutes to have action. Here's what a standard hockey betting line looks like:

New York Rangers
     +155   +1.5/-185   Over 5.5/+105
Vegas Golden Knights
     -175   -1.5/+165   Under 5.5/-125

The first column is the "money line" to win the game, including OT and shootout. You can bet $100 on the Rangers to win $155, or $175 on the Golden Knights to win $100.

The next column is the "puck line," which adds a goal handicap. In this case, you can take the Rangers getting one-and-a-half goals betting $185 to win $100, or the Golden Knights giving one-and-a-half betting $100 to win $165.

On the right is the "total," the total goals scored. This line is "shaded" to the under, so you'd bet $125 to win $100 U/5.5 and $100 to win $105 O/5.5.

If this game were to end Golden Knights 3-2, the winning bets would be Golden Knights on the money line, Rangers on the puck line, and the under. ♣

Chapter 8
The Cup

It's not a massive trophy. It stands only three feet tall and weighs 34.5 pounds. Its base is made up of five rings that hold the names of *all* previous Stanley Cup-winning teams *and* their players. Hockey fans refer to it affectionately as Lord Stanley's Cup, after Frederick Arthur Stanley, 16th Earl of Derby.

While he was serving as Governor General of Canada, Frederick Stanley was titled Lord Stanley of Preston. He purchased a decorative silver bowl from a silversmith in London for $48.67 to use as the prize for the top amateur hockey team in Canada. He had "Dominion Hockey Challenge Cup" engraved on the outside rim on one side and "From Stanley of Preston" on the other.

The first team awarded the Stanley Cup was the Montreal Amateur Athletic Association in 1893. For the next 33 years, the Cup made its way through various amateur and professional hockey leagues. Any team could challenge the previous winner of the Cup through a board of trustees appointed by Lord Stanley. Some leagues folded and others merged into the National Hockey League in 1926. Since then, no team outside the NHL has played for the Cup, as none of their challenges was ever accepted by the board of trustees.

To this day, the trophy is still owned by the board of trustees, although in 1947, they granted "control" of the trophy to the NHL.

The Stanley Cup trophy is unique in the world of North American sports. It's the only major-sports championship trophy that isn't re-made each year. The winning team is allowed to keep the Cup for 100 days, enabling the parade and other championship traditions. In 1994, the New York Rangers started a tradition in which each team member possesses the Cup for a day. When the Cup goes back to the trustees, it's engraved with that year's winners.

Although the trophy has taken a few different forms in the last 120-plus years, the actual cup at the top of the base today is the same one that Lord Stanley himself purchased in 1892—on the Original trophy, that is. There are actually three versions of the current Stanley Cup trophy: the Original Dominion Hockey Challenge Cup from 1892, the Presentation Cup authenticated in 1963, and the Permanent Cup (1993) that sits in the Hockey Hall of Fame whenever the Presentation Cup isn't available to be displayed.

The Presentation Cup is the one hoisted by players after winning. This Cup was commissioned in secret. It wasn't revealed that the Original had been replaced until three years afterward. The Original has been on display in the Vault Room at the Hockey Hall of Fame ever since.

As for 2018, welcome to the George McPhee Stanley Cup Finals.

In the 2017-2018 season of one surprise after another, the team that George McPhee built from scratch at the beginning of the season played for the Stanley Cup against the team he built in his 17-year tenure in Washington, D.C. Brandon Schlager, writing for *Sporting News*, summed it up nicely, "McPhee might be the first GM in professional sports to have influenced two competing championship finalists so heavily." And in the words of Thom Loverro of the *Washington Times*, "McPhee has more fingerprints on these teams than there are on all the plates at an all-you-can-eat Vegas buffet."

Amazingly, though McPhee left the Capitals organization a full four years earlier, 13 players who took the ice on Monday May 28 for Washington were drafted or otherwise acquired under George's rein as general manager for the Capitals. For all intents and purposes, the Stanley Cup pitted George's old team against George's new team.

This was the third consecutive year that a team made

its debut in the Stanley Cup Finals. Debutant teams own an all-time series record of 11-17 in the Finals, with the last three instances ending in defeat: The Nashville Predators (2017) and San Jose Sharks (2016) both lost in six games to the Pittsburgh Penguins, while the Ottawa Senators (2007) lost in five games to the Anaheim Ducks. The Tampa Bay Lightning (2004) were the last team to win the Stanley Cup in their first trip to the Finals.

Stanley Cup Finals, Game 1, Washington Capitals at T-Mobile Arena

The pregame entertainment was worthy of Donn Arden himself, Las Vegas' best-known choreographer and producer of old-time extravaganzas, such as *Lido de Paris, Jubilee!,* and *Hello Hollywood Hello.* The lavish show at T-Mobile came complete with faux flaming arrows, special ice effects, a fully costumed knight on skates dropping from the sky, a short sword fight, the castle flaming and smoking and the Knight Line pounding on drums up at the Fortress, and the voice-over by a woman with, of course, a British accent. Then, for the real surprise, boxing announcer Michael Buffer introduced the starting lineups for the Stanley Cup Finals, Game 1, at T-Mobile.

This might not have happened in Columbus (no offense meant, Blue Jackets).

If the appearance by Buffer was to suggest that we were about to see a heavyweight championship boxing match, for which Vegas is famous, consider that mission accomplished—except the teams mostly traded goals instead of punches.

In Game 1 of the Stanley Cup Finals between the Vegas Golden Knights and the Washington Capitals, the four lead changes were the most ever in the 100-year history of the Cup.

Washington blew leads of 2-1 and 4-3. Vegas blew leads of 1-0 and 3-2. The only time a team led by two goals was when Tomas Nosek scored an empty-netter with just 2.7 seconds left in the game, giving Vegas a 6-4 win and a 1-0 lead in the series. It was the second goal of the game for the player who also scored the first-ever goal at Vegas' first-ever home game at T-Mobile on October 10.

The VGK's first-ever Stanley Cup Finals game had T-Mobile Arena rocking from the pre-game opening to the final buzzer. During the season and playoffs, just when you thought the decibels couldn't possibly get any higher, the Vegas crowd somehow seemed to raise them game after game and it had a positive effect on the team. In this game, the VGK used that energy to overcome the Washington lead two different times.

In the previous six Finals, the team that won Game 1 went on to win the Cup. In the history of the Stanley Cup, teams that emerged victorious from Game 1 won the Stanley Cup 78% of the time.

The actual Michael Buffer portion of the game unfolded in the third period when Tom Wilson ran over Jonathan Marchessault in the neutral zone, well after Marchy had passed the puck and was defenseless, completely unprepared for a hit. The hit was late, unnecessary, even border-line dirty — par for the course when the Philadelphia Flyers were intimidating their way to back-to-back Stanley Cup championships in the 1973-1974 and 1974-1975 seasons. But the league left that era of "old-time hockey" behind. Wilson had already been suspended for three games during these playoffs for breaking the jaw of Pittsburgh Penguins' rookie Zach Aston-Reese in Round 2 Game 3. The silver lining: In my opinion, Wilson's hit energized Vegas. They responded like a team that played with and for one another, all 18 skat-ers, without exception.

Amazingly, no penalty was initially called on the hit. Once play was stopped, Brayden McNabb was so incensed, he threw a punch at Wilson. Deryk Engelland also attempted to get at Wilson. Meanwhile, David Perron cross-checked the Capitals' star and captain, Alex Ovechkin, sending him flying to the ice. Perron was taking matters into his own hands and making a statement: If you dare manhandle one of our top players, look out; we're coming right back at one of yours.

The four on-ice officials gathered in front of the scorer's table. In the NHL rule book, only a referee can call a minor penalty. A linesman can only inform a referee of an egre-gious play that might warrant a five-minute major or more. But only a two-minute minor was assessed against Wilson for interference. David Perron got two for cross-checking.

When Washington scored a first-period goal, it was the first goal Vegas had surrendered in the first 20 minutes of the previous seven home playoff games; they'd held the L.A. Kings, San Jose Sharks, and Winnipeg Jets scoreless in every first period played at T-Mobile. Before Nosek's empty-net goal, the 10th of the game, eight of the nine goals were at even strength. Vegas scored the only power-play goal of the game when Colin Miller opened the scoring at 7:15 of the first period. It was Miller's third goal of the playoffs.

Washington had two shots on goal in the first 14 minutes of play. Then, in the blink of an eye, the Capitals scored their first goal on just their third shot on Fleury. Luca Sbisa failed to clear the puck out of the defensive zone, leading to a goal by Brett Connolly, his fifth of the playoffs. Nicklas Backstrom scored Washington's second goal on the fifth shot at Fleury a mere 42 seconds later to take a 2-1 lead.

William Karlsson salvaged the first period, scoring with 1:41 left; his seventh of the playoffs tied the score at 2-2. Both teams were no doubt happy to see the first period end, as the wheels seemed to come off both buses during different parts of the period.

I hardly expected four goals in the first period or 10 goals in the game. We all knew that Fleury had been spectacular all season long, but especially during the playoffs, and Braden Holtby hadn't given up a goal in more than 160 minutes, logging back-to-back shutouts in Games 6 and 7 against Tampa Bay. It was a very sloppy start for both teams.

Vegas' fourth line of Tomas Nosek, Pierre-Édouard Bellemare, and Ryan Reaves gave Washington fits all night with a relentless forecheck and they had three goals and a +8 for the night.

Reaves now had a two-game goal streak after scoring the series clincher to win the Western Conference against

Winnipeg. His goal tied the game just 1:31 after Tom Wilson put Washington ahead 4-3 when Fleury, losing the puck, dragged Wilson's shot into the net with his left skate. On Nosek's second goal, he blocked a slap shot from Ovechkin with 10 seconds left in the game, chased down a clearing pass from Perron, and slid it into the open net for the 6-4 final score for Game 1.

With Holtby pulled for an extra skater and the clock at 44 seconds left, the Capitals had a glorious scoring chance, when Lars Eller was alone in front of Fleury. Brayden McNabb managed to get his stick on Eller's, preventing his shot.

The VGK rendered Alex Ovechkin a non-factor. He picked up an assist on Wilson's goal, but that was only after Fleury put the puck into the net himself. Ovi mustered two shots on goal. His four hits were also minimal for him.

Keeping Alex out of the game would be key to Vegas getting to four wins before Washington did. One of the reasons Ovechkin might have had an off game was that he didn't enjoy his Momma Lucia's chicken parmesan with plain pasta and four different sauces that he eats every game day at 11 a.m. With Vegas having home-ice advantage, Alex would get his favorite meal a possible total of three times from Momma Lucia in Bethesda, Maryland. Limiting the "Great Eight" to just three Momma Lucia meals at most might be all that was needed.

Vegas owned the best home record in the playoffs at 7-1. In eight games, they'd averaged 3.88 goals per game at T-Mobile, while surrendering 2.

I wasn't predicting that Game 2 would be another scoring frenzy, as both teams looked like their multiple days off had an effect on the defensive side of the game. Clearing attempts out of the zone were a challenge and both Fleury and Holtby seemed to lose the invincibility they'd displayed in the games leading up to the Finals.

Five different VGK players scored: Colin Miller on the power play (his 3rd), William Karlsson (7), Reilly Smith (3), Ryan Reaves (2), Tomas Nosek (2, 3).

Game 2 was now a must-win for Washington. The last thing the Capitals wanted was to have to win four of the remaining five games, especially against a now-proven team like Vegas.

Record: Vegas 1, Washington 0

Stanley Cup Finals, Game 2, Washington Capitals at T-Mobile Arena

Throughout Vegas' first 16 games in these playoffs, a number of incredible saves were made and until Game 2, for the most part they were made by Marc-André Fleury. In this game, Braden Holtby made what might be the save of his life.

As soon as I saw it, I started writing my blog for Las VegasAdvisor.com, in which I said that if Washington went on to win the Stanley Cup, it would be memorialized as "The Save."

With the clock winding down to just under two minutes and Vegas trailing 3-2, a pass into Washington's zone took a crazy bounce off the end boards. The puck came back out through the crease, past Holtby, and onto the stick of Cody Eakin. Following the path of the puck, Holtby slid from right to left to prepare for the shot. Eakin, however, slid the puck across to Alex Tuch, who had a wide-open net.

The entire arena leapt out of their seats. The thousands assembled in Toshiba Plaza jumped up and down, already celebrating, believing that Alex Tuch had scored and saved the day for the Knights, who for the second game in a row failed to play Knight-like hockey.

Somehow, however, Holtby dove across and just managed to get the paddle portion of his stick in front of the goal to stop Tuch's sure shot, which would have tied the score and most likely sent the game into overtime.

Fleury was pulled for an extra skater for the remaining 1:59, but Tuch's opportunity was as close as the Knights came. The final score, 3-2 in favor of Washington, tied the series at 1-1. This loss was the VGK's first at home in regulation in the playoffs.

This was a must-win for Washington. Going down 2-0 to Vegas and having to win four of the five remaining games would be all but insurmountable, especially since the Capitals had won only four of their previous nine games at home, while Vegas had a respectful 6-2 road record. So you'd have expected Washington to come out with a lot of energy and attempt to take the crowd right out of the game.

Instead, the first 10 minutes were the only 10 of the 60 that the VGK played like we'd all become accustomed to; they were the quicker team. When Luca Sbisa sent an alley-oop pass into the Washington zone, defenseman Dmitry Orlov reached to glove it and start back in the opposite direction. James Neal, also tracking Sbisa's pass, knocked the puck out of mid-air, skated a few strides to the faceoff circle, and wristed a perfect shot over Holtby's left shoulder to give Vegas the 1-0 lead 7:58 into the game.

Just like in Game 1 when Vegas scored first, Washington answered right back with 2:33 left in the first period, then added another 5:38 into the second period. When the Capitals scored their third unanswered goal, they took a commanding 3-1 lead. That goal was scored by Brooks Orpik, ending a monumental 220-game streak, dating back to February 20, 2016, including 39 post-season games, in which he failed to put the puck in the net. His last post-season goal was way back on April 21, 2014, when he played for the Pittsburgh Penguins and was a teammate of Marc-André Fleury.

The three goals that Washington scored were all off east-to-west passes that took advantage of Fleury's aggressive posture in coming out to cut the shooter's angle.

In Game 1, a hit on Jonathan Marchessault galvanized the Knights into a come-from-behind victory after playing a lackluster game. In Game 2, a similar situation occurred when Brayden McNabb crushed Evgeny Kuznetsov along the boards at center ice. Kuznetsov, the Caps leading scorer in the playoffs, immediately left the ice, hunched over and clutching his left arm; he didn't return.

The hit seemed to bring the Caps to life, giving them a purpose. Moving up Lars Eller to fill Kuznetsov's spot also paid dividends: Eller scored Washington's first goal, had primary assists on the team's two other goals, and wound up with three points, a +1 for the night and six hits, a team high in the game.

Alex Ovechkin, who was almost invisible in Game 1, was much more engaged; he scored a power-play goal and had five hits.

Washington had eight giveaways in Game 1, many of which were caused by Vegas' relentless forecheck. The Caps cut that in half with only four giveaways, while the VGK's forecheck for the most part was missing in action.

When the third period started, Vegas trailed by a goal. Contrary to expectations, during a 10-minute span in the third, the Knights were held without a shot. Even with a 5-on-3 advantage, they seemed to look for the perfect opportunity, instead of just getting some rubber on Holtby; they registered a single shot with the two-man advantage. That's unacceptable in any game, but in a pivotal Stanley Cup Finals game, it was devastating.

Winning Game 2 would have pretty much sealed the deal for Vegas in their attempt to hoist the Cup in their inaugural season. Now it was a best-of-five series with three of the remaining games in Washington.

Game 2's result was the first Stanley Cup Finals loss for the VGK franchise. Ironically, it was also the first win in Stanley Cup Finals history for Washington. In the Capitals only other appearance in the finals in 1998, they were swept 4-0 by the Detroit Red Wings.

If there was a silver lining to this black cloud, it was that Vegas hadn't played well in the first two games, but were tied 1-1; they lost in this game only because of The Save.

Record: Vegas 1, Washington 1

Stanley Cup Finals, Game 3, Capitals in Washington

In a game that Washington had to win, they played exactly like that.

The Capitals set the tempo of Game 3 early. In the first period, Washington won 13 of the 18 faceoffs and blocked 15 shots, four by defenseman John Carlson and two by Alex Ovechkin. When one of the best offensive players in the entire NHL is blocking shots, that speaks volumes about his commitment to do whatever it takes to win the Stanley Cup. Ovechkin also had three shots on goal in the first period in eight attempts and he logged two hits. He was ready. Vegas lacked that intensity.

Once again, Marc-André Fleury was the only reason the score was 0-0 after the first 20 minutes. He kept Washington off the scoreboard and the crowd out of the game.

Things changed early in the second period. Vegas failed on multiple chances to clear the puck out of the zone and it wound up on Ovechkin's stick, always a dangerous proposition for the opposing team. With one skate on the ice and his other leg on the back of Brayden McNabb, Ovi somehow lifted the puck with a backhand shot over the outstretched Fleury for the first goal of the game.

The Golden Knights had relied on their forecheck all season long and throughout the first three rounds of the playoffs for their success, but couldn't maintain it in the Finals. In this game, Braden Holtby was aggressive in going behind the net and moving the puck to his defensemen, which neutralized any attempt of a forecheck by the Golden Knights.

Indeed, Vegas' lone goal was Holtby's only mistake in the entire game.

All of his clearing passes in the first two periods were up and around the boards, both on Holtby's forehand and backhand, and he seemed to gain confidence in handling the puck as the game went on. Suddenly, he tried to show Vegas a different clearing look. Instead of going around the boards, he attempted to clear it up the middle of the ice. After Pierre-Édouard Bellemare got his stick on the pass, Tomas Nosek quickly picked it up and scored uncontested, with Holtby caught behind the net. That closed Washington's lead to one goal 3:29 into the third period and it felt like Vegas might have a chance to steal this game with a little puck luck.

Shea Theodore had a game that I'm 100% sure he'd like to forget. On both Washington's second goal and its back-breaking third goal with just 6:07 left in the game, Theodore's defensive play was less than stellar. He also created a situation that put Fleury in no-man's land outside the crease, forcing the goalie into taking a tripping penalty. Vegas dodged a bullet on that penalty. Actually, neither team capitalized on six power-play opportunities: Washington went 0-4 and Vegas went 0-2.

Of course, Theodore wasn't the only reason that Vegas lost the game 3-1 and now trailed 2-1 in games. When your best offensive players in a game are in the fourth line, you have offensive issues. Except for Marchessault, the number-one line of Karlsson, Smith, and Marchessault was almost invisible the entire game. The second line of Perron, Haula, and Neal was a -9, as all three were on the ice for Washington's three goals. Neither Perron nor Neal even registered a shot on goal.

In all their playoff games, including the multiple over-time periods, Vegas trailed in only 162 minutes and 43 seconds. Totaled up, that was less than three games out of the 16 they'd played thus far. In the last two games, they trailed 73:16 of 120 minutes.

Truth be told, Vegas didn't play well in the first three games of the series. They were lucky to be behind by only one game. Was it nerves? Were they worn out by the time they encountered a revved-up Washington? Was it just one or two missed opportunities? Or were the Capitals that much better as a team? How big was The Save that Holtby made in Game 2 now?

In my opinion, these two teams were evenly matched. Washington's forwards were outplaying Vegas' forwards. Holtby wasn't exactly outplaying Fleury; he just wasn't seeing as many shots. In this game, Washington blocked 26 shots, while Vegas blocked nine and managed only 22 shots on Holtby.

By the looks of the post-game crowd's reaction, it appeared that the Washington fans believed this was a best-of-three series, rather than a best-of-seven. By no means was Vegas out of this series. I mean, this was the first time the Knights had lost two in a row in the entire post-season. The last time the Knights trailed in a series, they won the next four games, defeating the Winnipeg Jets in five after losing the first.

In his post-game interview Coach Gallant was asked if Monday's Game 4 is a must-win for Vegas his response was, "Every game is a must-win when you're playing for the Stanley Cup."

With this loss, the Golden Knights were suddenly in the unfamiliar playoff position of having to win three of the four remaining games in the Stanley Cup Finals.

Game 4, the 101st game in Vegas Golden Knights franchise history, was now the biggest game that Vegas had ever played.

Record: Washington 2, Vegas 1

Stanley Cup Finals, Game 4, Capitals in Washington

It was *so* frustrating to have come this far and be faced with a task that now seemed unlikely. But was it? After all, we were talking about the Vegas Golden Knights. The unlikely started in October and continued right up until May 30, with Vegas suffering its first loss in the Stanley Cup Finals in Game 2 by virtue of The Save. I wondered if we'd all look back on that as the turning point of this magical run.

If the Golden Knights had won Game 2, the mindsets of both teams would have been completely different. Washington's task would have been to win four of the remaining five games, with two at T-Mobile where the VGK had been an almost irresistible force for eight months. This might have been demoralizing to a team that had a pedigree of playoff failure in its 44-year history. The other side of this coin would have been a team that had defied all logic in their brief existence and proved many, if not all, hockey pundits wrong.

Now, for the first time this year, the VGK were facing adversity.

Impossible? No.

Unlikely? Unfortunately, yes.

But one thing was perfectly clear: The Vegas Golden Knights had to win Game 4. If not …

Only one team in NHL history came back when trailing a Stanley Cup Finals series three games to one — the 1942 Toronto Maple Leafs. The other 32 teams, faced with what Vegas was now looking at, failed to accomplish what Toronto did.

Then again, the VGK broke NHL records the entire season, some of them 100 years old. Toronto's comeback was *only* 76 years ago.

Granted, it was deeply disheartening to suffer only three losses total in the first three rounds out of 15 games and now have three losses in the round that determined who would hoist the ultimate prize. Up until Game 4, the last time the VGK lost three games in a row was all the way back at the end of November. They'd never lost four in a row.

You never want to trail in a playoff series, especially 3-1. But if there was one team to which Vegas wanted to be down 3-1, it was the Washington Capitals. Here are just a few of their playoff collapses over the years.

1985: In a best-of-five series, Washington led 2-0, only to lose the next three games to the New York Islanders.

1987: They led the New York Islanders 3-1 and lost the next three.

1992: They led the Pittsburgh Penguins 3-1 and lost Games 5, 6, and 7.

1995: Another blown 3-1 series lead to the Penguins.

1996: After winning the first two games against Pittsburgh, they lost four in a row.

2010: They blew a 3-1 series lead to the Montreal Canadiens.

Knowing what they were up against, in Game 4, the Knights played their best up to that point in the series, especially in the first 10 minutes. They had the Capitals on their heels. Marc-André Fleury had his share of good fortune with the post and crossbars during the first three rounds. In Game 4, Braden Holtby was the beneficiary.

Vegas had 30 shots on Holtby, while Washington managed to score six goals on just 23 shots on Fleury. By no means am I blaming Fleury for all of those goals, in which lost coverages and good bounces played a part. Washington's three power-play goals in five attempts really put Vegas in a hole. The fact that the Knights went 0-4 on their power play also didn't help their cause. Once again, it appeared that Vegas was looking for the perfect shot, instead of just getting it on net, then looking for a deflection or rebound.

Washington did a good job of limiting the shooting lanes and blocked 24 shots, only two fewer than in Game 3.

Vegas was much more engaged in a game they knew they needed to win. They had 71 shot attempts, compared to 41 by Washington.

The momentum of the game changed after James Neal

missed a wide-open net just 4:31 seconds into the first period with the VGK on the power play. Vegas seemed to control games when they scored early. But Washington scored first. Actually, they scored three times in 9:45 to take a commanding 3-0 lead in the first period. Washington scored once in the second period to take a 4-0 lead.

Vegas appeared to regain some life with two goals in the third, by James Neal and Reilly Smith, to cut the lead to two with 7:34 left to play.

However, Washington responded quickly when Michal Kempny scored only 1:13 later. Brett Connolly closed the scoring with Washington's third power-play goal with just 1:09 left in the game. Final score: 6-2.

The Washington power play had made the difference up until this point in this series, scoring four goals in 12 attempts. Actually, it made the difference throughout the playoffs, with 21 power-play goals in 23 playoff games so far.

Now, there was no longer any room for error. Vegas was faced with the task of having to play near-perfect hockey in Game 5 to beat a very good Washington team. Still, one shift at a time, one period at a time: Win Game 5, then deal with Game 6. A win would certainly open the door of the closet that was filled with Washington's playoff skeletons.

Bottom line: It wasn't impossible, not with this team. They lifted an entire city when it was as low as it had ever gone. In Game 5, they'd again feed off the energy of their loyal fans who would rock T-Mobile.

It wasn't supposed to end in Game 5 in Las Vegas.

Record: Washington 3, Vegas 1

Stanley Cup Finals, Game 5,
Washington Capitals at T-Mobile Arena

But it did. In just 2:31, the sports story of all stories came to a screeching halt.

The unexpected never did materialize. The movie that *will* be made won't have the perfect Hollywood ending, not like the 1981 *Miracle on Ice* TV flick or 2004's *Miracle* feature film about the 1980 U.S. Olympics hockey team. It'll have to be more like *Moneyball*, where the Oakland A's lose early in the post-season and that part of the story is told in "epilogue titles," the end text that will gloss over the four losses in a row to Washington as quick cuts of the season highlights—Marchessault's sliding stretching goal, Neal's backhand from his knees, Tuch's breakaway through three defenders, Reaves crushing the Flames' TJ Brody—cross the big screen.

But it's still a tale for the ages, an instant legend that won't be soon forgotten.

The Vegas Golden Knights empowered an entire city just by being themselves. They proved to be the epitome of what a team is. They forced the non-believers to believe. They turned the entire NHL upside down.

But in the end, they came up three games short of doing the impossible and winning the Stanley Cup when they fell in Game 5 of the Finals to the Washington Capitals by a score of 4-3.

After a scoreless first period, both teams traded goals. Jakub Vrana scored on a breakaway 6:24 into the second period to give Washington a 1-0 lead. Vegas responded quickly when former Washington Capital Nate Schmidt scored.

Alex Ovechkin, Washington's captain and soon-to-be Conn Smythe Award winner (the trophy given to the player judged most valuable to his team during the NHL playoffs), scored a power-play goal (while Brayden McNabb was in the penalty box for tripping Ovechkin 23 seconds earlier) to take a 2-1 lead.

Vegas scored two additional goals in the second period, one at 12:56 by David Perron, who was pushed into Braden Holtby. Washington challenged the goal, claiming interference. The challenge denied, the score was now tied at 2-2.

With Ovechkin off for tripping, Reilly Smith scored on a power-play with just 29 seconds left in the second period, giving the VGK a 3-2 lead entering the third.

But in a matter of two minutes and 31 seconds, Washington scored two goals to regain a lead they wouldn't relinquish. Devante Smith-Pelly scored at the 9:25 mark; his third goal in three straight games tied the score at 3-3. Just 2:31 later, Lars Eller found a puck that dribbled through Fleury's pads after he made the original save. The Stanley Cup's winning goal was in the net.

The Washington power play scored only once, but it played an important role in winning the 2018 Stanley Cup. The Capitals scored 22 PPGs in 75 attempts (29.3%). Only three previous teams with at least 60 attempts had a better percentage: the 1981 New York Islanders (37.8%), the 1982 Islanders (29.9%), and the 1994 Toronto Maple Leafs (29.7%).

The VGK power play during the playoffs was 12 goals in 65 attempts (18.4%), with three out of 14 in the Finals. Washington scored five PPG in 16 attempts in the Finals.

In the first three playoff rounds, Marc-André Fleury yielded only 27 goals in 15 games. In the Finals, Washington scored 20 goals in five games. Vegas scored 14.

What made this loss disappointing was the reality that both third-period goals by Washington could have been avoided. They came off giveaways in the Golden Knights' own zone.

But that wasn't why the VGK lost in the Stanley Cup Finals. In the end, they were beaten by a better team, especially in the last four games.

Ironically, the Golden Knights closed out a season of setting one record after another with one final record—it was the first time they'd ever lost four games in a row.

It was Washington's time, make no mistake about it. But the Vegas Golden Knights had nothing to be ashamed of.

There's no need to single out who committed the giveaways. This was a team effort that started on Oct 6, 2017, and ended eight months later on June 7, 2018. They won as a team, they shocked the entire NHL as a team, and they lost as a team. They're beloved by fans in the city that they galvanized, and all over the United States, and in countries around the world.

We in Las Vegas were all privileged to witness a true team effort for 102 games. We were unbelievably lucky to play for the Stanley Cup in our first season. Washington, in their 44-year history, had only been there once before and four established franchises have never played in the Stanley Cup Finals.

My Three Stars of the Game, the Season, the Post-Season, and Next Season: 1) The entire VGK team, 2) the 18,000 fans who found a way to get into T-Mobile Arena, and 3) the 2.3 million residents of Las Vegas who bonded over this team.

The huge T-Mobile crowd stood as one. With a last roaring ovation, the whole world sent the Vegas Golden Knights to the locker room to let the Washington Capitals celebrate the Stanley Cup.

I'll give John Katsilometes of the *Las Vegas Review-Journal* the final word as he described the VGK's exit. "Vegas Strong. Vegas Born. Vegas Golden Knights. We never saw it coming, we might never experience it again, but this team made this town proud. Vegas Proud."

Ovechkin's Quest

Thirty-two-year-old Alexander Mikhailovich Ovechkin was born in Moscow and began his professional hockey career at age 16 with Dynamo Moscow in the Russian Super League. A standout from day one, he was drafted by the Florida Panthers in 2003 while he was still 17; his birthday was two days after the cutoff date. The Panthers tried to argue that with leap years, Ovechkin qualified, but the NHL didn't buy it. Instead, he was drafted the following year, first round first pick, by none other than George McPhee, general manager at the time of the Washington Capitals.

Ovechkin, whose nicknames are "Ovi" and the "Great Eight," is regarded as one of the greatest ice hockey players, and possibly the greatest pure goal scorer, of the modern NHL. The list of his individual achievements is as long as a hockey stick, but here's just a small sample.

Alex Ovechkin has led the NHL in goal scoring (for which the Rocket Richard Trophy is awarded) seven times; he's tied for the most times in NHL history with Bobby Hull. He first did so in the 2007-2008 season, when he recorded an astonishing 65 goals and 112 points. That year he led the league in points, winning the Art Ross Trophy; he also won the Hart Memorial Trophy as the league's most valuable player and the Lester B. Pearson Award, voted the best player by the NHL Players' Association. And he only got better over the next 10 years!

However, the list was missing three items: the Prince of Wales Trophy awarded to the Eastern Conference Champion team, the Conn Smyth Trophy awarded to the Stanley Cup

Finals most valuable player, and most importantly, the Stanley Cup itself.

As the face of the Capitals for more than a decade, Ovechkin took the lion's share of the blame for his team's failures in the post-season, which included three straight exits during the second round, two of them dealt by Marc-André Fleury's Pittsburgh Penguins.

But Alex Ovechkin slayed all three of his demons in May and June of 2018. From Game 1 of Round 1 of the playoffs, he commanded the ice like a man possessed, hitting, flying to loose pucks, dropping to the ice to body-block shots—setting an example that the rest of his team had no choice but to follow. In doing so, he became the 16th player in the history of the NHL to play at least 1,000 regular-season games before winning his first Stanley Cup; that he played those 1,000-plus games for the same team made him the second player ever to do that.

And when he was finally handed the Cup—*his* Cup—he clutched it like he might never let it go. Quest completed!

Though I was somewhat heartbroken when the Vegas Golden Knights were defeated in the Stanley Cup Finals, it was much easier to accept that it was at the hands of a true champion and his team. I also appreciated that the Capitals set a 100-year NHL record of their own: the first team ever to win the Stanley Cup after trailing in all four playoff series.

But best of all, and this comes from the deepest recesses in my hockey heart, was that the Washington Capitals took out a full-page ad in the *Las Vegas Review-Journal* to congratulate the Golden Knights on achieving "the most successful inaugural season in professional sports." And they added, "It was an honor to compete against you in the Stanley Cup Finals."

To me, that was more than an enormous display of respect and class. It was also the rarest of tributes for a sporting-event victor. There was, in the end, no loser. ♣

Chapter 9
The Records

The Vegas Golden Knights set so many records for a first-year expansion team that they fill this entire chapter. But before I get to those, I want to highlight a number of defining moments that epitomize this team, this season, and what they brought to Las Vegas.

In the first game of the 2017-2018 season, the Dallas Stars players lined up behind the Golden Knights to support the team and the city. The hitting in the game seemed subdued, as if the two teams were simply too raw for anything but a clean contest.

Likewise, at the VGK's first game at T-Mobile October 10, the visiting Arizona Coyotes again lined up behind the Knights. The introductions to the hometown fans were followed by 58 seconds of silence, one second for each life lost just a week and a half prior. The names of all the victims were projected on the ice as the Knight Tron counted down the 58 seconds. There wasn't a dry eye in the house as everyone realized that each second represented another name on the ice, another life that was unjustly taken.

Two minutes and 31 seconds into the home opener, Tomas Nosek scored the first goal at T-Mobile Arena, inciting a raucous ovation from the Vegas crowd. Less than two minutes later, Deryk Engelland scored on a one-timer from the point. The Knights never looked back from this moment, which defined the entire season.

During the VGK's fourth game, Detroit Red Wing Anthony Mantha crashed into goalie Marc-André Fleury during a rush; it looked like Mantha's knee beaned Fleury in the noggin. Fleury was slow to get up, clearly shaken; he finished the game, but was done playing for 25 more.

In the same game, the Red Wings' Tomas Tatar delivered a low (questionable) body-check that sent Erik Haula head over heels. Haula threw down his gloves and Tatar obliged. It was the Golden Knights' first fight and the crowd erupted in support as Haula stuck up for himself, his team, and his city. By all accounts, Haula lost the fight, but in the penalty box he was laughing and on camera, it looked like he was saying, "It was my first one." Of course it was. This team was all about firsts. Whether he knew it or not, Haula, win or lose, had just exemplified the spirit of this who-the-f***-do-you-think-you-are expansion team in only its fourth game. What made it even more defining was that Tomas Tatar was traded to the Golden Knights just before the deadline at the end of February—and Haula and Tatar became teammates. They joked about their altercation, the heat of the moment, how neither of them was much into fighting, that it was in the past, and they both looked forward to playing together.

Before the season, the Golden Knights were expected to be cellar dwellers, but wound up surprising everyone by winning their first three games. But now, with Fleury out and with no timetable for his return, it surely spelled the end of the season for Vegas and had to be another defining moment. Didn't it?

Of course, Malcolm Subban, an untested waiver pick-up, came in and led the Knights to two more wins before also getting hurt. Third-string goalie and AHL call-up Oscar Dansk finished the game, leading Vegas to another victory in overtime. Dansk led the team to two more victories before going down and out during a road game. Fourth-stringer Max Lagacé took the ice. Talk about a defining moment! The only other goalie in the VGK organization was 19-year-old Dylan Ferguson, who was under an entry-level contract as a prospect and was playing with the Kamloops Blazers of the Western Hockey League. Reportedly, he had to leave a dinner with friends to catch a flight to New York, where the next night he suited up as the backup netminder against the Rangers.

Ferguson saw ice time in relief of Lagacé in the last 9:10 of a game in Edmonton. He even made a save on Connor McDavid, preventing a hat trick. That made Ferguson the fifth goalie to play for Vegas in little more than a month.

In two ways, Fleury's absence helped define the team. For one, the surprising depth and talent of the backup goaltenders combined for a remarkable record of 16-8-1 while he was out. For another, the entire team stepped up in front of them. When Fleury returned, he came back to an even stronger group, which had played so well without him that it confounded *everyone*. And now the Knights had their star player back.

A personal defining moment arrived on the Dad Trip, where most of the Knights' players were traveling with their fathers, a fine NHL tradition. In the game at Nashville, Malcolm Subban was the Knights' goalie, while his older brother, PK, filled his role as a star defenseman for the Predators, with their father in the stands. The shootout went six rounds, but Malcolm emerged victorious.

Next, Marc-André Fleury faced his old team, the Pittsburgh Penguins, at T-Mobile. The build-up to this game had national attention. Penguins' star Sidney Crosby told a reporter that Fleury is usually "pretty vocal" during games. "If he's back there hootin' and hollerin', it's probably not going good for us." Well, Fleury was hootin' and hollerin' throughout the game; he even ventured 30 feet from the net to the top of the faceoff circle to make a daring diving poke-check on Conor Sheary. Fleury led the Golden Knights to a 2-1 victory that night, once again proving the legitimacy of his new team — at the expense of the old one.

The entire month of December was one long defining moment. The Knights went 11-1-1, with victories over Nashville, Pittsburgh, Tampa Bay, Washington, Toronto, and L.A., plus two over Anaheim, all teams that made the playoffs later in the season.

The last victory in December and 2017 came against Toronto at home on New Year's Eve, where William Karlsson made history with the Golden Knights' first hat trick. Karlsson's third goal was one of the most impressive empty-netters of the season: He won a footrace to the puck by diving, stretching out his prone body, and reaching out his stick to knock in the goal around the Leafs' would-be defender. And Vegas was already up by two!

On February 1, 2018, in a preview of the Western Conference Championship series, the Knights and Winnipeg Jets were tied 2-2 in a 60-minute slugfest that was going into overtime. Twice during OT, the puck ended up in the Vegas crease behind Fleury, causing frantic scrambles in front of the net. The first time, Vegas defenseman Colin Miller practically tackled a Jet to keep the puck out. The second scramble ended with Fleury out of position and Erik Haula lying across the goal line to protect the net. The puck escaped the crease and was rushed to the Knight's zone where David Perron scored the game winner, ending a wild night in Winnipeg.

The last home game of the season came against division rival San Jose Sharks. The Sharks had put the Knights away in overtime just a week prior, causing a race for the lead in the Pacific Division. With the score tied 2-2 in the third period, the Knights found themselves down a man. Not only did they kill the penalty, but William Karlsson intercepted a pass, raced toward the Sharks' net, put the puck between his legs, and sailed it over Martin Jones. It won the game and was the shot of the year, and it came shorthanded. What a way to end the season at home.

Vegas' 51st and final victory of the year came in a shootout in Vancouver. It was the first game after NHL legends Henrik and Daniel Sedin announced they were retiring. After the final buzzer, the Knights stayed on the ice to show respect for the Sedins, 18-year veterans, as they took in a well-deserved ovation from the crowd. The identical twins shook hands with each Knights' player before leaving the ice. It was a class act all around; shows of sportsmanship like this are rarely seen in sports outside of hockey.

Now for all those records.

The Vegas Golden Knights started with a bang: They became the only expansion team in NHL history to win their first three games. In the process, a record that few noticed was that Marc-André Fleury, in the VGK's first game against Dallas, made the most saves ever in an expansion team's first win: 45.

By winning five of their first of six games, they tied a 100-year-old record, joining the 1917-18 Montreal Canadiens as the only other franchise in the history of the league to start its first season 5-1-0. And one of the victories for the Canadiens was a forfeit against the Montreal Wanderers as a result of a fire that burned Westmount Arena to the ground on Jan. 2, 1918. In my opinion, the record is owned by the VGK—as they actually had to *win* five out of the six.

In the following game, the Knights broke another NHL record: the first expansion team in the history of the game to win six of their first seven games.

Two wins later, their five-game winning streak tied them with the two teams in 100 years that had a similar streak to start their inaugural seasons: the 1926-1927 New

York Rangers and the 1979-1980 Edmonton Oilers.

Even after three losses in a row on the road, the Knights became the second expansion team in NHL history playing the fewest games before achieving their ninth win.

In the loss to the Toronto Maple Leafs on November 6, 2017, the Golden Knights missed a chance to set their sixth record: A win would have made them the first expansion team in NHL history to win 10 in just 14 games played. Oh well.

It took another seven games for the VGK to tie a century-old record held by the Toronto Arenas in the 1917-1918 season: an eight-game winning streak at home by an expansion team in its first year.

With the Thanksgiving weekend 4-2 win over the Arizona Coyotes, the Knights became the fastest NHL team to achieve 15 wins in its inaugural season. The record had been held by the New York Rangers in the 1926-1927 season. It took the Rangers 25 games to reach 15 wins. The VGK got there in 22.

In their game against the Anaheim Ducks at T-Mobile, Vegas became the first expansion team in the entire history of the league to post 11 wins in just 13 home games.

Three games later, their 20 total wins broke another 100-year-old NHL record, becoming the fastest team to record 20 wins—out of just 31 games—in their inaugural season.

Next record to be broken: the fastest expansion team to win 24 games. Here are the records for the previous expansion teams in their first 34 games:

Philadelphia Flyers, 1967-1968: 17-12-5

L.A. Kings, 1967-1968: 16-15-3

Florida Panthers, 1993-1994: 14-15-5

Quebec Nordiques (now Colorado Avalanche), 1979-1980: 14-15-5

Vegas Golden Knights, 2017-2018: 24-9-2 (70.6%)

In the second-to-last game of 2017 against the L.A. Kings, the Knights established a new record as the first team in its inaugural NHL season to rack up a six-game winning streak (they were 10-0-1 in 11 games).

In the very next game on New Year's Eve at T-Mobile, the Knights won their 11th game in December to break another 100-year-old NHL record for the most wins by a first-year team that month. Their record in December was 11-1-1.

And the new year not only kept the string going, but tied a record that was extended to *all* the major sports by winning eight games in a row in their first year. That was held solely by the 1976-1977 Denver Nuggets of the NBA. Ho hum—it was only 40 years old.

In the league's number-two Knights' 4-1 victory over the number-one Tampa Bay Lightning on January 18, the Knights logged their 30th win and tied with four other teams to win 30 games in their inaugural NHL season. At the time, Anaheim and Florida held the record for most wins in their first seasons with 33 in 84 games.

They tied *that* record against the Calgary Flames in the first game after the All-Star break, just 49 games into an 82-game season. Then they broke it two nights and one game later, on the road, against the Winnipeg Jets, in overtime.

With the home win against the Chicago Blackhawks in game 56, their 20th in 26 home games, the VGK tied both the 1967-68 L.A. Kings and the 1979-80 Hartford Whalers for 20 home wins in the first season.

Another game, another broken record. By this point in the season, it was starting to sound like a broken record!

In the February 21 contest against the Calgary Flames, the VGK's 7-3 victory gave them their 84th point of the season, breaking a 24-year-old expansion-team record set by the Florida Panthers in the 1993-1994 season. The win was also the VGK's 23rd victory in 29 home games, which broke another NHL expansion record, this one 38 years after the 1979-1980 Hartford Whalers won 22 of the 40 games they played at home.

In beating the Red Wings in Detroit on March 8, the Knights tied another one: their 19th road victory. They now shared it with the 1993-1994 Anaheim Ducks. The very next game, on March 10 against the Buffalo Sabres, the VGK broke the road-wins record (20) in an inaugural year. The Ducks had held it for 24 years.

Though the Knights lost in overtime to the Colorado Avalanche in the 75th game, their point got them to 101 for the season and they owned the record for an expansion team breaking the 100-point mark most quickly. It took the Edmonton Oilers three tries to break 100 points; they hit 111 in 1981-82, their third season. The New York Islanders reached 101 points in 1975-76, their fourth season.

With their win against the Avalanche in the next game

at home, the Golden Knights became the first expansion team ever to qualify for the Stanley Cup Playoffs in their inaugural season. Only two expansion teams had ever made the playoffs in their first year, but they weren't brand new teams put together just three months before the season started, as were the VGK. The 1968-69 Hartford Whalers and the 1979-80 Edmonton Oilers were established teams from the World Hockey Association when they joined the NHL. Also, since the first six expansion teams that joined the original six NHL teams were all put in the same division, it allowed four of them to make the playoffs. So does that count? Vegas, for all intents and purposes, is the only real expansion team having to compete against established teams to make the playoffs in its first try.

And in its last home game of the season, against the San Jose Sharks on March 31, 2018, the Golden Knights became the first modern-era expansion team from *all four* North American professional sports leagues to start from scratch and finish first in its division (excluding mergers and all-expansion divisions).

At the end of the regular season, the Knights' record of 51-24-7 set another NHL milestone for the best win-loss totals for a first-year expansion franchise. Also, they were the NHL's first expansion team ever to earn as many as 109 points in its first season.

In the first playoff game against the L.A. Kings, Vegas wound up as the fourth team in its inaugural season to win a shutout in a postseason game. The other three teams were the 1927 New York Rangers, the 1968 St. Louis Blues, and ironically the L.A. Kings.

In Game 6 of Round 2 against the San Jose Sharks, the Vegas Golden Knights became the third first-year expansion team to win their first two playoff rounds. Actually, it was really only two teams. When the St. Louis Blues accomplished it in 1968, they played their first two rounds against the other five expansion teams that entered the league the year the NHL doubled to 12 teams. So one of the six teams was guaranteed to win two rounds. The other team that actually accomplished this was the Toronto Arenas — exactly 100 years ago in 1918.

In Game 3 of the Western Conference Championship, in a rare individual record, Jonathan Marchessault became the first player in the NHL's entire history to score a goal in the first minute and the last minute of the same playoff game.

In winning the series 4-1 against the Winnipeg Jets, the Vegas Golden Knights became the second expansion team in the NHL, NFL, NBA, and MLB since 1960 to reach a championship series in its first season. Back in 1967-68, the St. Louis Blues also achieved that feat.

By winning the Western Conference Championship series as the visiting team in Winnipeg, the VGK became the seventh team in NHL history to win the first three rounds of a season's playoffs on the road. Five of the previous six teams went on to win the Stanley Cup.

Not a record, but poetic justice indeed: In Round 1 of these playoffs, Brayden McNabb, a former L.A. King, scored the winning goal against his former team in the series-clinching game. In Round 2, Ryan Carpenter had an assist on the series-clinching goal against his former team, the San Jose Sharks. And in Round 3 against the Winnipeg

Jets, Ryan Reaves, a Winnipeg native, scored the game-winning goal to send the Vegas Golden Knights to the Stanley Cup Finals.

In Game 1 of the Finals, the four lead changes were the most ever in the 100-year history of the Cup. There had been six games in which the lead changed three times. The last was in Game 1 of the 2010 Finals, Philadelphia at Chicago. The others took place in 1982's Game 1, Vancouver at the New York Islanders; 1980's Game 1, New York Islanders at Philadelphia; 1976's Game 4, Montreal at Philadelphia; 1973's Game 5, Chicago at Montreal' and 1971's Game 4, Chicago at Montreal.

Finally and ironically, in a season of setting one record after another, the Golden Knights set another franchise record in Game 5 of the Finals: It was the first time this team had ever lost four games in a row.

In the end, the VGK were the expansion-team version of Wayne Gretzky, who broke and/or set almost every NHL scoring record, most of which stand to this day. And most of the expansion records that Vegas broke this season will remain for a long time, if not forever.

Finally, all four nominees from the Vegas Golden Knights for NHL awards won — a clean sweep of the Awards ceremony before the 2017-2018 season could be officially closed.

George McPhee accepted the prize for General Manager of the Year.

Gerard Gallant won the Jack Adams Award for Coach of the Year.

William Karlsson took home the Lady Byng Trophy, awarded to the player who exhibited the best sportsmanship and gentlemanly conduct, combined with a high standard of playing ability.

And Deryk Engelland will hang on his wall the Mark Messier Leadership Award, presented to the player who exemplifies great leadership qualities to his team on and off the ice and plays a leading role in his community in growing the game of hockey.

It was a fitting finale to the extraordinary season and all-consuming saga of the Vegas Golden Knights in their first year.

The Vegas Guy and the Vegas Golden Knights

by John L. Smith

[John L. Smith is one of Las Vegas' most beloved writers. A former sportswriter and columnist for the *Las Vegas Review-Journal*, he's the author of *Running Scared—The Life and Treacherous Times of Las Vegas' Casino King*, *No Limit—The Rise and Fall of Las Vegas' Stratosphere Tower*, *Of Rats and Men—Oscar Goodman's Life from Mob Mouthpiece to Mayor of Las Vegas*, *Sharks in the Desert—The Founding Fathers and Current Kings of Las Vegas*, and many others. I'm honored that we can reprint this column by him, which sums up a prevailing opinion around Las Vegas about the outcome of the Stanley Cup Finals—though I don't happen to share it.]

I ran into the Vegas Guy just the other day. To my surprise, instead of his dealer's black-and-whites, he wore a Vegas Golden Knights cap and a replica of goaltender Marc-André Fleury's No. 29 jersey.

You know the Vegas Guy. Why, you may even be the Vegas Guy. The Vegas Guy knows what day it is, pal. He knows the score and the bottom line. He's like Las Vegas. He never gives a sucker an even break. He gets the best of it. That's because the Vegas Guy only backs winners.

The Vegas Guy loved Jerry Tarkanian and his UNLV Runnin' Rebels. He didn't care all that much whether the coach was an outlaw or Mother Teresa. He just liked the fact that his teams won, what, 90% of their games? But when the Runnin' Rebels experienced a rare off year, the Vegas Guy bad-mouthed the team and swore off attending games at the Thomas and Mack Center.

And when, just a couple years ago, a guy named Bill Foley revealed his long-term plan to have a National Hockey League team based in Las Vegas, the Vegas Guy laughed until tears ran down his face. Foley was crazy. Didn't he know Vegas only backs winners? Didn't he know the most popular use for ice in Las Vegas is in a margarita?

But Foley persisted. He persuaded the NHL to take a chance on an odds-against town and that led to a shimmering arena on MGM Resorts International property and a major sports franchise Las Vegas could call its own.

When he learned the team's roster would be full of players left unprotected by the rest of the league, the Vegas Guy nodded knowingly. "See? They've got losers written all over them. The only thing they got from their old ball clubs was a bus ticket out of town." And even when they showed early promise, our local cynic wasn't convinced it would last.

He laughed again when Foley announced that the team would be called the Golden Knights. It would be coached by a guy named Gallant.

"What is this, some fairy tale? Maybe they should play their home games at the Excalibur? A team called the Golden Knights with a coach named Gallant, are you kidding? What, Prince Valiant wasn't available?"

Then, after the night of October 1, with Las Vegas staggered to its core, the Golden Knights skated to the rescue. They paid nightly tribute to the fallen and played their hearts out for a heartsick community. That dedication was reciprocated. A relationship was born that pierced the collective cynicism of one of the most cynical places on the planet.

But a funny thing happened on the way to a fairy-tale ending. Against the talented Washington Capitals, a franchise that had spent more than four decades chasing a Stanley Cup, the Golden Knights were all too human. The home team lost at home despite the loudest fans in the league and enough theatrics and pyrotechnics to light up the Strip.

At the risk of being mugged by Knights fans everywhere, I think it's a good thing the team didn't win it all in its first season. It would have made the feat feel too easy. We'd have become like those out-of-towners who hit a jackpot or a string of lucky blackjack hands on their first trip to Las Vegas. We would have been chasing a high that might never come again and would never be happy just to experience the moment.

If the Golden Knights help Las Vegas make the transition into a community in full, one that roots for a common home team and takes pride in southern Nevada over distant hometowns scattered across the globe, then there will be something much greater to celebrate than the outcome of a hockey game.

"Besides, there's always next year, right?" the Vegas Guy says, a tear in his eye and a strange sensation swelling in his heart, one later diagnosed as a sudden case of community pride. ✤

Epilogue

The Vegas Golden Knights play in a city known for having an edge in its games, turning visitors and locals who play those games into underdogs praying for the long shot, the jackpot, the cold hard cash that finally, conclusively, returns as easy money.

In *Sports Illustrated*, Charlotte Wilder wrote about "sports innocence, a false sense of normal," the kind of easy-money inaugural season that spoiled or even blinded Las Vegas fans. It was a common refrain, from the sadder but wiser hockey mavens offering a gentle reality check to the doubters who were back in force after the Finals.

They said, "They're marked now. They won't sneak up on anyone next year. No team in the league will underestimate the lowly expansion club."

They said, "The Knights will end up victims of their own success. They came in and gave the fans a great run, but they can't repeat it."

They said, "It'll be interesting to see how rabid the

Vegas fan base is on a cold and rainy Tuesday in February if the Knights are mired in a losing streak and out of the playoffs."

They even said, "The fact that so many season-ticket holders sold their seats to Caps fans for Game Five in the Finals was exactly why the Golden Knights had such a sweet set-up. The arena was new. The draft was rigged. The refs were lenient with them and stringent with their rivals. It was all so they'd win and be a shiny new marketing tool for the league and the game."

Hm.

I wouldn't presume to try and predict what the future has in store for anyone or anything, but I can say this: A relationship like the one between the Vegas Golden Knights and Las Vegas is essentially unknown in all the hockey cities in the world. It began under the direst circumstance, around which the VGK wrapped themselves in a way that forever tied them to it. Their presence as Las Vegas' home team couldn't help but keep the memory of the events on October 1 alive — almost as a rallying cry. Because of that alone, I'm all in. I was from day one. And I will be till the end — bitter, sweet, or anything in between. And it's not only me.

For tens of thousands of fans, this season wasn't just a season, even a first season. It was a deeply emotional experience. It was downright riveting, even for long-time hockey fans. The story just kept on getting better and better, chapter after chapter, like a book you just cannot put down.

These last words of this epic tale don't culminate in the feel-good fairy-tale climax, the one that everyone, except the Washington Capitals and the sports books managers would have loved to witness.

Yes, Washington was the better team in the Finals. But the VGK provided the kind of competition that inspired the Caps to play the best hockey in their 44-year history, break the so-called playoff jinx, and take the Cup back to their own (troubled) city. That was why the team took out a full-page ad in the Knights' local newspaper, thanking them for being a worthy opponent.

In the end, this was a situation that almost can't exist in sports where, for there to be a winner, there has to be a loser. Whether the Vegas Golden Knights won or lost was, amazingly enough for a major-league sports franchise, almost beside the point. For the VGK just to be *in* the Stanley Cup Finals promotes an argument that *both* teams in hockey's championship series *were* winners.

I'll give the final sentence and sentiment to Mike "Doc" Emrick, the most recognizable voice in hockey, having called the play by play on every major network, and a number of minor ones, for more than 40 years.

"The Golden Knights will be preceded by the word 'since' at the end of all future references. Because no one has accomplished what they did, all the achievements of first-year teams to come will be followed by '… since the Vegas Golden Knights of 2017-2018.'"

Index

A

Adidas 35
Adirondack Red Wings 38
AHL. *See* American Hockey
    League
Albany Devils 65
Ali, Muhammad 104
Allen, Jake 105
Allen, Kevin 223
American Hockey League 3, 38,
    48, 50, 52, 58, 61, 64, 66, 68,
    72, 77
Anaheim Ducks 20, 60, 70, 87,
    124, 125, 131, 141, 173, 175,
    304, 333, 335
Anderson, Craig 182
Andrews, Chris 295, 296
Anschutz Entertainment Group
    (AEG) 15
Aoki, Steve 16
Arden, Donn 304
Arizona Coyotes 4, 9, 20, 68, 92,
    93, 97, 98, 126, 130, 201,
    323, 327, 333
Armia, Joel 269
Art Ross Trophy 324
Aston-Reese, Zach 306
Atlanta Thrashers 15

B

Bakersfield Condors 58
Bark-André Furry 232
Belfour, Ed 250
Bellemare, Hannah 48
Bellemare, Pierre-Édouard 47, 87,
    143, 185, 190, 250, 307, 314
Bemidji State University 58
Bet on Sports 299
Bettman, Gary 8, 11, 14, 16, 27
Bischoff, Jake 84, 85

Bishop, Ben 127, 152
Black Knights 32
Black Knight Sports and
    Entertainment 32
Bobrovsky, Seregi 186
Boedker, Mikkel 260
Boehlke, Ken 84
Bond, Enne 258
Bonk, Radek 9
Borden, Sam 293
Boston Bruins 74, 75, 79, 100,
    102, 113
Boston College 78
Bowling Green State University
    48
Brassard, Derick 265
Brody, TJ 194
Brooks, Kenny 84
Brown, Dustin 181
Bubolz, Kerry 231
Buffalo Sabres 46, 49, 64, 103,
    161, 188, 189, 190, 335
Buffer, Michael 304
Burns, Brent 198, 271
Burrows, Alexander 182
Byfuglien, Dustin 269, 271, 277,
    282

C

Calgary Flames 52, 158, 174–
    178, 193, 210, 334–335
Campbell, Jack "Soupy" 181
Campoli, Nick 84
Carlson, John 313
Carlyle, Randy 125
Carolina Hurricanes 39, 50, 55,
    136, 154, 155
Carpenter, Ryan 48, 148, 163,
    166, 170, 175, 262, 267, 274,
    284, 337

Carrier, William 46, 49, 131, 174, 202, 238, 241, 256, 265
Chiarot, Ben 269
Chicago Blackhawks 51, 70, 107, 120, 147, 169, 208, 335
Chicago White Sox 292
Chicago Wolves 58, 61, 70, 77, 79, 85, 87, 101, 208
Christenson, Pat 222
City National Arena 31, 95–96, 215, 232
City National Bank 31
Clarkson University 35
Clifford, Kyle 62, 181
Coach of the Year 40, 155, 339
College of Saint Rose 35
Colorado Avalanche 75, 84, 87, 109, 120, 199, 334, 335
Columbus Blue Jackets 14, 28, 38, 58, 60, 62, 84, 120, 144, 156, 185
Connecticut Whale 62
Connolly, Brett 307
Conn Smyth Trophy 324
Cotsonika, Nick 26
Couture, Logan 199
Covers.com 294
Cowell, Simon 293
Craven, Murray 13, 22, 23, 30
Crosby, Sidney 70, 164
Cruz, Tommy 176, 185, 208

D
Dallas Stars 67, 74, 91, 98, 127, 128, 135, 141, 152, 161, 168, 327
Dangerfield, Rodney 80
Dansk, Oscar 4, 55, 87, 105, 108, 109, 111
Day the Bookies Wept, The 290
Deadspin 36
Dell, Aaron 250

Detroit Red Wings 25, 38, 50, 55, 68, 76, 99, 186, 195, 312
Dewey, Todd 293
DigitalSport.com 228
Di Giuseppe, Phillip 136
Dillon, Brenden 254
Dion, Céline 230
Dominion Hockey Challenge Cup 2
Doughty, Drew 143, 239, 241, 243, 245, 247, 271
Duchene, Matt 199
Dugan, Jack 84
Duke, Reid 84, 85
Dumba, Matt 57, 78

E
Eakin, Cody 47, 49–50, 123, 141, 187, 211, 243, 250, 262, 267, 310
ECHL 3, 61
Edmonton Oilers 53, 58, 62, 120, 121, 150, 151, 170, 173, 207, 209, 220, 333, 335, 336
Eller, Lars 308, 311, 321
Elvenes, Lucas 84
Elvises, The 234
Emrick, Mike "Doc" 345
Engelland, Deryk 50, 54, 87, 94, 97–98, 103, 116, 128, 136, 138, 189, 194, 240, 253, 257, 278, 285, 306, 328, 339
ESPN 288

F
Fanatics.com 215
fans, hockey 1, 81, 106, 132, 136, 139, 168, 188, 217, 237, 242, 289, 301
Fantenberg, Oscar 244
Fashion Show Mall 215
Ferguson, Dylan 3, 55, 85, 111, 116, 120, 329

Ferrall, Scott 249
Fidelity National Title Insurance
  Company 12
Fiesta Hotel-Casino 8
fighting, NHL 80–82
FlashSeats 222
Fleury, Marc-André 3, 46, 56, 69,
  76, 92, 100, 131, 135, 136,
  137, 140, 142, 145, 146, 147,
  149, 151, 153, 159, 163, 166,
  170, 178, 183, 184, 187, 189,
  190, 191, 193, 195, 199, 201,
  202, 211, 239, 242, 244, 246,
  248, 249, 250, 251, 253, 255,
  256, 259, 263, 264, 268, 270,
  274, 275, 276, 278, 279, 281,
  284, 285, 307, 309, 311, 313,
  314, 322, 328, 329, 330, 332
Florida Panthers 39, 40, 55, 62,
  63, 70, 74, 107, 138, 153,
  154, 220, 324, 334, 335
Folded Flag Foundation 17
Foley, William 11, 12, 18, 21, 31,
  34, 37, 205, 221, 283
Forbes 27, 51, 297
Forbort, Derek 142, 241
Founding 50 17
Frolik, Michael 159
Fuhr, Grant 201

G
Gaborik, Marion 142
Gallant, Gerard 40, 41, 51, 73,
  77, 81, 93, 97, 108, 120, 129,
  135, 138, 141, 151, 154, 176,
  183, 184, 197, 200, 202, 207,
  208, 210, 238, 242, 246, 260,
  261, 262, 265, 266, 270, 273,
  274, 276, 316, 339
Gay, Jason 102, 228
GC Technology 292
Gibson, John 124, 125, 131, 141,
  174

Glass, Cody 84, 85, 87
Gold Coast Casino 89
Golden Knights Yearbook 31
Golden Misfits. See Vegas Golden
  Knights
Golden Nugget Hotel-Casino 296
Goodman, Oscar 14, 106
Gordie Howe Hat Trick 177
Graham, Dirk 38
Grand Rapid Griffins 68
Gravel, Alexandra 64
Green, Trent 292
Gretzky, Brent 9
Gretzky, Wayne 207

H
Hague, Nicholas 84
Halak, Jaroslav 157
Hamonic, Travis 177
Hangover 107
Hartford Wolf Pack 61
Hart Memorial Trophy 324
Hasek, Dominic 163
hat trick 86, 127, 143, 177, 195,
  276, 329, 330
Haula, Erik 57, 58, 78, 87, 99,
  114, 122, 127, 132, 134, 159,
  160, 167, 186, 189, 191, 197,
  241, 243, 250, 257, 269, 277,
  315, 328, 331
Hefner, Hugh 293
Hellebuyck, Connor 119, 271, 272,
  274, 276, 277, 278, 282, 284
Heller, Steven 36
Hertl, Tomas 253, 256
Hickey, Shawn 231
Hobey Baker Award 24
Hockey Hall of Fame 81
Holtby, Braden 307, 308, 309,
  310, 311, 312, 313, 314, 315,
  318, 321
Houston Rockets 7
Howe, Gordie 177

Hughes, Cameron 229
Hull, Bobby 324
Hull, Brett 161
Hunt, Brad 58, 157, 169
Hyka, Tomas 85, 86, 87, 178
Hyman, Zach 3, 116

I

Imagine Dragon 225
Iowa Stars 67

J

Jack Adams Award 39, 40, 339
Jacksonville Jaguars 13
Jagr, Jaromir 154
Jankowski, Mark 211
Johnson, Carnell 227
Johnson, Drew 233
Jones, Ben 84
Jones, Martin 59, 126, 167, 198,
    206, 206–207, 249–250, 252,
    254, 258, 263, 266–267, 331

K

Kamloops Blazers 329
Kane, Evander 250, 255
Kane, Patrick 154
Kantowski, Ron 227
Karlsson, Erik 114, 273
Karlsson, William 51, 57, 59–60,
    74, 87, 106, 114, 120, 122,
    123, 127, 143, 156, 157, 166,
    167, 168, 170, 175, 179, 181,
    183, 195, 203, 206, 210, 243,
    246, 252, 253, 257, 267, 271,
    272, 307, 309, 330, 331, 339
Katsilometes, John 323
Kelly, Mike 39
Kempny, Michal 319
Kezirian, Doug 288
Khabibulin, Nikolai 249
King Clancy Memorial Trophy 53
Knight Line 226

Kolesar, Keegan 87
Konegay, Jay 289
Kontinental Hockey League 101
Kootenay Ice 64
Kopitar, Anze 181, 182, 244, 247
Korpisalo, Joonos 186
Koutelas, Reed 228
Kraemer, Mackenzie 291
Kuznetsov, Evgeny 311

L

Lady Byng Trophy 339
Lagacé, Max 5, 55, 61, 87, 111,
    112, 113, 114, 115, 116, 118,
    121, 122, 123, 125, 126, 129,
    134, 181, 191, 329
Laine, Patrik 59, 269, 273
L.A. Kings 15, 20, 49, 56, 58, 62,
    64, 65, 66, 85, 87, 107, 122,
    123, 124, 125, 133, 142, 180,
    181, 211, 216, 217, 238, 241,
    243, 248, 253, 257, 268, 270,
    281, 306, 334, 335, 336
Lamborghini Aventador Roadster
    63
Lamborghini Las Vegas 63
Landeskog, Gabe 200
Larosée, Véronique 54
Las Vegas 51s 10, 19
LasVegasAdvisor.com 33, 162,
    213, 309
Las Vegas Arena. *See* T-Mobile
    Arena
Las Vegas Events 222
Las Vegas Founding 50 16
Las Vegas Ice Center 79, 83
Las Vegas Review-Journal 32, 227,
    323, 325
Las Vegas Sun 32
Las Vegas Thunder 9
Las Vegas Wranglers 10, 52
L.A. Times 296
Le Castle Vania 227

Lehtonen, Kari 92
Leicester City Foxes 292
Leschyshyn, Curtis 84
Leschyshyn, Jake 84
Lester B. Pearson Award 324
Lewis, Kevin 213
Lil Jon 225
Lindberg, Oscar 62, 98, 206
Lindberg, Tobias 179
Little, Bryan 284
Logic 225
Loverro, Thom 303
Lowell Lock Monsters 52
Lowry, Adam 278
Lundqvist, Henrik 112
LVSportsBiz.com 222

M
MacDonald, Blair 207
MacKenzie River Pizza, Grill and
   Pub 95
Madison Square Garden 1
Malone, Joe 207
Maloof, family 11, 21, 22, 234,
   283
   Colleen 7
   Gavin 7, 8
   George, Jr. 8, 16, 24
   George, Sr. 7
   Joe 7, 8
   Joe G. 7
Manchester Monarchs 66
Mandalay Bay 89
Manson, Josh 77
Manteris, Art 296
Mantha, Anthony 55, 100
Marchessault, Jonathan 46, 51,
   59, 62, 63, 64, 74, 87, 99,
   114, 122, 126, 159, 166, 167,
   168, 179, 183, 200, 201, 202,
   203, 240, 244, 246, 250, 254,
   256, 267, 269, 275, 276, 278,
   281, 305, 311, 320, 337

Mark Messier Leadership Award
   53, 339
Matthews, Auston 115
Maurice, Paul 270
Mayweather, Floyd 16
McComb, Clint 226
McDavid, Connor 53, 120, 150,
   170, 209, 329
McKrimmon, Kelly 25
McNabb, Brayden 46, 51, 64, 73,
   87, 128, 146, 167, 168, 194,
   245, 247, 259, 272, 306, 308,
   311, 313, 321, 337
McPhee, George 24, 27, 29, 36,
   37, 41, 44, 46, 50, 51, 52, 66,
   72, 76, 81, 86, 171, 179, 265,
   274, 283, 303, 324, 338
Meier, Timo 253, 260
Merrill, Jon 66, 137, 261
MGM Resorts 15, 215
Miller, Colin 66, 87, 105, 191,
   209, 210, 252, 256, 284, 307,
   309, 331
Miller, Tony 296
Minnesota North Stars 38
Minnesota Twins 292
Minnesota Wild 14, 28, 57, 58,
   78, 128, 162, 173, 192
Miracle 320
Miracle on Ice 320
Mojave Desert 178
Moneyball 320
Montreal Canadiens 39, 110,
   116, 171, 173, 207, 318, 332
Moose Jaw Warriors 52
Mount Kilimanjaro 72
Murphy, Connor 148
Muzzin, Jake 241, 243
Myers, Tyler 281

N
Nashville Predators 58, 67, 76,
   109, 132, 145, 151, 223, 304

National Hockey League 1, 3, 4, 5, 8, 9, 14, 15, 18, 19, 20, 25, 28, 51, 52, 132, 154, 171, 215, 256, 287, 302, 341
NBC Sports Network 266
Neal, James 46, 63, 68, 91, 92, 98, 99, 109, 115, 120, 134, 137, 151, 153, 154, 166, 167, 168, 190, 197, 203, 241, 243, 257, 277, 311, 315, 318, 320
Negreanu, Daniel 17
Neuvirth, Michal 168
Nevada Storm 96
New England Patriots 5
New Jersey Devils 24, 65, 183, 191, 282
New Mexico 7
New York Islanders 25, 39, 84, 110, 157, 173, 317, 318, 322, 335, 338
New York Jets 292
New York-New York Hotel-Casino 23, 93, 219, 223, 230, 298
New York Rangers 1, 4, 24, 61, 62, 70, 102, 112, 148, 208, 241, 302, 333, 336
New York Times, The 35, 293
NHL. See National Hockey League
NHL.com 23, 26
NHL Network 266
Nosek, Tomas 46, 68, 97, 127, 169, 262, 265, 273, 274, 281, 305, 307, 309, 314, 328
Nugent-Hopkins, Ryan 120

O
Oklahoma City Barons 58
Olympics 178
Ontario Hockey League 67
Ontario Juniors 70
Orchard, Lee 226

Orpik, Brooks 311
Orr, Bobby 272
Osgood, Chris 285
Ottawa Senators 12, 20, 71, 114, 115, 182, 183, 199, 273, 304
Ovechkin, Alex 25, 59, 60, 154, 203, 233, 235, 306, 308, 312, 313, 321, 324, 325, 326

P
Pabst Blue Ribbon 7
Paddock, Stephen 5, 88, 204
Palat, Ondrej 153
Parise, Zach 192
Patera, Jiri 84
Perron, David 68, 69, 87, 103, 120, 122, 131, 135, 159, 169, 202, 273, 306, 321, 331
Philadelphia Eagles 5
Philadelphia Flyers 47, 107, 168, 169, 190, 282, 306, 334
Pickard, Calvin 75
Pirri, Brandon 70, 208, 210
Pittsburgh Penguins 52, 54, 56, 67, 70, 110, 137, 140, 166, 304, 306, 311, 318, 325, 330
pizza 96
Players Tribune, The 54, 69
Plymouth Whalers 67
President Trophy 140
Prince of Wales Trophy 324
PropSwap 293

Q
Quebec City 19
Quebec Major Junior Hockey League 39, 49, 61, 62, 68
Quebec Remparts 62
Quick, Jonathan 123, 180, 181, 240, 241, 242, 243, 244, 246, 247, 270

R

Raanta, Antti 92
Rask, Tuukka 79, 101
Reading Royals 52
Reaves, Ryan 49, 70, 71, 81, 179, 180, 181, 194, 206, 238, 239, 265, 266, 278, 281, 285, 307, 309, 320, 338
Rensselaer Polytechnic Institute 70
Rheaume, Manon 9
Rinne, Pekka 56, 134, 152
Rittich, David 175
Rivkin, Eddie 118
Roarke, Shawn P. 31
Rochester Americans 64
Rocket Richard Trophy 210, 324
Rodman, Blair 299
Rogers, Mike 207
Rondbjerg, Jonas 84
rookie camp 85
Rosen, Dan 13, 22, 23, 43
Route 91 Harvest Festival 5, 88, 89
Runnin' Rebels 10
Russian Super League 324
Russo, Michael 17

S

salary cap 28, 74, 80
San Diego Padres 292
San Jose Barracuda 48
San Jose Sharks 20, 48, 56, 59, 62, 79, 87, 125, 167, 192, 197, 198, 203, 204, 224, 238, 242, 248, 255, 261, 264, 267, 279, 281, 290, 304, 306, 331, 336, 337
Saros, Juuse 152
Sbisa, Lauren Anaka 72
Sbisa, Luca 46, 71, 87, 115, 185, 187, 202, 261, 281, 285, 307, 310

Scheifele, Mark 60, 276, 277, 278
Schlager, Brandon 29, 303
Schmidt, Nate 46, 64, 72, 73, 87, 92, 185, 187, 254, 267, 272, 277, 281, 321
Schram, Carol 27, 51
Scucci, Bob 296
Seattle 19
Sedin, Henrik and Daniel 331
Shattuck-Saint Mary's 57
Sheary, Conor 330
Sherman, Jeff 291
Shipachyov, Vadim 100, 214
shootout 106, 116
Shunock, Mark 226
Siegel, Benjamin "Bugsy" 233
Silver, Nate 19
Simbal, Jason 288
SinBin.com 84
Sisolak, Steve 16
Smith, John L. 340
Smith, Mike 159, 193
Smith-Pelly, Devante 321
Smith, Reilly 59, 63, 74, 75, 87, 105, 106, 116, 120, 122, 123, 134, 136, 148, 169, 176, 179, 183, 185, 187, 190, 202, 246, 256, 271, 275, 282, 309, 321
Snel, Alan 222
sniper, hockey 106
South Point Hotel-Casino 230, 292, 296
Sporting News 29, 303
Sports Illustrated 37, 343
Staal, Eric 57, 128
Stalock, Alex 192
Stanley Cup 1, 24, 27, 171, 185, 248
Finals 25, 301–323
history of 303
Stanley, Lord Frederick Arthur 1, 301
Station Casinos 232, 296, 298

Stevens, Derek 16
St. Louis Blues 49, 58, 69, 70,
    105, 203, 265, 336, 337
St. Louis Rams 292
Stoughton, Blaine 207
StubHub 221
Subban, Jordan 133
Subban, Malcolm 3, 53, 55, 75,
    76, 101, 105, 122, 123, 126,
    127, 128, 129, 131, 133, 134,
    135, 141, 145, 148, 153, 154,
    185, 191, 196, 197, 203, 211,
    329, 330
Subban, PK 76, 133, 330
Summerlin 26, 86
Super Bowl 5, 292
Suzuki, Nick 84, 85
Swedish Hockey League 47, 60

T
Talbot, Cam 210
Tampa Bay Lightning 20, 38, 55,
    62, 77, 107, 139, 140, 152,
    197, 225, 290, 334
Tatar, Tomas 76, 185, 187, 197,
    198, 208, 260, 262, 265, 273,
    274, 281, 328
theathletic.com 17
Then One Day 296
Theodore, Shea 52, 77, 141, 174,
    205, 206, 209, 238, 240, 254,
    257, 274, 314
"The Save" 309, 312, 315, 316
Thompson, Rocky 85
TickPick 225
T-Mobile Arena 14, 18, 23, 68,
    87, 88, 92, 100, 102, 107,
    110, 119, 137, 139, 149, 170,
    172, 179, 197, 203, 205, 215,
    218, 219, 222, 223, 226, 232,
    233, 234, 238, 248, 273, 304,
    316
Toews, Jonathan 154

Toronto Maple Leafs 3, 17, 75,
    115, 143, 201, 317, 322, 333
Tortorella, John 157
Toshiba Plaza 223
Toyota Sports Center 85
Tuch, Alex 57, 58, 77, 78, 79, 84,
    85, 87, 100, 101, 103, 114,
    123, 132, 135, 163, 177, 187,
    189, 201, 202, 206, 208, 214,
    240, 241, 250, 259, 260, 262,
    263, 269, 278, 284, 310, 320
Tuch, Carl 78
Tuch, Luke 79
Tyson, Mike 16

U
United States Military Academy at
    West Point 12
University of Central Florida 35
University of Michigan 65
University of Minnesota 57
USA Today 223
U.S. Hockey League 57, 72
U.S. National Development Team
    65, 78
U.S. Patent and Trademark Office
    35

V
Vaccaro, Jimmy 289
Vancouver Canucks 20, 24, 86,
    122, 207
Vandal, Vanessa 69
Vanek, Tomas 154
Vatanen, Sami 77
Vegas Golden Knights 67, 139
    City National Arena 31, 86
    Clarence S. Campbell Bowl and
        286
    Dad Trip 133, 330
    defining moments 332
    development camp 85

doubters and 56, 140, 142, 209, 275, 280, 281, 285, 317, 343, 344

expansion draft 27, 29, 58, 67, 290

fans 9, 22, 46, 79, 84, 93, 139, 152, 179, 194, 203, 264, 273, 323, 342

developing base 10, 19, 102, 343

visiting teams of 15, 19, 27, 56, 102, 108, 164, 280, 289, 298, 315

worldwide 258

gambling on 123, 287–298

games

playoffs 237–286

preseason 88–94

regular season 97–212

Stanley Cup Finals 301–323

Golden Misfits 60, 246, 264

Gordie Howe Hat Trick 177

hat trick 86, 127, 144, 195, 276, 330

home ice. *See* T-Mobile Arena

home-ice advantage 119, 202, 207, 220, 221, 247

home opener 94

Junior Golden Knights 96

"knightmare" 254

Knight Tron 227, 228, 327

largest crowd 207

last home game 207

league lead and 145, 167, 171, 173

making playoffs 201

mass shooting and 5, 94, 285

merchandise of 37, 217

naming of 35

ownership. *See* Foley, William and Maloof, family

penalty kill 159

pink flamingoes 233

players 45–79

playoffs

L.A. Kings 237–247

San Jose Sharks 248–268

Winnipeg Jets 268–286

power play 159, 190, 240, 272, 322

practice facility. *See* City National Arena

records set 339

rookie camp 85

season-ticket holders 230, 344

season-ticket sales 18, 219, 222

shootouts 116, 132, 134, 136, 189, 209, 330, 331

television ratings 217

trademark dispute 35

uniform 37

Vegas flu 19, 119, 140

Vegas hangover. *See* Vegas flu

#VGKWorldwide 258

Vow program 222

Vegas oddsmakers 107, 298

Vezina Trophy 101

"VGKUltimatefan" 231

Villiers, Lady Constance 1

Vivid 225

Vlasic, Marc-Edouard 267

W

Wall Street Journal 102, 228

Warner, Kurt 292

War Room 161

Washington Capitals 25, 29, 50, 56, 72, 140, 162, 203, 225, 281, 305, 317, 320, 323, 324, 325, 338, 342, 345

Washington Post 36

Washington Times 303

watching hockey 104

Wayne Gretzky Estates 13

Western Hockey League 50, 77, 111

Westgate Las Vegas 289, 291
West Point. *See* United States
   Military Academy
Wheeler, Blake 74
Whitecloud, Zach 210
Wilder, Charlotte 343
Wilkes-Barre/Scranton Penguins
   52
William Hill 291
Wilson, Tom 305
Winnipeg Jets 56, 68, 118, 119,
   120, 129, 204, 268, 272, 273,
   276, 280, 283, 306, 315, 331,
   335, 337, 338

Wong, Tyler 86, 87
World Hockey Association 20
World Hockey League 52, 64
Worth magazine 14

Y
Yanick Dupre Memorial Award
   48

Z
Zhukov, Maksim 84
Zucker, Jason 96, 192

About the Authors

During Joseph Pane's 18 years in Vegas, he has shared his passion for hockey online, in print, and on radio and TV. His blog, Knights on Ice, at LasVegasAdvisor.com gave Joe the opportunity to cover, in detail, every game the Golden Knights played in their inaugural year, which is the basis for this book.

Deke Castleman has been the editor of Las Vegas-based Huntington Press, publisher of this book, since 1991. Using Joe's extensive coverage of the 102 games and his technical expertise, along with Andrew's player profiles and other contributions, he wrote, indexed, and oversaw production of this book over a span of eight weeks.

Andrew Uyal is a Las Vegas author and casino insider. He and his family have taken an avid interest in hockey and their new home team, attending games, participating in fan events, and becoming immersed in the VGK culture. Starting with the very first game in Dallas, they spent many a "family knight" watching and cheering for their beloved Golden Knights. His book is *Blackjack Insiders*.

Visit
LasVegasAdvisor.com

to read Joe Pane's Knights on Ice blog
and for all the latest on gambling and Las Vegas

Free features include:

- Question of the Day (casinos/gambling)
- Active message boards (all things Las Vegas)
- Up-to-the-minute casino-promotions announcements
- Blogs and ongoing updates on sports betting, blackjack, video poker, poker, and more

Become a *Las Vegas Advisor* Member and get our exclusive coupons and members-only discounts.

About Huntington Press

Huntington Press is a specialty publisher of Las Vegas- and gambling-related books and periodicals, including the award-winning consumer newsletter, *Anthony Curtis' Las Vegas Advisor*.

Huntington Press
3665 Procyon Street
Las Vegas, Nevada 89103
LasVegasAdvisor.com
e-mail: books@huntingtonpress.com